CONSCIOUSNESS

— FROM —

ZOMBIES TO ANGELS

THE SHADOW AND THE LIGHT
OF KNOWING WHO YOU ARE

CHRISTIAN DE QUINCEY, PH.D.

Park Street Press
Rochester, Vermont

Park Street Press
One Park Street
Rochester, Vermont 05767
www.ParkStPress.com

Park Street Press is a division of Inner Traditions International

Library of Congress Cataloging-in-Publication Data
De Quincey, Christian.
  Consciousness from zombies to angels : the shadow and the light of knowing who you are / Christian de Quincey.
    p. cm.
  Includes bibliographical references (p.   ) and index.
  ISBN 978-1-59477-253-5
  1. Consciousness. I. Title.
  B808.9.D39 2009
  126—dc22

                                                                2008035087

Printed and bound in the United States by Lake Book Manufacturing

10 9 8 7 6 5 4 3 2 1

Text design and layout by Virginia Scott Bowman
This book was typeset in Garamond Premier Pro and Agenda with Trajan Pro, Gil Sans, and Agenda as display typefaces

To send correspondence to the author of this book, mail a first-class letter to the author c/o Inner Traditions • Bear & Company, One Park Street, Rochester, VT 05767, and we will forward the communication.

To all sentient beings who enjoy what it's like to be . . . especially those who have the courage and wisdom to embrace and love their shadow.

CONSCIOUSNESS
—— FROM ——
ZOMBIES TO ANGELS

"This is the guide to consciousness that millions have been waiting for. In clear, nontechnical language, Christian de Quincey guides us through the labyrinth of the mind. This is one of the best books on consciousness to emerge in years."

LARRY DOSSEY, M.D., AUTHOR OF *HEALING WORDS*
AND *THE POWER OF PREMONITIONS*

"It's a rare book that pushes the frontiers of science, philosophy, and spirituality all at the same time. Christian de Quincey has done just that. With an inviting mix of deep insight, compassion, and humor, he shows us how our inner light shines with brilliance only when we embrace all of who we are, including our darkest shadows."

GAY HENDRICKS, AUTHOR OF *FIVE WISHES:*
HOW ANSWERING ONE SIMPLE QUESTION CAN
MAKE YOUR DREAMS COME TRUE
AND *CONSCIOUS LOVING:*
THE JOURNEY TO CO-COMMITMENT

"This is an amazing book. Dr. de Quincey is the first among pure philosophers to intuit and understand the subtleties of consciousness."

AMIT GOSWAMI, AUTHOR OF *PHYSICS OF THE SOUL*
AND *GOD IS NOT DEAD*

"Christian de Quincey delivers a masterful synthesis of ancient wisdom and cutting-edge insight, a warm and rare work revealing the secrets of self-knowledge. Read and awaken to the wondrous potential of your human consciousness."

OBADIAH HARRIS, PRESIDENT OF THE
UNIVERSITY OF PHILOSOPHICAL RESEARCH

"Christian de Quincey has given us a rare gem of a book. It's truly beautifully written, is simple and readable, and is profound and meaningful. Anyone who has ever wondered about mind and consciousness, and about who we really are and how we are related, should read this book. It is informative and thought provoking. And that's the classical mark of all inspired philosophers."

ERVIN LASZLO, AUTHOR OF *QUANTUM SHIFT IN THE GLOBAL BRAIN* AND *SCIENCE AND THE AKASHIC FIELD*

"Finally, a book that unites the evolution of consciousness with conscious evolution. As we stand at the threshold to a new world, Christian de Quincey raises the conversation about consciousness to a whole new level. In clear and simple language, he educates, entertains, and inspires. *Consciousness from Zombies to Angels* is an owner's manual to that final frontier where science and spirit meet."

MICHAEL DOWD, AUTHOR OF *THANK GOD FOR EVOLUTION*

"The hard problem of consciousness has never been presented in an easier and more illuminating way. Christian de Quincey has achieved a miracle of popularization and has also broken new philosophical ground—and the combination is an even greater miracle."

NICHOLAS HUMPHREY, PROFESSOR OF PSYCHOLOGY, LONDON SCHOOL OF ECONOMICS, AND AUTHOR OF *SEEING RED: A STUDY IN CONSCIOUSNESS*

"In this breakthrough book, philosopher and spiritual mentor Christian de Quincey uses a rare mix of humor and intelligence to launch us on the way to personal and collective transformation."

JAMES TWYMAN, AUTHOR OF *THE ART OF SPIRITUAL PEACEMAKING* AND *THE MOSES CODE*

"A must-read for anyone who wants to know more about consciousness. Lucid and comprehensive, profound and inspiring. Christian de Quincey tackles the hard problems of mind head-on, offering deep insights into our essential nature."

PETER RUSSELL, AUTHOR OF *THE GLOBAL BRAIN* AND *FROM SCIENCE TO GOD*

CONTENTS

ACKNOWLEDGMENTS

This book has been inspired by what I have learned from a great many people. Here, I simply want to thank all my students, readers, and audiences over the years who have given feedback on my ideas by asking often penetrating and challenging questions.

Learning always involves heartfelt exchanges. Every time I stand in front of a class or present at conferences, the most engaging and satisfying moments come during the Q&A sessions. As much as I enjoy spending long hours preparing the structure of my talks and graphics for my presentations, it all comes alive in the spontaneity of dialogue.

These exchanges—via e-mail as well as face to face—have helped me in a number of ways. First, I continually have to rethink my own assumptions and beliefs. Second, as I refine my work I am always looking for the simplest, most direct language to express profound, complex, and important ideas. This book, then, uses simple words to bring to light some of the deepest mysteries of life.

I also want to thank the editors and designers at Inner Traditions International for their contributions—especially Jon Graham, who immediately saw the potential for a "user's guide" to consciousness; Anne Dillon, for her enthusiastic and very helpful editing suggestions; and to Rob Meadows and his creative team in Marketing.

Of course, I am deeply appreciative and grateful for support from

Reba, Oblio, Pecos, and Tatchi, who share my space and life even when I retreat into my den to think, meditate, and write.

Finally, I want to thank all the authors, scholars, and sages whose work I have drawn on, or with whom I have discussed these ideas—including L. Frank Baum, Thomas Nagel, David Chalmers, Nick Humphrey, Peter Russell, Eric Weiss, Andrew Newberg, Dan Lloyd, Albert Einstein, Niels Bohr, David Bohm, Wolfgang Pauli, Carl Jung, Stuart Hameroff, Ken Wilber, Amit Goswami, Arthur Young, Hendrik Casimir, Ervin Laszlo, Alfred North Whitehead, René Descartes, Giordano Bruno, Sir Francis Bacon, Immanuel Kant, Arnold Keyserling, Ronald D. Moore, Lee Nichol, Jean Gebser, Debbie Ford, Lao Tzu, and Buddha.

As always, thanks, too, to the countless sentient beings with whom we share this wondrous world and on whom we all depend—not forgetting any zombies who might also be walking among us!

STEPPING INTO
CONSCIOUSNESS

*Consciousness, the final frontier. These are the voyages
of the great ship* Psyche. *Our mission: To explore strange
new worlds within. To seek out new possibilities and new
horizons. To boldly go where no science has gone before.*

INSPIRED BY THE CREATORS OF *STAR TREK*

Everybody has a mind, yet few of us really know how to talk about it. If asked about its nature, we quickly discover the limitations of language.

If asked how it works, we either talk about the brain, about behavior—or we are left scratching our heads.

If we wonder how to develop this ghostly faculty, launching ourselves to new mental or spiritual heights, again we are often at a loss for words.

The talk today in philosophy of mind is how to crack the "hard problem"—to explain how consciousness is related to matter, how brains scintillate with mental events.

Shelf-loads of books claim to "explain" or "rediscover" the nature of consciousness, but they are mostly too technical or fail to deliver on their promise.

In this book, the most difficult problems in consciousness are unpacked and presented in simple, nontechnical language, so that even a philosophical zombie can finally understand what's been missing. This step-by-step "owner's guide" sorts out the tangles of philosophical and scientific efforts at exploring the mind and leads us to the threshold of spiritual awareness.

Reading this book is likely to challenge some of your basic assumptions about who you are, about the world you live in, and how it all fits together. Even though I've tried to write about these important issues in an easy and engaging way, at times you will be called on to think more carefully and deeply than is often the case in our increasingly fast-paced lives. Getting to where we want to go takes some work. But I'm confident that the benefits will more than repay the self-discipline and effort.

I teach philosophy and consciousness studies as a career. And over the years I've realized how challenging philosophy is for many people—even though it deals with the most profound questions about what it means to be human. And then there's science. Without some background in physics or biology, many people also find science challenging, even scary. But, of course, it need not be. You do not need to be a philosopher or a scientist to understand the ideas and insights presented here.

In the pages that follow, I have done my best to capture the essence of philosophy and science as they grapple with questions surrounding the most important aspect of everyone's life: *our own consciousness.* However, philosophy and science are not the only roads leading to this "final frontier." For thousands of years, the world's spiritual traditions have focused on exploring and developing the potentials and possibilities of consciousness aimed at making our lives more satisfying, peaceful, and enlightened.

This book honors and draws on all three of these great traditions: philosophy, science, and spirituality. For reasons that will become clear as we move ahead, we begin with philosophy in order to lay the groundwork for how to think clearly and coherently about what is probably the toughest, and often the most confusing, question of all: *What is consciousness and how does it work in the world?* We then turn to science to see how, or if, understanding what goes on in our brains can help us come to terms with the perennial mystery of mind.

For those of you who have not been exposed to very much philosophy or science, these foundational chapters may require additional attention. But trust me: Having covered the basics, you will be well prepared for the final leap—looking at consciousness through the lens of spiritual wisdom.

What I hope to show is that every one of us has the essentials to be a philosopher, scientist, and mystic. Each of us comes into the world with four special "gifts"—different ways of knowing about ourselves and our world. I call these "The Philosopher's Gift" of reason, "The Scientist's Gift" of observing, "The Shaman's Gift" of feeling, and "The Mystic's Gift" of intuition. (For simplicity, I have blended together "The Shaman's Gift" and "The Mystic's Gift" in this book.) Using these gifts of knowing, we can build a bridge from philosophy through science to spirituality, leading to knowledge and understanding of life's greatest mystery: *consciousness.*

In a nutshell, then, here's a quick map of the journey that lies ahead:

In chapters 1–3 in part 1, The Philosopher's Gift, you will learn how clear thinking opens the way to understanding and talking about what consciousness is.

In chapters 4–9 in part 2, The Scientist's Gift, you will learn why investigating the brain is important, and why knowing what goes on in that fascinating "three-pound universe" is not the same as understanding our minds.

In chapters 10–14 in part 3, The Mystic's Gift, you will learn how to finally emerge into that silent clearing of consciousness, rich with meaning and purpose, as revealed by the world's great mystics and sages.

Part 4 brings together a selection of "Consciousness Dialogues" to more deeply explore important themes from this book.

CONSCIOUSNESS IN DIALOGUE

One of the greatest satisfactions of being an author and public speaker is the feedback I get from people who have read my books, attended a talk, heard me on the radio, visited my website, or taken one of my classes. I get a lot of e-mails, and, thankfully, I'm often challenged to defend or clarify something I've written or said. It keeps me on my toes. Sometimes a real gem of a question whizzes through cyberspace and gets me thinking deeper and more carefully about an idea I've put out there.

I've collected these "gems" over the years, and have created an archive of "MindBytes"—a series of questions and answers organized under headings such as "God," "Energy," "Cosmos," "Evolution," "Miracles," "Quantum," "Time," "Beliefs," and, of course, "Consciousness." I view them as "learning nuggets," little consciousness dialogues that highlight important questions. These "MindBytes" are typically short and to the point, and I have included examples at the end of each chapter.

SEVEN STEPS TO TRANSFORMING YOUR LIFE

This book offers three gifts of consciousness—three ways to explore *what it is, how it works,* and *why it's important.* To receive these gifts, I invite you to embark upon a short journey of seven simple steps that we will take together as we explore the territory ahead.

Step 1: Watch Your Language

Step 2: Identify the Problem

Step 3: Learn How to Look

Step 4: Recognize Your Patterns

Step 5: Know Thyself

Step 6: Embrace Your Shadow

Step 7: Practice Transformation

These steps will lead us through philosophy's hardest problem, science's final frontier, and mysticism's deepest mystery.

THE
WIZARD'S GIFT

Zombies are not bad. Angels are not good. And you, my friend, are neither.

I don't mean you don't have a mix of vices and virtues—of course you do. You're human. But I know you are neither a zombie nor an angel, simply because you have a body and a mind. Because you're human.

You see, the problem with zombies is that they are exactly like us in every way, down to every cell and atom, but *they don't have any consciousness.* Zombies have no souls. Angels, on the other hand, are exactly the reverse: they are pure awareness but *have no body.* They are free-floating spirits or souls.

And, you may ask, just how do I know all this? Good question. So let's get it cleared up right off the bat. I admit it: As far as I know, I've never met a zombie or an angel. But I've read about them, and this is what I learned: zombies have *no* spirit, angels are *all* spirit. It's part of our mythology. And since I'm a philosopher, prone to all kinds of imaginings and speculations, I got to wondering: *Can zombies and angels help us know more about ourselves?* Can they help us understand the relationship between body and soul, matter and mind, energy and consciousness—and the shadow and the light of being human?*

I discovered that they can. And that's what I want to share with you in these pages. So, we're off to meet the wizard—not from Oz, but the Wizard of Za.

In *The Wizard of Oz,* Dorothy skips along the Yellow Brick Road with the Cowardly Lion, the Tin Man, and the Scarecrow. They all want something from the Wizard: Dorothy wants to find her way back to Kansas, the Cowardly Lion wants courage, the Tin Man wants a heart, and the Scarecrow wants a brain. On our journey, though, we have different companions, Zombie and Angel, and each wants something different. Zombie wants a mind, Angel wants a body.

And we . . . what do we want? Well, like Dorothy, we also want to find our way home—we want to know our place in life, in the world, in the cosmos. Perhaps more than anything else, we want to know three things: *Who are we? How are we related? Why are we here?* Getting answers to these three questions is the business of philosophy, of science, and of spirituality. What they all share in common is the mystery of *consciousness*—the connection between experience and existence.

Without a doubt these are deep questions, and have puzzled the wisest minds and souls throughout history. Yet the great mysteries remain. Why, then, should you expect to find answers here? Quite simply: you won't. At least, you won't find any *final* answers. This book offers you something else. It guides you gently into the mysteries of philosophy, science, and mysticism, and shows you how to *understand the questions* in new ways. It untangles knots, allowing you to think

---

*In another sense, you are also *both* a zombie and an angel—simply because you *are* human. If you think of zombies representing the dark, shadow side of human nature (all the fear, shame, anger, pain, and grief we all suppress to some degree) and think of angels as representing our brilliant and magnificent qualities (many of which, by the way, we also suppress) then the human psyche teems with hidden zombies and angels. On the road to transformation, we inevitably encounter the shadow and the light of who we truly are.

and feel more clearly. By understanding the questions, answers will gradually and naturally unfold.

So, that's what we're up to. And, thankfully, we have helpful allies to guide us on this journey. Along the way, we will learn a lot from Zombie and Angel, and their friends, Android and Ghost.

Meanwhile, at a crossroads, we bump into Dorothy and her gang. We walk with them awhile until we reach a fork in the road—one way leading to Oz, the other to Za.

Our groups compare notes. Why would the Scarecrow want a brain and Zombie want a mind? Are they not they same thing? Well no, they're not, and for a very simple reason: You can see and touch a brain because it fills up the space inside the skull. It is made of matter in the form of cells, molecules, and atoms—physical stuff. But you cannot see or touch a mind because it's not made of "stuff"—mental events like thoughts, desires, wishes, and feelings don't take up any space. So what *are* they made of? (Minds and brains are closely related, of course, but, as we shall see later, that's another story.)

This difference between brains and minds is precisely why the Scarecrow and Zombie don't ask for the same thing. Open up a scarecrow's head and you'll find nothing but straw—no brain. But open up a zombie's head and you'll find a perfectly normal brain—normal, except for the fact that there are no thoughts or feelings going on. The Scarecrow wants a brain so that he can think intelligent thoughts. And Zombie, more than anything else, wants to be able to *feel*.

The Tin Man and Angel share a common bond, too. One wants a beating heart to brighten up his clanking armor with the sparkle of life. The other, Angel, wants a flesh and blood body so she can touch the Earth, and move about our world, experiencing joys and tribulations with the rest of us human beings.

At some point in our lives, we've all probably seen an angel or a zombie on the silver screen. And like everything else in Hollywood, they have their time in the limelight as trends come and go. But their histories began long before the movies.

According to different religious mythologies, angels populate a region or dimension somewhere between Heaven and Earth. Their main job description is to serve as messengers, mediating between God and humans—a kind of celestial UPS.

Zombies, on the other hand, are mythical creatures from a specific place on Earth—the Caribbean island of Haiti. Known as the "living dead," they are supposed to be victims of voodoo, corpses revived by magic and able to walk about in a trance doing all sorts of nefarious things at the bidding of their spellbinding masters. While scientific evidence for angels is nonexistent, some scientists say zombies do really exist, but that they are people drugged into a state resembling death, and then brought "back to life" in a deep and permanent trance.

Real or mythical, the point about zombies is that they are humans who have been robbed of their consciousness. They cannot think, they cannot feel, they have no emotions, no free will, no desires, wishes, beliefs or opinions, no point of view, no experiences of any kind—in a nutshell, *there's nobody home.*

Zombies, then, are simply mindless humans. All their bodily functions work normally, controlled by the chemistry of the brain. They can do just about anything you or I can do—but they have no consciousness, no inner lives. They stare out blankly at the world, empty of all feeling. In fact, you could say they are just machines made of meat.

IS THERE ANYBODY HOME?

Whether such creatures actually exist is a matter for anthropologists to investigate. But how would they know for sure? How could they know that somebody was or was not a zombie? What would be the test? Since minds, unlike brains, cannot be seen, touched, smelled, heard, or tasted, they cannot be detected or investigated by any physical instruments. A brain scan can show us only what's going on in a brain—there is no such thing as a "mind scan." No blinking lights or needles dancing on a dial can pick up the presence of consciousness.

In normal life, whether or not someone has consciousness is hardly ever a question, let alone a problem. However, it can become an issue of grave concern in cases where a loved one is in a coma, and may be suffering in a silent, painful hell. Less dramatically, the question of whether anyone has consciousness (other than you, of course) remains open philosophically.

Think about it: How could you tell if the person in front of you tingles with consciousness? If zombies can do everything you and I can do—including smile or grimace, or even speak words such as "I am conscious" or "I am in pain"—they may behave as normal people but inside would actually be empty of all feeling and experience. The person closest to you, for all you know, could be a zombie that just appears normal. How, then, could you ever tell a zombie from a real person?

This might sound like the kind of question only children, teenagers, or science-fiction writers would fantasize about. But, strange as it may seem, it is a question that many grown philosophers talk about today. It is one of the hottest debates in the field called "philosophy of mind." Philosophers, however, are not interested in whether zombies actually exist. They are interested in the logical possibility of such creatures—creatures just like us in every physical way, except that they have no minds. Philosophers call them *philosophical zombies.*

ZOMBIES AND MIND GAMES

What's the point, you may ask, of playing mind games (philosophers prefer to call them "thought experiments"—sounds more serious), conjuring up fantastic philosophical zombies? Why on Earth would you or I be interested? What's it got to do with real life? Well here's one reason why: if philosophical zombies are even possible—creatures with brains but without minds—then it means that just having a brain is not the same as having a mind. And this means that brains do not equal minds.

You may not think that's a big deal, but many philosophers do.

One of the big questions in philosophy of mind is: "Does mind equal brain?" Is consciousness nothing but the chemistry of nerve cells? Now the mere possible existence of philosophical zombies tells us "no"—minds do not equal brains (since as a philosophical zombie you can have a brain but have no mind). This is big news in philosophy, and it could be big news for you and me—particularly if we like the idea of consciousness continuing to exist after the body dies.

If your brain equals your mind, then when your brain dies, that's it chum—end of story for you. But if mind is not identical to brain (and we now know it isn't), then the way is open for your mind to survive, even when your brain is dead. All this because of the possibility of philosophical zombies. Neat, eh?

Now, it's not too difficult to imagine such a possibility, is it? After all, we could easily imagine Dorothy meeting such a zombie on the Yellow Brick Road. To you and me, philosophical zombies are a cause for hope because they open the way for consciousness to exist apart from the brain—and therefore for some aspect of us (our "inner self") to continue to exist after our brain and body die. But to a philosopher, the mere fact that we can imagine such a thing is a cause for concern. It raises the uncomfortable question of whether anyone really has a mind. Don't be silly, you may say. Of course people have minds. How else could we think and dream, imagine and desire, make choices and intentions, and feel pain or pleasure, or do any of the many wondrous things that give us humans such rich interior lives if we didn't have minds? You simply can't have mental events without minds.

And I would agree. It does seem silly to doubt—even sillier to deny—that people have minds as well as brains. Why even raise the question? Well, I've raised the issue of "philosophical zombies" here because there's something very strange going on in philosophy today. One of the most puzzling things I've noticed about philosophers who study the mind is that some of them believe we are, indeed, all empty-headed zombies—creatures without consciousness, without any subjective experience. I happen to think otherwise.

THE WIZARD'S GIFT

This book, then, is the "wizard's gift" to all such philosophical zombies.

Without a brain, the Scarecrow is a dummy—he couldn't figure anything out. Without a mind, Zombie is worse than a dummy—he is, we could say, "soulless."

Because you already have a brain and can figure out all sorts of things, you don't need a book on "consciousness for *dummies*." But you might want a book on consciousness that goes right to the heart of the mystery—a book so direct that even a "zombie" could understand it. This is what I've tried to write: an introduction to consciousness for regular folk who want to know more about the mind—what it is, how it works, and why it's important.

As a book that takes consciousness seriously, it is also for "philosophical zombies"—people who have trouble understanding how anyone could have a mind that was more than a brain. The wizard's gift to any zombie is a mind that knows it is real—consciousness that knows itself and the full-bodied joy of experiencing experience moment by moment by moment.

And so we're off to see the Wizard, on a journey that will guide us to the three gifts of consciousness—the philosopher's "what?" the scientist's "how?" and the mystic's "why?

PART I

THE PHILOSOPHER'S GIFT

What Is It?

1

MEANING AND
THE MYSTERY OF LIFE

Have you ever stopped to think about your own mind? I mean really *get to know it*. If you're at all like me, you probably tried this as a kid, but it felt a bit like trying to catch your own shadow. Somehow, it always managed to be just out of reach. Like me, you might have asked your parents strange questions such as "Where did my mind come from?" or "Where does it go when I fall asleep?" Of course, they couldn't tell you. In fact, chances are, they felt a little uncomfortable and left you with the impression that this is not the kind of thing normal kids spend their time doing. So you stopped thinking about your mind and moved on to other, much more important, things. Yes?

You might have turned to playing Lego and gone on to become an engineer; or you might have splashed around with finger paints and later became an artist or interior designer. Well I didn't. I stayed with the question, and, for my sins, ended up becoming a philosopher.

You see, I continued to wonder about my own consciousness. In fact, it became my passion. In my teens and twenties, I scoured books on psychology, philosophy, and evolution trying to find answers to questions like "What is consciousness?" and "Where in the great unfolding of evolution did mind first appear?" When I couldn't find what I was looking for in bookstores or libraries, I decided to go to college to find out. Eventually, I found a career.

Over the years, I've met many fascinating and well-informed people who share my passion. We've discussed consciousness at conferences and workshops, published scholarly papers and books, and one of the things I noticed was *how much confusion* surrounds the topic. At cocktail parties I'm often asked what I do for a living, and when I say I explore, teach, and write about consciousness one of two things tends to happen: either it's a conversation stopper or a conversation starter (usually the former). Most people don't know what to say when the topic of consciousness comes up. They tend to get uncomfortable (just as my parents did) when asked to think about their own mind. But sometimes people are fascinated and want to know more. And we sink into deep and rich conversations. However, pretty soon it's clear that, just as with the scholars, ordinary folk get confused and don't know quite what to say. I often end up feeling the way I did as a kid—as if we are all just chasing our shadows.

And that's not so far off the mark. When it comes to consciousness, I see three kinds of people: shadow chasers, shadow catchers, and shadow avoiders. The fact that you are reading this book tells me you are unlikely to be a shadow avoider. More than likely, you are a shadow chaser, just like me, wondering if it is possible to ever actually catch up with yourself and become a shadow catcher. As you will come to see later on, the notion of catching or *embracing* our shadow is one of the most important steps we can take; that's what this book is about.

I wanted to write something that would help shadow chasers become shadow catchers, a book that lays out steps we can all take to know our own minds from the inside out, as well as from outside in. If you are interested in exploring the greatest mystery in life, hold tight. We are about to set off on a grand adventure. Think of these first few chapters as a kind of gymnasium for the mind. I'm going to ask you to do a little workout, exercising your mental muscles for the task ahead. You are about to do some philosophy, but, I promise you, it will be quite different from any philosophy course you might have taken in college. I've done my best to make this user-friendly "philosophy without tears" that will prepare you well for the exciting challenge of getting to know your own mind. Along the way, you are likely to find that it is not what you think it is. Indeed, as I hope to show, *you are not who you think you are.*

Getting to know your own mind is perhaps the best recipe for creating a rich, satisfying, and powerful life. To succeed, however, you will need to understand the difference between mystification and mystery. I cannot—and don't want to—promise a way to remove mystery; but I do promise that if you pay attention to important and sometimes subtle distinctions in the pages that follow, you will be equipped to cut through the mystification. Mystery is a feeling, usually involving a sense of awe and humility in the face of *something greater.* Mystification, on the other hand, involves *confused thinking* and is something we carelessly create.

Our first move, then, is to unwrap the Philosopher's Gift—to make sure our adventurer's kit has the basic equipment we need for the journey. Most of all, we need to check that the precision tools of language and clear thinking are nice and sharp, so we can begin to slice through the thicket of mystification and confusion that surrounds the word *consciousness.* Without that, without some basic distinctions, we are unlikely to make much headway. So, get ready, we are about to engage your "inner philosopher."

Philosophers are like deep-sea divers: they plunge into the ocean of language, pushing far beneath the surface to hunt for the rock-bottom meanings of words and ideas. But good philosophers don't stay down for too long. Having pried loose important nuggets of meaning, they return to the surface and offer us their polished gems. Now that you've slipped into your philosopher's wetsuit, let's dive right in by looking at the meaning of meaning itself.

STEP 1: WATCH YOUR LANGUAGE

THE MEANING OF MEANING

First things first: In any conversation, but particularly about consciousness, clarity depends on getting our meanings straight because words can mean many different things to different people. From the start, then, we need to realize there are two different kinds of meaning: one is about language, the other is about life.

Symbolic Meaning

As we know, philosophers search for meaning in language—they explore how words and ideas can refer to other words and ideas or represent things in the world. For instance, take the familiar word *ball;* it's a sound or image that refers to a spherical object. No big deal. But have you noticed that the word *ball* is not itself spherical. It's just a string of letters. Words can be very different from the things they mean.

Words are *symbols,* they point to, or signify, something else. Language, philosophers are fond of reminding us, is a symbolic system.

"And your point is?" I hear you ask. Well, I have to admit that sometimes philosophers are masters of the obvious. But, when you least expect it, the obvious can turn out not to be so obvious after all. And that's when philosophers shine. The hidden "gem" we are hunting for here is, as I said, about the difference between language and life. And, as you will see later on, this difference is crucial when we look at what we *believe* and what is *real.*

So hold your breath, be patient. We are building a bridge between philosophy, science, and spirituality, step by careful step. Trust me: it will all hold together in the end.

I am saying that the philosopher's kind of meaning is a very useful gift to master when we want to make ourselves clearly understood, especially about difficult, abstract ideas and concepts—such as "consciousness," "energy," "mind," and "matter."

But there is another kind of meaning—far more important for many of us.

Experienced Meaning

Sages and mystics search for a different, deeper kind of meaning. They explore whether life and the universe have meaning. For them, meaning is not a question of which words refer to which things but what meaning do individual lives and the whole cosmos have *in themselves.* This kind of meaning is *intrinsic*—it is "built in," not merely symbolic, and comes naturally with consciousness. It is *experienced* as something worthwhile in itself and helps give life purpose and value.

The two kinds of meaning do have something in common: both refer to what is beyond themselves. In language, words have meaning because they refer to things. In life—as it is actually, concretely lived and experienced—we get meaning from participating in the greater whole, whether in time or space, or beyond.

Thus, although your life has *intrinsic* meaning—that is, it is meaningful just as it is—it gets its richness from interconnectedness and interdependence with the world around it.

In *Radical Knowing,* I offered the following definition: *"Meaning is the experienced fit between self and its environment."*[1] For instance, if we feel disconnected from the whole (whether life as a whole, the universe as a whole, or existence as a whole) we feel that life has lost its meaning. The more we feel connected with the whole, the more we experience life to be rich with meaning and possibilities.

The first kind of meaning is philosophical and depends on *symbolic* connections grasped by reason. The second kind is psychological, mystical, or spiritual and depends on *experienced* connections revealed through intuition or mystical insight.

This is not to say that philosophers never concern themselves with the deeper kind of meaning—many do, especially those who follow in the tradition of Socrates and Plato. But when writing or talking about the deeper kind of meaning, they pay close attention to symbolic meaning. It is one thing to *experience* meaning; it is something else to *talk* about it. That's when we make use of the philosopher's gift of reason.

THE MEANING OF LIFE

When I say: "Meaning is the experienced fit between self and non-self," the key word is *experienced*. It is not enough just to fit in; you have to *feel* yourself fitting in. By contrast, in machines things just fit into other things, like cogs meshing together. For life to have meaning, though, you need to do more than simply physically fit into your environment, like a hand into a glove. That would be merely *functional* fit. Don't get me wrong: functional fit is important, too. We need it to stay healthy and alive. But we want to do more than just survive. We want to also enjoy life, to experience satisfaction and accomplishment, to *feel* our relationships with others. For this, we need to *experience fitting in.* Your life has meaning depending on your experience of fitting in.

So, ask yourself: "How do I fit in?" Do you experience yourself fitting into your *body*? How comfortable are you in your own skin? Do you like the way it looks? Do you like its shape, its color, its weight, its degree of agility, its youth or age? How about your *family*? How well do you relate to your spouse, parents, brothers, sisters, cousins, and so on? What about your local *community*—how well do you get along with your neighbors, shopkeepers, police, traffic wardens, school board, or businesses? How do you feel about your *gender* or your *nationality*? How well do you fit into your *race,* or get along with people of other races? And then there's the issue of your *species,* how it impacts the environment and the survival of other species: Are you at peace with that? Or take the *planet* as a whole: Do you feel at home everywhere you go, in cities, other countries, forests, deserts, ice fields, out on the ocean, deep underground, or beneath the sea? How do you feel about your local climate? Does it suit you? What is your relationship to thunderstorms, hurricanes, tsunamis, volcanoes, earthquakes, floods, or drought? And, finally, when you look out into the sky at night, teeming with countless billions of stars and galaxies: Are you even aware of your place in the Milky Way, and its position among the gazillions of other galaxies? Do you feel at home in the universe? Do you fit into the cosmos—at one with all that is?

These are examples of levels of meaning that surround you. We are all embedded in circles of meaning.

If you feel you fit in all the way—if your experience of relationship between "self" and "other" extends all the way out from your own skin to embrace the entire cosmos—you are among the fortunate ones. You know directly what the mystics of the ages have been telling us about union with the divine, the Creative Ultimate. "Your" consciousness is fully integrated with the consciousness of the cosmos. You are enlightened, a Buddha. If, however, you fall short of this, then, like me, you have work to do.

Assuming you are not only interested in spiritual experience but also want to understand your own consciousness so you can talk about it at the dinner table, or teach it or write about it, then you will need to cultivate your god-given Philosopher's Gift of reason and language.

"But it's all just clever semantics," you protest. Well, then, this is the perfect place to finesse our terminology.

THE ANTICS OF SEMANTICS

I'm often amused when I hear people dismiss a nuanced discussion with the disclaimer "it's just semantics." Yes, of course, it is. That's just the point. "Semantics" is all about what words (or other signs or symbols) mean—about how we *use words*.

If you and I are going to communicate—especially about "consciousness," "thought," "belief," "intention," and so on—then it will help a great deal if we get clear on how we use our words. But that's only half of the process. Once we are both clear on what we mean, then we need to let each other know what we mean. We don't have to agree on the meaning; we just need to know what each other means.

That done, we can communicate effectively. Semantics? You bet. Very important.

Over the years, it has become clear to me that many people in the New Thought/New Age movements do not know exactly what they mean when they use words such as *thought* or *consciousness*. Certainly, these words are often used without much consistency or precision—and sometimes in contradictory ways, even within the same group, and even by individuals in the same conversation (or, worse, within the same sentence). No wonder it's hard to get to the bottom of such "metaphysical" talk. And that's another layer of difficulty: when it comes down to it, language is just not capable of grasping or expressing ineffable realities. And, for the most part, that's what we're dealing with here: metaphysical ineffables.

As the ancient Chinese sage said: "The Tao that is spoken is not the true Tao." That's true. However, it doesn't let us off the hook (sorry!). If we do choose to speak about metaphysical mysteries such as consciousness or the relationship between thought and reality, then we really need to take responsibility to do our level best to use our gifts of reason and language as effectively and as appropriately as we can. We do this by being clear about the meanings of the words we use.

Now, with this in mind, let's untangle a knot that often causes great confusion—the distinction between "consciousness" and "energy"—and how they relate to one another.

ENERGY TALK

Despite what you might have read or heard, *consciousness is not a form of energy*. That's a major, and very common, misconception—a kind of "physics envy"—a hangover from centuries-old science. It dates from the time when most of the scientific world believed that the laws of physics handed down to us by Isaac Newton could tell us everything we needed to know about reality. Of course, nothing could be further from the truth.

Nevertheless, many scientists, and far more folks in the New Age community, continue to hold on to the notion that everything that exists must be some form of energy—including consciousness. But, as you will learn in this book, that cannot be so. For reasons we will explore in detail later on, consciousness and energy are two radically different aspects of the world.

Why? Why would I insist that it's a mistake to discuss consciousness using "energy talk"? Well, for now, let's just realize the simple fact that all forms of energy are spread out in space. Consciousness, however, doesn't hang out in *any kind* of space. You can't see it, touch it, hear it, smell or taste it. It's just not that kind of thing. In fact, it's not *any kind* of thing.

It's is an important distinction to get. If you miss this, you run the risk of wandering off into the jungles of confusion that have kept many people in the dark about consciousness for so long. We, however, are sniffing the air, and we've picked up the scent. We're on a trail, and we want to stay on track. We want to follow the steps that will take us from shadow chaser to shadow catcher.

So bear with me for now, and take a moment to consider a simple equation. I promise you it's the only kind of equation you'll come across in this book. And the beauty is, you don't need to know any math.

I came up with this equation a few years ago before a trip back home to Ireland. I try to visit the old country at least once a year, usually around Christmas. Invariably, as we sit around the dinner table, the conversation turns to "what are you up to these days?" My typical response is, "Well, I'm still teaching consciousness studies, and writing articles and books about consciousness." Then, as almost always happens when I'm met with glazed eyes, I try to explain just what it is that I do, and I begin with the word *consciousness* itself. Determined to find a way to communicate what I'm up to, in words that even my mother would understand, I hit upon the following equation:

The World = Things + Experiences of Things

That's it. That takes care of all that exists. By "world" I mean the entire universe, nothing left out. "Things" are all the objects that populate the world—from apples and angels to zucchinis and zombies, and everything in between. Objects may be physical things (for example, all the stuff you see around you) or nonphysical things (such as thoughts, beliefs, dreams, wishes, and so on).

But the world doesn't consist only of these things. It also contains beings who know and feel, who *experience,* these things. You and me, for instance. But our experiences are not themselves *things*. They don't exist in space, like tables and chairs, mountains and mice, apples and zucchinis. Right? You can't see or touch or measure an experience. Even more to the point: Experience is what *knows* or is *aware of* anything, and awareness of a thing is not the thing. Your awareness of the book you are holding exists in your mind (it's nonphysical); but the book exists in physical space, right there in your physical hands. You are the *subject who knows,* but your awareness is not itself an object.

Okay, as you probably guessed, despite my best intentions, I had already lost my poor ol' mum. She just wasn't interested in these fine distinctions. If I'm in danger of losing you too, all you have to do is keep in mind that *energy,* which is what things are made of, is extended in space, it is *physical;* while *consciousness,* which has no extension in space, is *nonphysical.* Things connect and interact by exchanging energy (*mechanism*), consciousness connects by sharing *meaning.*

To help make this less abstract, here's a personal question: "How do you connect?" Well, like the rest of us, you connect in two fundamental ways—*physically,* through media such as phones, radio, TV, books, Internet. All these modes of connection and communication occur through exchanges of energy—through *mechanisms.* However, this is not the only way you connect and communicate. You also relate to others *nonphysically,* for example, through empathy, compassion, feelings, synchronicity—in other words through shared experience, through *meaning.* There is a world of difference between connections through meaning and connections through mechanism.

The table below summarizes key differences between meaning and mechanism.

Mechanism and Meaning	
Mechanism	**Meaning**
Exchanges of energy	Shared experiences
Energy is physical	Experience is nonphysical
Matter/energy has extension	Consciousness has intention
Moves through space	Not located in space
Mechanisms are measured	Meaning is felt
Mechanism has functional fit (like cogs in a wheel)	Meaning is experienced fit (between self and not-self)

Whether you realize it or not, if you use words such as "vibrations," "waves," "frequencies," "fields," or even the current favorite, "nonlocality," when talking about consciousness, you are using "energy talk." You are trying to squeeze mind into the mechanisms of matter. But mind or consciousness is not even remotely like a machine. So why use the language of physics to describe it? When was the last time you went to see an engineer because you were feeling depressed or wanted to improve your relationship? *Huh?* Therapists are not engineers (even though many still use energy talk).

Energy talk is for machines; much better to use "consciousness talk" for consciousness. When I make this point at lectures, someone in the audience usually pipes up: "But if we stop using words like 'energy,' 'vibrations,' or 'fields,' we'd have to invent a new language for talking about consciousness or the mind."

At that point, I usually remind people that, on the contrary, we do already have a very rich vocabulary for consciousness—for example, words such as "meaning," "intention," "purpose," "attention," and "feeling." And that's just for openers. Here are some other words specific to mind or consciousness (see table below).

Mind Talk	
Understanding	Affirming
Thinking	Denying
Perceiving	Willing
Wanting	Refusing
Remembering	Imagining
Anticipating	Valuing
Believing	Judging
Doubting	Creating
Desire	Awareness
Hoping	Courage
Caring	Feeling
Affection	Experience
Fearing	Choosing
Conspiring	Sensing
Intelligence	Observing
Wisdom	Loving

None of these words or qualities is reducible to physics, to energy talk. From now on, let's get in the habit of using "mind talk" for consciousness, and we'll find it much easier to think and talk and write more clearly about this deep and intimate mystery.

HEALING ENERGY

"What do you mean consciousness isn't energy?" I often get this question from students and others who practice some form of energy healing (whether it's Reiki, network chiropractic, therapeutic touch, or even intentional prayer). Usually, the question is thrown at me with a barb of indignation, as if my assertion that consciousness is not energy undermines their work and passion.

After all, many of them have experienced or witnessed startling recoveries and other healing effects. I do not deny that, nor do I wish to detract from their well-intentioned service. *However . . .*

I do want to draw attention to what I believe is a useful and important distinction. I can sum it up best in two simple sentences: *Consciousness is not the same as energy;* and *Consciousness and energy always go together.* You never have one without the other. You cannot separate them. But they are not identical. Unity is not identity.

So, yes, when someone practices "energy healing," it may well be that at times some kind of energy transfer is taking place. Something travels between healer and healee. It may even be a form of subtle energy, for instance what the Chinese call *ch'i,* the Indians *prana,* Japanese *ki,* and Polynesians *mana.* Whatever form of energy it is, if it travels from one person to another then it necessarily travels through space. *It is physical.*

But if the healing involves "quantum nonlocality," then it most certainly does not move through space, and does not involve any energy exchange. Many healers report that distance is no obstacle to their healing art. It makes no difference whether the recipient is just a few inches or half a world away. The effects are often claimed to happen instantaneously. None of this can be explained using "energy talk." *Something nonphysical is going on.*

Here's what I think is happening: As I pointed out above, we are all connected in two fundamental ways—*physically* through energy exchanges (mechanism) and *nonphysically* through shared experience in consciousness (meaning). Energy exchanges must pass through space, and therefore they take time to occur. They cannot be instantaneous. Even if a healer lays hands on someone, it takes some small amount of time for energy to travel from the healing hands to the point of repair.

Remember, however, consciousness is not an object or a thing. It does not exist in space in any way whatsoever. It is not merely "nonlocal," it is *nonlocated*. Space makes no difference to consciousness. None whatsoever. Healing through consciousness, through *sharing meaning*, therefore, can happen instantaneously, whether the parties involved are in the same room or even on the same planet!

When an "energy healer" expresses an intention to heal, the *meaning* of the healing in the healer's consciousness is accessed by, and *shared with* the consciousness in the cells and molecules of the recipient's body. *They are connected through consciousness.*

Now, since consciousness and energy always go together, the "healing meaning" in the energy/body of the healer is *experienced* by the energy/body of the recipient. And since consciousness is the intrinsic capacity of matter/energy to move and direct itself with purpose, the change in consciousness, the shift in *meaning*, redirects and reorganizes the energy in the recipient's body toward a restoration of wholeness and health.

"Energy healing," then is really mostly *consciousness healing*. It is the shared intention and meaning to heal that shifts the energy. When there is not enough time for energy to flow from one person to another, healing can still occur through shared meaning. *Consciousness knows. Energy flows.* Consciousness is aware of, and directs the flowing of energy in alignment with expressed and shared intention. Energy does not need to flow from healer to recipient for a healing to happen. All that's required is a sharing of meaning in consciousness so that the energy in the recipient's body is redirected.

Bottom line: Better to use "meaning/consciousness talk" rather than "energy/mechanism talk" to describe intentional healing at a distance.

In the next chapter, we will look more closely at the meaning of consciousness and see why catching hold of it in a net of language is so difficult; why, despite being ever-present, it remains so elusive.

Getting to Know Consciousness

Q: *I am convinced that logic, reason, and science will not take me to wisdom and higher consciousness.*

A: Quite right. Science won't even get you started on that journey because it focuses exclusively on the *objective* physical world. And philosophy, as currently practiced in the Western world, deals with symbolic language and conceptual abstractions. None of these is sufficient for exploring the realms of feeling and intuition. A *comprehensive* exploration of consciousness will require nonsensory and *extra*-rational ways of knowing—beyond science and philosophy (as currently practiced).

That's what we are unveiling here, using our "four gifts of knowing."

2

HONING CONSCIOUSNESS

Consciousness, as we all know, is our most intimate reality—yet, paradoxically, once we think about it, it is also our deepest mystery.

To give you an idea of the journey ahead, I'll begin with a couple of quotes from previous adventurers in this field.

> Consciousness is a fascinating but elusive phenomenon: it is impossible to specify what it is, what it does, or why it evolved. Nothing worth reading has been written about it.[1]

> Consciousness is a word worn smooth by a million tongues. Depending upon the figure of speech chosen it is a state of being, a substance, a process, a place, an epiphenomenon, an emergent aspect of matter, or the only true reality.[2]

It's no surprise, then, why so many people think that trying to capture consciousness is a slippery proposition. However, the challenge need not be so daunting—if we pay attention to how we use our words.

When I teach Consciousness Studies, often on the first day of class I ask students what consciousness means to them. They call out, popcorn style, a medley of words that run the gamut from "awareness" or "mindfulness," to "life" or "energy." Some say it is "being awake," while others shout out it is "being itself," or "spirit." Still others hesitate, and after some encouragement, softly say, "it's who I am," or, more bravely, "it's emptiness" or "nothingness."

After fifteen or twenty minutes, the blackboard is littered with multiple, often contradictory, meanings. I then point to the tangled word salad and say, "Take a look. This one simple word means so many different things to different people. No wonder we get confused when trying to talk about it."

Typically someone then asks me: "Well, how do *you* define consciousness?"

"I don't," I respond. "Notice I didn't ask you to *define* consciousness. I specifically asked what it *meant* to you."

I then go on to explain that I avoid offering a definition of consciousness for a couple of reasons. First, to define means to "put a boundary around" or "to limit" something. But I think it is far too premature for us to decide in advance whether consciousness has any limits. Certainly, we learn from many of the world's great spiritual traditions that it is infinite, totally free, and without constraint. Second, definitions are statements of (presumed) objective fact. A dictionary definition is fixed and public. But consciousness is not objective; it is *subjective*. Furthermore, if you look up the definition of a word, it tends to carry authoritative weight, implying this is the correct or right meaning. But who decides?

I think defining consciousness, therefore, is a little arrogant. I don't assume that I have the one and only "right" meaning or that mine trumps yours. Not at all. However, if we wish to communicate, I do think it is important to be as clear as possible about the meaning we do use. And so I tell my students that I will spend the following class giving a presentation that clarifies what I *mean* when I use the word "consciousness." They don't have to agree with me, but it is important for them to understand what I mean.

And that is true for you, too.

CONSCIOUSNESS

So, to be clear from the get-go, here's what I mean by "consciousness": it is the ability or capacity to *know* (experience), to be *aware of* (subjectivity), and to *feel* (sentience), along with the ability to create and express *intentions* and make *choices*. These are all *nonphysical* aspects of reality.

If you can feel anything, or have a point of view, you have consciousness (which rules out zombies). You are sentient, a subject experiencing the world from your own unique perspective. Consciousness, therefore, includes experience, subjectivity, interiority. It is what-it-feels-like from "within."

Besides the capacity for (1) *sentience* (feeling), and (2) *subjectivity* (awareness), consciousness is what enables any body (3) to *know* anything (the source of knowledge); (4) to be for anything or be about anything else (the source of *intentionality*); (5) to *choose* anything (the source of value); (6) to have self-direction (the source of *purpose*); and (7) to be for itself (to have intrinsic *meaning*).

In short, consciousness is the ground or context of all mental or psychic phenomena—such as feelings, sensations, perceptions, ideas, thoughts, desires, beliefs, wishes, intentions, and will.

That's what it is. But it also gets its meaning in contrast to what it's not.

Two Basic Meanings

I've noticed that when discussing "consciousness," professionals and lay people alike often find themselves talking in circles because they mean quite different things. It's essentially a difference between *psychological* and *philosophical* meanings.

For some people, "consciousness" means more or less being awake, alert, aroused, aware—or, simply, being conscious as distinct from being unconscious. This is the psychological-psychoanalytic meaning as used in Freudian, Jungian, and many other psychologies. It is the kind of distinction we each encounter every morning—the difference between being asleep and waking up.

But if this is what we mean by "consciousness," how then do we account for the difference between a sleeping person and, say, a rock (or a dead person)? It is not sufficient to say that both the sleeping person and the rock are unconscious in the same way. While it is true that neither is awake, it is not true to say that both lack all psychic or sentient capacity.

The sleeping person is *un*conscious, but the rock is *non*conscious. The unconscious person's body still responds to stimuli, it still senses and feels—it still has a psychic life—but the rock does not.

There is a world of difference between being unconscious and being non-conscious. At night, you want to slip into unconsciousness. Sleeping and dreaming are good for you. But you don't *ever* want to be nonconscious! You can wake up from being unconscious (even comatose people sometimes revive). But you won't wake up from being nonconscious (when you're dead, it's for keeps).

Given this crucial distinction, the word "consciousness" has two fundamentally different meanings—one is the opposite of "unconscious," and the other is the opposite of "nonconscious."

For a clear understanding of many puzzles and problems in psychology and philosophy, we need to know which meaning of "consciousness" is implied in each context. If we don't keep this distinction in mind, we leave ourselves open to all kinds of confusions. In fact, many professional psychologists and philosophers frequently switch back and forth between these two meanings— sometimes even within the same sentence! No surprise, then, that debates and discussions about consciousness often end up in a fog of misunderstanding.

Consciousness and Pet Rocks

Picture a playful puppy chasing his tail, jumping around and yapping with excitement. He's wide awake. Okay, now picture a sleeping dog, dreaming, paws twitching as he chases an imaginary rabbit.

The difference between these two images sums up the *psychological* distinction between "conscious" and "unconscious." Quite simply, the puppy is awake, alert, attentive, aroused, while the dog is asleep, "lost to the world," as we say.

By contrast, an example of the *philosophical* distinction is the difference between, on one hand, either the playful puppy or the sleeping dog, and, on the other, a rock. Both the puppy and the dog have some form of consciousness going on (the puppy is alert, active, and aware, the dog is dreaming), while the rock has nothing going on (it is neither alert nor dreaming), it just lies there; it just is—*nonconscious.*

Both the wide-awake puppy and the sleeping dog can *feel*—it feels like something to be either one, each has a *subjective* point of view. If you could put yourself in the puppy/dog's place—if you could *become* that animal—you would continue to have some experience of how the world appears to you; you would continue to have some *phenomenology.* However, if you could become the rock, the entire world would be lost to you because rocks have no awareness, no phenomenology—the world does not "appear" for the rock. Rocks have no feeling: There is nothing it is like to be a rock. It has no point of view of its own, no subjectivity; it is merely an object among other objects (which know nothing of each other). If you could put yourself in the rock's place you would cease to *experience* anything.

Yes, I know, some of you are quite partial to rocks, and may wonder why I keep picking on our geological cousins. Actually, I have nothing against pebbles, stones, boulders, or mountainous chunks of granite. We (philosophers) use the example of rocks to illustrate a distinction that depends for its effect on commonsense assumptions. We *assume* that rocks are insentient. Whether rocks *actually* have or don't have consciousness is not the issue. Either way, the word "consciousness" gets its meaning *in contrast* to its opposite.

It's like trying to make sense of words such as "being" or "existence." Even though "nonbeing" or "nonexistence" cannot actually exist (how could something that has no existence exist?), we give meaning to the word "existence" by *contrasting* it with its opposite. That's how language works. I'm just using the hypothetical example of nonconscious rocks to illustrate my point about the philosophical meaning of consciousness. I promise, if you want to snuggle up to your favorite pet pebble and coo sweet nothings, I won't tell a soul.

Okay, then, let's get back to the two basic meanings of our favorite word. Cultivate awareness of this distinction and you will greatly enhance your clarity and coherence when reading or writing or thinking or talking about consciousness. In fact, I'd go as far as to say: *If you are serious about studying consciousness, getting clear on the difference between the psychological and philosophical meanings should be your first step.*

It boils down to this: "Consciousness" means there is *something it feels like* to be a sentient being (you, for example); "nonconsciousness" means there is *nothing it is like* to be an insentient being (a rock, for example).*

THE IMPORTANCE OF EXPERIENCE

Ultimately, of course, grasping the distinction requires that you or I actually *experience* (not just conceptualize) what it is like to be a sentient being. Without an actual experience of consciousness—knowing firsthand *what it feels like* to be—the distinction will elude us. Its full force cannot be captured merely rationally or cognitively. So, if you

---

*It is fascinating to me how many people get all agitated and excited at the suggestion that rocks don't feel anything. Just in case you are one of these good folks, I've included a short discussion of the subtleties involved in this rocky debate (see Consciousness Dialogue 4, Rocks and Network Consciousness, in part 4).

happen to be one of those philosophical zombies I mentioned earlier (who thinks consciousness is some kind of "folk fiction"), you won't know what I'm talking about. To you, *everything* is like a rock (though why on Earth you would be reading—or *pretending to be thinking*—about consciousness beats me).

Over the years, as I've read the literature and attended conferences, it has become clear to me that there are two kinds of philosophers of mind: those who *think and talk* about consciousness and those who actually spend time *experiencing* it—and then talk or write about it. This difference between experiential and rational knowing, I suspect, lies at the root of why philosophers are divided into these two camps: those to whom the reality of consciousness, subjectivity, and first-person experience is obvious; and those who deny the reality of consciousness, or try to explain subjectivity or consciousness in physical terms. Philosophers from the first camp must be tempted to ask philosophers in the second camp: "What is it like to be someone who doesn't experience what it is like to be someone?"

Well, would you believe that exploring this question will take you to the heart of three of the most debated issues in philosophy of mind—issues that keep many modern philosophers busy scratching their heads:

1. Zombies and the problem of *other minds*—How can we know that someone else has a mind (or not)?
2. Angels, ghosts and the *mind-body* problem—Can minds exist apart from bodies, and how can the two interact?
3. Androids and the problem of *free will*—Do we really have choice or are all our actions determined?

Becoming familiar with these problems will provide a valuable foundation for understanding what philosophers know about the mind—important for anyone involved in consciousness studies. That's what the next three chapters explore.

Sleepwalking Zombies

Q: *Philosopher David Chalmers claims that the world could have been inhabited by zombies who have no consciousness but still exhibit traits that we conscious critters do. Many scientists who study consciousness dismiss this claim. But don't zombies exist in real life—such as the Haitian zombies called "sleepwalkers"? If so, then the scientists are mistaken and Chalmers is justified. But I never once saw him mention sleepwalkers, and I think they'd help his case.*

A: I think you might have misunderstood the point Chalmers was making. He (and others) is talking about *philosophical* zombies—not real-life Haitian zombies. To revisit our earlier discussion in this book, philosophical zombies are merely *theoretical* constructs. It is irrelevant whether zombies actually exist or not. Philosophy is about *possibilities*, not actualities. Science explores the *actual* world (are there really zombies?) while philosophy explores *possible* worlds (are mindless zombies conceivable?).

Chalmers' point is that utterly mindless philosophical zombies are conceivable. We can imagine a creature exactly the same as one of us in every physical detail—right down to the molecules, atoms, and quanta—except there's *nobody home*, no mind, no consciousness, no experience, no subjectivity, no sentience whatsoever. The lights are totally out. Such a creature would have a brain *exactly* like ours in every physical respect—but they would be brains without consciousness. Chalmers uses this "thought experiment" to make the point that brains cannot equal minds. Why? Because a zombie brain is *exactly* like ours, but without a mind. Therefore our brains must be more than purely physical objects and events—consciousness must be "something" in addition to the physical brain.

Now, this is not at all the case with real zombies (the "sleepwalkers" you mention). These unfortunate people do exist (medical science shows that they have been drugged). They lack self-awareness, and walk around in a deep trance or dream state. They lack consciousness in the *psychological* sense (meaning they are *un*conscious). But they do not lack consciousness in the *philosophical* sense (meaning they are not *non*conscious). Real zombies still have unconscious mental processes going on; they still have experiences. Their cells, their molecules, their atoms, their quarks and quanta, still "tingle with experience." This is in stark contrast to the philosophical zombies, which have zero consciousness at any level of organization.

3

ZOMBIES AND OTHER
PROBLEMS

You've just finished watching a Hollywood movie, *Revenge of the Zombies*. Feeling a little scared as you walk out of the theater, your unease is heightened by a strange thought: perhaps your partner is not what you assume. After all, in the movie, it turned out that one of the lovers was a zombie who seduced and then killed his partner. But, hey, it was only a movie! This is real life, right? As you walk along, you think about this more, and it dawns on you that you're not at all sure how you could tell if your partner was a real person.

How would you know—I mean *really* know—that the person walking beside you is not a zombie? In the film, the sophisticated zombie looked and behaved *exactly* the way a normal human does: his flesh was soft and warm, he spoke with perfect diction, and made all the right responses. It certainly *seemed* for all the world that he was a normal person. Until . . .

And your partner certainly *seems* normal, too—right? But how do you know *for sure* that there is truly somebody home, someone tingling with consciousness and experience? It could be that your partner just makes all the right sounds and gestures but is empty of all experience and feeling. How could you tell if the other has a mind?

STEP 2: IDENTIFY THE PROBLEM

Here's the problem:

THE PROBLEM OF OTHER MINDS

The only experiences you can ever have are your own. This is obvious once you think about it: let's say it was possible for you to have someone else's experience: the only way that could happen is for *you* to experience their experience (otherwise, how would you know about it?). But that would instantly make it *your* experience. You'd have no way of distinguishing your experience from anyone else's.

Can you ever know what it's like to have someone else's experience, or even if they have any? Trying to figure this out is known as "the problem of other minds." Philosopher Thomas Nagel called attention to this in a famous essay "What Is It Like to Be a Bat?" and in a wonderful little book *What Does It All Mean?* In *Radical Nature*, I wrote:

> Experience is a private affair, the exclusive privilege of your unique point of view. Nobody else can have direct access to the feelings, sensations, perceptions, ideas, thoughts, volitions, desires, fears, hopes, wishes and all the other phenomena that flow through your experience. The only way anyone could have any knowledge of what it is like to be you, living your life as you experience it from within your own subjective domain, is if you tell them, or if they observe your behavior.
>
> But you may deceive people by what you say, and they may misobserve or misinterpret how you behave. Even if you speak your mind truthfully, and even if others are skilled observers of behavior there is still no way that others can be certain that what you say or how you behave is an accurate and reliable reflection or representation of your

experience. And even if these were accurate, others could access only their own private experience of how your speech or behavior affects them. *There is no way for another person to know whether their experience matches yours.*[1]

When Nagel asked "What is it like to be a bat?" he was pointing to the problem of knowing what goes on in the mind of some other animal (or even in another human), and he concluded (as do most philosophers today) that the question cannot be answered. The problem of other minds is insoluble. All we can ever know are the experiences that flit through our own subjective consciousness. Subjectivity is such a private affair, I can never know what it is like to be any other being other than myself. Isn't this really a form of solipsism—the view that only I exist, and everything else is my invention?

Actually, Nagel's view does not lead to true solipsism because it allows for the reality of other conscious beings, of other centers of subjectivity besides one's own. However, it is a first cousin of solipsism because this view assumes that the only way I can know anything about your consciousness (or the consciousness of any other creature) is if you *tell me*. In other words, by sending me some kind of signal. But signals such as words, spoken or written, are at best *objective reports* of a subjective experience. And, by definition, anything objective cannot be the same as something subjective. And so the impasse: We can never know, *firsthand,* what it is like to be a bat (or anyone else). And, besides, what if you were really a zombie or a computerized android programmed to tell me what it is "like" to be you? How could I tell the difference between the real thing and a facsimile, a *simulation* of consciousness?

While modern philosophers almost unanimously agree that there is no way to solve the problem of other minds, I don't go along with them. In *Radical Knowing*, I explained why. Knowing other minds is a "problem" only if we accept a very narrow definition of selfhood or "subjectivity," inherited from the seventeenth-century French philosopher René Descartes. This is the idea that individual consciousness (yours or mine, for instance) is sealed up and insulated from everyone else's. It's an *atomistic* view of consciousness and assumes that the only way we can ever communicate and know anything about each other's minds is by *telling each other* through language or some other symbols.

In other words, we form relationships when our isolated "atomic" selves exchange linguistic tokens. We sometimes even refer to the "chemistry" of relationships. I happen to take a very different view. Unlike Descartes (and many modern philosophers), I don't accept that we are basically isolated, atomic "bubbles of consciousness" that happen to come together and form relationships. Quite the reverse in fact: I think our deepest and truest nature is *relationship* and that our sense of individual selfhood arises from our networks of relationships—with *everything*. We are not isolated "atomic" beings; rather, we are profoundly interconnected *interbeings*. I will say more about this later on when we come to look at the Shaman's Gift and how it can serve us on the path to transformation.

ARE ANDROIDS CONSCIOUS?

You've seen the movies and TV shows, futuristic scenarios where science and technology have advanced so far that humans can build sophisticated computer brains, plug them into humanoid bodies made of lifelike silicon flesh, and let them loose among the population. Perhaps they "live" among us right now? How could you tell—I mean *really* tell, *for sure?*

If science could create realistic androids that look like us, move like us, talk like us, even smell like us, wouldn't that qualify not just as artificial life, but as true *artificial intelligence?*

If so, then androids would be like zombies-in-reverse—because, unlike our empty-headed flesh-and-blood insentient cousins, androids would have "artificial" consciousness. They would not only think, but also feel. They might even believe in God. We'll come back to the mind-boggling implications of this in chapter 11, when we meet the Cylons, those superhuman androids from the hit TV series *Battlestar Galactica.*

But just because it looks like us, walks like us, and squawks like us, would an android really be able to think and feel like us? This is the billion-dollar question at the heart of the cognitive science scramble to develop artificial intelligence, or A.I.

From the charming nineteenth-century tale *Pinocchio* by Italian author Carlo Collodi, immortalized on screen by Disney, to the eleven-year-old "David" in the Kubrick-Spielberg fiasco *A.I.,* to Neo's nemesis in the box-office smash *The Matrix,* our culture has been enthralled by the sweet pathos of not-quite-human androids longing to be real, or by flipside scenarios of all-too-human heroes battling to prove they are real and not just the creations of some overwhelming artificial intelligence manipulating virtual reality. The pathos and the paradoxes seem to stir something deep in our psyches, some primal insecurity about the status of our own humanity and our relationship to the gods we believe or suspect may run our lives from behind the scenes. It's a story as old as the Olympian odysseys of Homer and the great metaphysical-spiritual epic of the Hindu *Bhagavad Gita.*

Throughout history, underlying all these narratives, we find a common theme—an unending fascination with the perplexing connection between consciousness and reality. Typically, the question is expressed in two main versions: *Is reality a creation of the mind?* or *Is the mind a product of reality?* In this book, we will explore a third option where mind and physical reality always go together, neither one creating or producing the illusion of the other.

Here, however, we will focus on one aspect of this conundrum—the race to develop artificial intelligence. Specifically, we want to know, not so much *is it possible,* but *how would we know?* In essence, it's exactly the same "problem of other minds" we face when trying to decide about the status of zombies. *How could you tell if an android is conscious?*

I posed this question in one of my classes, and a student piped up confidently: "Well, we can program a computer, a robot, or an automaton to have a goal—for example, to move around objects—and, with sufficient programming, it can achieve that goal over and over again, despite obstacles placed in its way. My mom even has a vacuum cleaner that can do this. Computers solve problems. That's artificial intelligence, isn't it?"

I pointed out the key words he used: having a "goal," and "programmed" to "solve" problems. I then asked: "Programmed by what or by whom?" The question was rhetorical. It's done by an *experiencing* human programmer, of course! The goal, the problem, and the solution exist only in the programmer's mind.

"Computers or robots don't 'solve' problems," I said. "They *compute*. And that's a mechanical operation based on *instructions* embedded in the machines by conscious human beings. The goals that computers achieve are not 'goals' for the *computer;* they are goals originating in the minds of humans. There is nothing it is like to be a computer."

"So, how do you define intelligence," another student wanted to know, not yet getting the point. "Isn't it simply the ability to solve problems? If so, then computers and androids would be intelligent—even if they're not actually conscious. Anyway, it is possible to measure intelligence because that's what IQ tests do. So isn't that a way to decide whether a computer or an android has artificial intelligence?"

"You simply cannot have intelligence if you don't have consciousness," I replied. "Intelligence is a characteristic of consciousness. Anyone who attempts to define intelligence as a 'problem-solving ability' and tries to avoid consciousness is likely to come up with something far removed from anything that the word 'intelligence' typically means."

I repeated that the very words "problem" and "solving" already imply consciousness. Nonexperiencing entities (such as rocks, beer cans, hammers) never experience problems and never discover solutions. A problem arises only when some experiencing organism has a goal or purpose in mind that is thwarted (or perceived to be thwarted). And only creatures with consciousness can have goals or purposes. Nothing purely physical can be intrinsically purposeful or goal-oriented.

"IQ tests don't measure intelligence," I pointed out, "they measure *behaviors.* The person interpreting the behavior then infers that there is some intelligence (or not) guiding the behavior."

AI investigators working with computers can, at best, design processes in their software and hardware that produce behaviors that *they* (the investigators) interpret as "intelligent" using *their own intelligence.* The best AI can do is *simulate* intelligence. It's not a good idea to mistake a simulation for the real thing. Just try *really* flying around the world playing with a flight simulator. You won't get very far. You can't actually live in virtual reality—you need physical cause and effect to feed, nourish, and maintain your body's health. It just doesn't work to confuse mental events with physical reality. Likewise, it doesn't make sense to equate nonphysical intelligence with physical behavior. A robot or android that is merely *acting* intelligent does not mean its own intelligence is guiding its actions.

It is important, then, not to make the error of equating "intelligence" (which is a *subjective* phenomenon) with "intelligent behavior," which is based on evaluations of *objective* actions. Because it is subjective, intelligence is not observable or measurable. There's simply no getting around that. As I keep saying, we don't have a *mindalyzer* to detect and measure mental events. Only consciousness can observe consciousness.

The student seemed a little confused, so I hit the bottom line: "Okay . . . here's my definition of *intelligence:* Having a purpose and the means to creatively move toward fulfilling that purpose."

Think about that. With consciousness, you can *discern possibilities* and formulate a *plan* to achieve a *chosen goal.* In the real world of physical events, you need to expend some amount of energy to reach your goal. You benefit from a *strategy* to optimize your use of energy as you move toward your objective. But, as you might have noticed, the physical world inevitably "conspires" to throw an obstacle or two in our way (technically, it's called "entropy"). Life just wouldn't be all that interesting if it were too easy, right? No pain, no gain, and all that. So you need to draw on your innate *creativity* to find ways around life's obstacles. That's intelligence: having a purpose and creatively moving toward it.

Notice that the words in italics in the above paragraph, all necessary ingredients of intelligence, require consciousness. Intelligence without consciousness—that is, artificial intelligence—is an oxymoron. The vision of building intelligent machines from parts that have no consciousness or intelligence is simply a mirage, a chimera. It would require a miracle. But the cognitive scientists who tinker with their digital toys in the vain hope of creating a Pinocchio or HAL don't believe in miracles. So they're stuck, plum out of luck.

But wait a minute. If intelligence and consciousness are subjective, and whatever is subjective is not observable by the senses or measurable in any objective way, then how the heck can you or I be so sure that a computer or an android *doesn't* have consciousness? Maybe the CogSci boys can, after all, construct a thinking, feeling android, but we just wouldn't know it? Hmmm.

As Thomas Nagle tried to show, it's impossible to ever tell for sure if any other creature besides yourself tingles with the spark of conscious experience.

Or so it seems. The way experience has been described so far—as *private* and *privileged*—is itself a reflection of a particular understanding of consciousness and the world around us. But there are other ways to understand this relationship.

The problem of other minds is insoluble only if we make two rather large (and highly questionable) assumptions. The first is *sensory empiricism,* the belief that the only valid route to knowledge is through the senses. The second is that *subjectivity* is necessarily confined to the experiences of separate, individual subjects or egos. This, as we saw above, is the view of consciousness handed down to us by René Descartes. We can call it "Cartesian subjectivity."

Clearly, knowledge of the world involves more than raw sensory data. We also *interpret* what the senses reveal. We *conceive* as well as *perceive.* In other words, we apply the Philosopher's Gift of reason and language to the Scientist's Gift of the senses. But by no means are these the only valid routes to knowledge.

We also have the Shaman's Gift of *alternative states of consciousness* (ASC) coupled with *participatory feeling,* and the Mystic's Gift of *intuition* accessed via *sacred silence.*

If you've ever had the opportunity to use your Shaman's Gift, involving an ASC, participating with the world through intense *feeling,* you will have had a direct experience that reveals the limitations of the Cartesian notion of "subjectivity." You will know that subjectivity is not, as Descartes believed, sealed up in the privacy of an individual mind, only to be communicated via sensory utterances such as language or other gestures. Quite the opposite, really: you will have realized that our sense of "subjectivity" is deeply intertwined with other sentient beings, with other subjects. *Subjectivity* is fundamentally *intersubjectivity.* We are not so much "individuals" as *interviduals.** We cocreate each other. And since my very being, my subjectivity, is a cocreation that involves all other sentient beings I am in relationship with (ultimately the entire cosmos), then part of my being is literally created by and shared with the "Other."

Do you see what this means? Part of who I am, or part of who you are, when we encounter a bat *is* that bat—because part of its being contributes to the creation of our being. So, yes, we can know what it is like to be a bat (or a cat, or gnat . . .). We can know the bat from the inside, because part of its "interiority" is part of who we are. By paying close attention to our own *being-in-relationship,* the "insoluble" problem of other minds is dissolved. And this applies not just to bats and other furry or feathered animals; it applies to inanimate things, too—such as molecules, atoms, and electrons.

---

*The term *interviduals* was suggested by one of my students, Andrew Miller.

What Is It Like to Be an Electron?

Q: *When you start ascribing sentience or consciousness to atoms or electrons I feel lost. Is there anything we can observe that indicates this? Are you seriously suggesting that electrons are intelligent?*

A: Good question. However, let's turn it around and ask what "observations" would or could "indicate" the presence of consciousness in *anything*—even in human beings? The plain fact is, as already noted, we do not possess a "consciousness meter" or "mindalyzer" for detecting consciousness. It is not "observable" *except by consciousness itself!*

So, there is *nothing* about the behavior of electrons that would indicate they possess consciousness. However, this is just as true for humans. There is *nothing* about human behavior that "indicates" we possess consciousness. We may act "intelligently" but all that's observed is "intelligent *behavior*"—not intelligence per se.

Cultural conditioning makes it difficult for modern Westerners to accept the idea that electrons could possess some kind of low-grade capacity for feeling or experience. This is not the case, however, in indigenous cultures where all of nature is imbued with spirit or consciousness at every level of being (right down to the smallest ingredients).

As for intelligence in electrons: My answer is an unequivocal *yes*. (For a detailed discussion of this topic, see *Radical Nature*.)

A MEETING OF MINDS

More important to you, however, is whether knowing-through-relationship can help you decide, once and for all, if your movie-going partner is a thinking, feeling human being, or just an attractive, mindless, zombie.

Despite your philosophical paranoia about zombies and androids, you take the risk and say to your partner: "What the heck. I like being with you. I like the way you look and feel to me," and, in the privacy of your own mind, you add: ". . . even if you happen to be a zombie who can't feel a thing." At least, that's what you think on this first date. Later on, of course, if your feelings deepen, it probably won't be enough that only *you* feel good in your friend's company. You will want your partner to feel something for you in return—not just act that way. Love is a two-way street, as the cliché goes. (Though if you can never know the difference, who cares?)

Okay, caution abandoned in the pursuit of love, lust, and science, you take action. When you get home you turn down the lights, put on some well-chosen mood music, throw cushions on the floor, and pull out your favorite drums. As you tap away, and start chanting, building up to a hypnotic rhythm, your consciousness begins to shift. You enter an alternative state. You pay extra close attention to your partner who is dancing wildly to the beat. You *feel* the rhythms from your hands and the sounds from your mouth ripple out across the room and merge with your partner's movements. For a timeless moment, you, the drums, the chanting, your partner, and the dance become one. *You are part of each other.* And at that moment you *know.* You know through *direct shared experience* that your partner is not a zombie. Intersubjectivity tells you what you need to know.

Your qualms are laid to rest. You both settle down on the cushions to share this moment of intimacy, and you know without a shadow of a doubt what it is like to be each other. You experience what it means to be *interbeings.* You know what it is like to be another. Q.E.D.

THE MIND-BODY PROBLEM

All this talk of zombies can be confusing. So you quit fantasizing and decide to get real, focusing on what common sense tells you.

"What's the one thing I know about consciousness?" you ask yourself. And you answer, "Well, whatever it is, it always comes wrapped in a body." Unless you believe in ghosts, angels, and spirits, that is. But more than that: Common sense says the one thing everybody knows about consciousness is that it is closely connected with the brain. Ever been knocked unconscious by a blow to the head? Ever seen someone in a coma? Ever got high on drugs? When the machinery of the brain is damaged or enhanced, consciousness is always affected, too. So perhaps the simplest explanation for how mind and brain are related is that the brain produces consciousness, or as one philosopher put it, consciousness is squirted from the brain.

But somehow, this doesn't seem quite right, either. For one thing, another line of common sense paints a very different picture: people throughout history have reported seeing or being influenced by angels or ghosts, and religious traditions for millennia all talk about spirits. These angels, ghosts, and spirits, according to the descriptions, are *disembodied,* they are not connected to bodies or brains. Angelic spirits, we are told, are completely free to roam independently of material bodies. Could it be that all such reports are based on illusions or some large-scale conspiracy? That claim seems ludicrous in the extreme. Besides, consciousness just doesn't *feel* like it's a brain or a body. In fact, if anything, it feels much more like the kind of thing a spirit is—something that has no precise location in space, indeed, something that doesn't occupy any space at all.

Perhaps the brain, rather than producing or transmitting consciousness, is more like a receiver—the way your TV set picks up and decodes invisible radio waves? Some people, particularly in the New Age community, talk of consciousness as though it were a kind of "subtle energy"—a kind of soul substance undetectable by normal physical instruments, yet perhaps with the kind of "vibration" that an immensely complex and subtle system like a brain would respond to. But, because of the reasons discussed earlier in this book, this view of consciousness doesn't seem to hold together.

So now we're faced with a new problem: If, as common sense seems to confirm, both brains and minds are real, how on Earth are they related? How can nonspatial minds interact with spatial brains?

In my other books, especially *Radical Nature,* I have explored the mind-matter relationship in great detail. So let's just cut to the chase here. There are four major worldviews that, in one form or another, have come into and gone out of favor over the centuries. It's hard to know which one can claim the greatest antiquity or longevity, though it's clear which one holds sway today—*materialism.* But let's begin with its older brother.

Dualism. This is the belief that reality is basically divided up into two separate and radically different realms: matter and mind. Remember our discussion in chapter 1 about the difference between energy and consciousness? Well, this is the same issue. Matter is not just the stuff you bump into, it also includes a bunch of other stuff you don't see, and can't even feel—most forms of electromagnetic energy (radio and X-rays, for example), as well as the forces that hold atoms together, and, the granddaddy of them all, gravity. The one thing that all matter-energy has in common is that, whatever its form, it is spread out in space. It has length and volume. *Matter has extension.* It is *physical* stuff.

Mind, on the other hand, is the exact opposite: it doesn't take up any space, because it has no extension. Our old friend René Descartes defined mind as a "thinking thing." Instead of imposing itself on reality by flexing extension, mind simply hangs out in nowhere contemplating the mysteries of creation. It is *nonphysical* stuff. Think of it this way: You can trip and stumble over matter, and you can make all kinds of wonderful things happen with energy. But mind is insubstantial like a ghost or an angel, pouring its entire being into thinking or feeling and willing.

Problem is: How can these two separate realities ever interact? How can weighty substantial matter and weightless insubstantial mind mix it up? If the brain is a machine made of meat, how does the ghost of mind get in there and make things happen? For four hundred years, ever since Descartes split mind from matter, *no one* has ever given a satisfactory explanation for the "ghost in the machine." Not even come close. It's a doggone godforsaken mystery. In fact, it's a *miracle.*

Yet, *something is happening.* Check it out. Every time you decide to move your arm (or some other part of your anatomy) it obliges. Right? *Somehow,* your mind makes the matter of your body move. But if your mind and your body really hung out in separate domains, they couldn't possibly ever come together to influence each other. Same thing happens the other way around: if you bang your head, or drink too much liquor, you hurt. *Somehow,* physical things happening in your head make you *feel* the pain. Well, goddarn it, *how?*

Since no one has the slightest idea, it's not surprising that dualism fell out of favor, and gave way to its successor . . .

Materialism. These days, this is the big brother of worldviews. It's top dog and not in the least bit bashful about its alpha status. Downright cocky, in fact. It claims that *all that exists* is matter or some form of physical energy. Dead, insentient stuff. Nothing as messy as mind to deal with, at least not until, after billions of years, creatures with complicated brains came along. Critters like you and me.

Here's the gospel according to materialism: In the beginning, was the big bang, and the bang was with energy. About fourteen billion years ago, an enormous burst of really, really hot energy came flaring forth from nowhere, and nowhen. As the eons slipped by, the universe cooled down, and eventually galaxies, stars, and solar systems began to form. And then, on a little speck of a planet in a remote and unremarkable corner of a pretty average galaxy called the Milky Way, something quite amazing happened: life appeared. But still no mind, no consciousness. No, it took yet another four-plus billion years of evolution for living cells to clump together, randomly of course, and form themselves into nervous systems and brains. Then lo! at some point in this great unfolding of evolution these squishy gelatinous lumps, sealed up inside boney skulls, squirted out consciousness. Amazing, indeed. More than amazing, really. *Miraculous.*

Problem is: How could a universe composed of *nothing but* "dead" insentient, wholly nonconscious matter ever evolve into stuff that now tingles with feelings, with sentience, with consciousness? Materialists ask us to believe that mind *emerged* from mindless matter. But they are utterly at a loss to even begin to explain how that could have happened. It's called "the hard problem." There's a great big gap in their "explanation," and they don't know what to do about it—except to tell us to wait and have faith. Sooner or later, when neuroscience finally figures out all the fine details of how the brain works, they promise to be able to give us the answer. Don't hold your breath. This "promissory materialism" is not the kind of promise I'd put much faith in. And for good reasons.

First, *no amount* of information about *physical* processes in the brain could *ever* explain how *nonphysical* mind could emerge. The problem is not a lack of *empirical* details; it's a lack of *ontological* logic. You simply can't get something from nothing. If there ever was a time when the universe consisted of *nothing but mindless matter,* then no matter how much matter evolved, all such a universe could ever produce would be more *mindless* matter. (See Consciousness Dialogue 2, Something for Nothing?, in part 4.)

It comes down to this: Materialists want us to have faith in a miracle—but miracles are precisely what materialism denies are possible. Checkmate.

Let's be explicit about why this is so embarrassing for science (or at least it should be). By definition, a "miracle" is a gap in explanation that resists *all* attempts to fill in. Miracles, then, are supernatural interventions into the natural course of events. If we *could* explain them, they wouldn't be miracles.

The logic is simple and clear: on the one hand, science denies miracles, yet, at the same time, it needs a miracle to account for the emergence of mind from matter. In other words, *for scientific materialism to be true, it must be false!* Yikes. In short, scientific materialism is reduced to absurdity. It makes no sense whatsoever.

That is, indeed, bad news for materialism. But it gets worse . . . as we will see in chapter 9, Science through the Looking Glass.

With the problem of interaction scuttling dualism, and the problem of emergence snarling materialism, what other options are there?

Idealism. This is the mirror image, the exact opposite, of materialism. It comes in two flavors—*maya* idealism, which claims that only consciousness or spirit is real, and that matter is an illusion; and *emanationism*, which says that pure consciousness creates the material world.

Let's take them one at a time. How could *pure* spirit ever create *real* matter? To say that matter "emanates" from spirit is just the flipside of materialism, which claims that real mind "emerges" from "pure" matter.

Problem is: This form of idealism stumbles into the same kind of logical gap that befuddles materialism—you can't get "something coming from nothing." There's simply no way to explain that. Bottom line: Emanationist idealism requires a miracle to plug the explanatory gap, just like materialism does. However, idealism doesn't deny the possibility of miracles—in fact, according to this worldview *everything* is a miracle. But if we invoke a miracle, then we give up the possibility of *explaining* the mind-matter relationship. And right now, since we're using the Philosopher's Gift, we are looking for explanations.

But what if we don't say that spirit creates *real* matter? What if there's just *pure spirit or consciousness*? That takes us to the *maya* hypothesis. According to this view, the material world isn't real, and that what we think is matter is really just forms dreamt up in the mind.

Problem is: No one who makes this claim actually lives in the world in a way consistent with the claim. Literally, they don't walk their talk. If you happen to know anyone who claims that matter is illusory, just keep a close eye on him or her. I bet you will see that they don't eat poisonous food, do drink water, wear clothes, live in houses, don't walk through walls or levitate, and avoid speeding cars when crossing the highway . . . in short, they treat matter as though it is very real indeed. I can't blame them. They really have no other option but to acknowledge the reality of the physical world. Matter is pretty insistent and stubborn about its own reality, or haven't you noticed?

I've got to admit, though, that this maya business is darn hard to refute—in fact it's impossible to prove wrong. Why? Because there's no way to step outside the mind to show that matter has any reality independent of the mind that knows it. The only way to know anything (including the reality or unreality of matter) is in consciousness. So, *logically,* maya idealism is pretty safe. But *pragmatically,* it is still a problem: when people claim one thing, but act or behave or perform in ways that contradict that claim, philosophers call it a "performative contradiction." And that's a red flag—it tells us "Something's not quite right. Keep looking for an alternative."

Panpsychism. And so we come to the fourth of our four worldviews on the mind-matter relationship. Like dualism, panpsychism acknowledges the reality of both matter and mind. But unlike dualism, it says they are *inseparable.* Matter and mind, energy and consciousness, always go together *all the way down.* At every level of reality, from animals down to atoms, matter/energy always possesses some degree of sentience. You can't have one without the other.

The attraction of this worldview is that it doesn't require any kind of miracle. Because it doesn't separate mind and matter, there is no need to explain how two radically different substances come together and interact. Matter is intrinsically sentient, and so instead of "interaction," we have matter/energy purposefully directing and moving itself from within. And because neither mind nor matter is reduced to the other, we avoid the problems of "emergence" and "emanation." Of course, since matter and mind are real, there is no performative contradiction.

Panpsychism is the only worldview that offers a coherent explanation of the relationship between mind and body.

Problem is: If all levels of the physical world have their own consciousness, this would mean that every cell, and every molecule and atom, in your body has its own "little consciousness." In that case, you'd have gazillions of little cellular, molecular, and atomic consciousnesses running around your body. So how come that's not what you experience? You experience yourself as a unique, single conscious "self." Right? How does this happen? What *binds* all your little consciousnesses together? This is called the "binding problem," and is often seen as the Achilles heel of panpsychism. However, a solution does exist.*

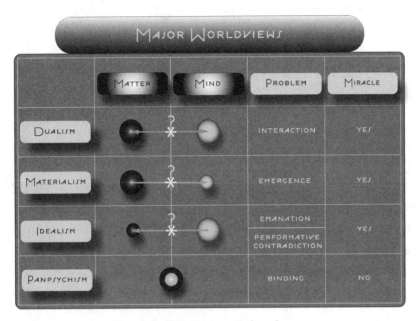

Major worldviews on mind and matter

And so we come to the final of the three key problems in Philosophy of Mind.

THE PROBLEM OF FREE WILL

I have dealt with this in detail in *Radical Nature* and will simply repeat it here.

Try this thought experiment: Suppose you are at the boardwalk with a friend and she buys two cones of ice cream—one is chocolate

---

*If you are interested, it is spelled out in *Radical Nature* (pp. 230–35).

flavored, the other is vanilla. She invites you to take one. But before doing so, she insists that you make your choice *completely independently* of all considerations you have about preferences (yours or hers) for one taste or another, or for size, shape, texture, or anything else. Her instruction is simply either to make your choice *prior to* all considerations, or to put aside, "bracket out," all such considerations that spring to mind, *and then choose.* You agree. And this raises three deeply interesting questions.

First, can you do so? Can you exercise a choice that is not determined by any of your conditioned preferences, beliefs, opinions, fears, hopes, wishes, and so on? The second question, once you have made your choice (let's say it was chocolate), is "Why did you choose chocolate?" At this point you may be tempted, by force of habit, to say something like "Well, I prefer chocolate." And your friend will remind you that that is not what you agreed to do. You agreed to choose *prior to* any considerations, or *after all considerations were bracketed.* So she takes back the cone and offers both to you again, with the original invitation to choose prior to or after all considerations are put aside. Feeling a little sheepish, you agree one more time, and you make your choice.

Now, since you successfully put aside all considerations and chose, it is clear that the answer to question one, is "yes," you can choose independently of all considerations. This time you chose vanilla. Again, your friend asks "Why did you choose vanilla?" And, feeling a little clever and creative now, you say "Because this time I wanted to be different?"

At which point, your friend immediately takes back the cone and points out that that is not what you agreed to do. "Wanting to be different is just another consideration," she points out. "The agreement was that you would choose *independently of all considerations.* Is our original agreement back on?" One more time you agree, and she offers you both cones (which are beginning to drip down the sides by now).

And so the situation unfolds, and each time you choose she asks you why you chose (either chocolate or vanilla), and each time you answer "Because . . ." And each time you answer "because" she quickly points out that you have broken the agreement. Eventually, frustrated and somewhat confused, you spontaneously make a choice, and when she asks why you made that particular choice, you equally spontaneously blurt out *because that's what I chose!* Bingo! She let's you eat the ice cream cone.

"That's right," she says, "you chose because you chose. Period. Which means, does it not, that there was no 'because' determining your choosing. You chose because you chose. *Your choosing was its own cause.*"

A green light of insight flashes in your mind: "Oh, I get it, my choice is not determined by anything other than the choice itself. In other words, my choice is unconstrained, it is *free.*" Making a choice is an act of free will, not determined by anything outside the agent who chooses.

Having gotten this far, your philosophical friend now asks you the third question: "The fact is you chose chocolate. Could you have chosen vanilla?"

You think about this for a moment. You want to be careful about your response. You think to yourself, "If I say no, I couldn't have chosen vanilla, that's the same as saying that I had to choose chocolate. But that would mean my choice wasn't free, which would be a contradiction." So you say to her, "Yes, I could have chosen vanilla."

She replies, "But the fact is you didn't choose vanilla, you chose chocolate. Why?"

Now sharp to the line of questioning, you respond "For no particular reason. I simply chose chocolate because I chose chocolate."

For no particular reason. You're feeling pretty smart now.

She has you repeat: "for no particular reason."

"In other words," she continues, "there was no reason for your choice."

"That's right," you say, pleased that you've got the swing of the inquiry.

"But," she comes back, "if there is *no reason* for your choice, isn't that the same as saying that what you call 'choice' *just happens?*" Suddenly, your insides have that old sinking feeling, you're beginning not to feel so smart after all.

She underlines the point: "If choice 'just happens,' that's the same as saying no one is responsible for it, *not even you.* It's like saying 'It's raining,' or 'accidents just happen.' How can choice be something that 'just happens'? Surely the whole point of any choice is that *you* make it, that you are the agent?"

Feeling uncomfortable and trapped by her logic, you mumble: "Choice just happens?" But you're not sure.

Choice means, as we saw earlier, that you are the agent, you are the cause—nothing else is. But now you are saying that because your choice is made for no particular reason (as you agreed), it "just happens," it has *no* cause. You are out of the picture of your own choice. How does that differ *experientially* from the situation where your choice is determined or conditioned? As far as you are concerned, logically if your "choices" just happen, if they are utterly random, you have no claim to agency. Similarly, if your choices don't just happen, if they are not random, they must be determined, and once again you have no claim to agency. Without agency, without the power or possibility to freely initiate action, what has become of your free will?

This is the core of the problem of free will: In a world of causes and determined effects, how can there be anything such as free will? On the one hand, it certainly feels that (barring extreme situations) we all have the experience of being free agents, able to exercise our own free will. Yet as soon as we explore its existential parameters we find that (1) free will means the self-as-agent is the cause; (2) but self-as-cause means without external or prior determination or consideration, that is, *without any reason;* (3) but an event that happens without any reason is the same as saying "it just happens"; (4)

and that's the same as saying "it's an accident," which means no one, including you, is responsible; (5) but if you are not responsible for your choices, then that is the same as saying you are not the agent of your choices; (6) and that contradicts premise (1). Which leaves two options, either (a) all your "choices" are effectively random, or (b) all your "choices" are effectively determined. Free will is refuted. It is an illusion; a persistent, universal illusion, but an illusion nonetheless— according to this analysis.

SELF-AGENCY AS UNCAUSED CAUSE

If this analysis is correct, free will is an illusion. However, if free will is not an illusion, this analysis must be in error. Does the above analysis contain an error, then?

Some philosophers (the determinists) say no, this analysis (or some variation of it) provides a devastating critique of the notion of free will. Other philosophers (the volitionists) insist that the analysis must be wrong because it flies in the face of one of our most intimate experiences: our ability to exercise volition. The volitionists rely on the notion that logic cannot override experience; that if logic and experience are in conflict, then experience must take priority. A third group, the rationalists, say that logic and experience cannot contradict one another. So if the experience of free will is a fact of our general experience of being healthy and whole human beings (which it clearly is), then it is not that logic as such is inferior, but that the logic of this particular argument must be faulty.

Where is the flaw? Let's take another look at premise (2): it asserts that "self-as-cause" means without prior determination or consideration, that is *without any reason*. Premise (3) then follows: "But an event that happens without any reason is the same as saying 'it just happens'." As we saw in the chocolate or vanilla thought experiment, choice was *independent of all considerations,* which means it happened without any prior cause. But if the selection, the physical act of taking the chocolate cone, was the *effect* of the choice, then the choice must have been the *cause* of the selection (a standard axiom of logic is that causes always precede effects). That is, the selection did have a cause—namely, your choice. But the choice itself had no cause, it had no prior reason compelling it (as we saw).

What does it mean to say "the choice itself had no cause"? Well, according to the earlier analysis it means that the choice "just happened," that it was random—which hardly counts as choice at all. But to insist on this line of argument is to ignore premise (1) "free will means the self-as-agent is the cause." Therefore, given this premise, it is not accurate to say that choice "just happens" without reason. There is a cause, there is a reason: *the self-as-agent*. But, and here is the important point, the self-as-agent does not provide a cause or reason *prior to* the act of choosing. The act of choice by the self-as-agent is a purely creative act, a spontaneous exercise of volition *right at the moment of choice*.

In this particular case, in the act of choice, choice-as-effect coincides with self-as-cause. (That is, in this unique case, cause *does not* precede effect. They are synchronous.) And this amounts to saying that choice is uncaused by anything external to the existential act of choice itself. For this to be true, choice and self must coincide. There is no dualism of agent and choice. Agency *is* the act of choosing.

In fact, this line of analysis leads to an axiom: "In any case where cause and effect coincide in time, there is an identity of agency and choice." A corollary is that "the identity of cause and effect *is* the self-as-agency." Self, as an occasion or instance of agency, *is* the creative act of choice. That is to say, the very essence or being of self (or consciousness) is the act of choice. *Self exists only as choice.*

Thus, the error in the initial analysis was ignoring premise (1), self-as-agency is the cause of choice, and assuming that choice "just happens" because there is no *external* cause. There was a cause: the *internal,* or coincidental, agency of the self exercising the choice.

Choice doesn't "just happen"; in fact, choice is the precise opposite of randomness. It is the injection of order into the flux of stochastic events. In short, choice is neither random nor determined—it is not random because it is a reduction of the random, and it is not determined because (as we saw) it was exercised prior to all considerations, external causes, and reasons.

However, a problem still remains. In the thought experiment described above, the agent (you) made your choice prior to all *conscious* considerations. It is entirely possible (and likely) that beneath the threshold of awareness, all sorts of unconscious psychological and physiological dynamics are at work *determining* your preferences and considerations. You may consciously bracket out all conscious considerations, but you cannot block out your *unconscious* biases. By definition, the contents and processes of the unconscious are not accessible to conscious awareness. (As soon as they rise to awareness, they are no longer unconscious.)

It remains possible, therefore, that your act of choosing the chocolate cone was not prior to all *unconscious* considerations. And you have no way of knowing whether your act of choice is *independent* of all such unconscious dynamics. Thus, the determinists argue, you have no way of refuting the claim that all your choices are determined by unconscious motivations and drives. This is true; but by the same token, the determinists have no way of confirming that any or all of your choices *are* determined by unconscious dynamics. The issue remains open.

That is what I wrote in *Radical Nature.* It tackles the free will verses determinism debate as a philosophical issue. However, I'd now like to add something that takes the issue beyond conventional Western philosophy and look at a question that is of greater concern in spirituality. It comes from one of my readers.

Choice and Consciousness

Q: *I have just reread* Radical Nature, *and I have a question: In your discussion of free will and choice, I understand you to say that the essence of self is the act of choice or choosing. How does this fit with the Buddhist notion of "choiceless awareness" or the notion of the "Witness" as the essence of the true self?*

A: Quite honestly, I'm not sure of this. I seem to oscillate—sometimes convinced that choice is essential to all forms of consciousness, and sometimes intuiting the Buddhist view. On balance, I'm inclined to come down on the side of "choice" rather than "choiceless" consciousness.

Here's why: What would be the point of consciousness that was purely witness? How could purely witnessing consciousness ever direct or purposefully shift attention?

Like most deep issues to do with consciousness, I think we encounter a paradox here: For consciousness to reach the stage of "pure" witness, it needs to make a choice (or a series of choices) to "let go," and simply "be." To achieve "choicelessness" requires an initial act of "choice."

Over the years, as I've meditated on this, I've come more and more to the intuition that really the issue is not "choice verses choicelessness" but rather who is choosing? Yes, I think for individual humans to reach "enlightenment" we need to let go of our personal (egoic) individual will (self-agency or choice). In doing so, we "relax" into the intersubjective communion of "universal consciousness" (call it "spirit" if you like). We relinquish personal choice (or perhaps the illusion of personal choice) and open up to the true source of self-agency or choice of the Creative Ultimate. "Our" choices may be manifestations or expressions, through us, of choices enacted by the Creative Ultimate (call it "Spirit," "Divinity," "God," if you prefer).

Bottom line: If choice was not intrinsic to consciousness, how could anything ever happen purposefully or creatively?

❖

Congratulations! You have now completed part 1, The Philosopher's Gift, and the first two steps on your journey into consciousness. Getting clear on the language you use to talk about mind or consciousness was the first step. Step 2 explored the three key problems in philosophy of mind, so you know what you need to know as you move ahead. These are the problem of other minds (how can you tell if a zombie, or anyone else, is conscious?); the mind-body problem (how are consciousness and matter related?); and the problem of free will (do we really make choices or is everything determined?).

You have seen why consciousness is not to be found in the physical universe. Physical things are made of energy and they occupy space; consciousness is nonphysical, is not a form of energy, and does not occupy space. You won't find mind by looking in matter, but you will find it *associated* with matter—particularly the brain.

In part 2 we now turn to the Scientist's Gift to see how using the senses in rigorous research may help us explore and understand the fine details of the brain. But knowing about the brain and nervous system is a far cry from knowing consciousness. I'm often called to task for emphasizing this point because, these days, a great many people are very excited about research in the cutting-edge field of neuroscience. Indeed, it does have a lofty mission (again, with apologies to *Star Trek*):

> Consciousness, the final frontier. These are the voyages of the great ship *Neuro*. Our mission: To explore strange new worlds within the brain. To seek out new structures and new connections with the mind. To boldly go where no science has gone before.

Neuroscience is striving ahead, regularly hitting the headlines with reports of new findings from the wondrous three-pound universe inside the skull. But there's a glitch in the mission. In step 3 we'll explore what the brain can tell us about the mind, focusing on a prime example of "mission overshoot" by a couple of neuroscientists who thought they had taken a picture of God.

PART II

THE SCIENTIST'S GIFT

How Does It Work?

HARDWIRED FOR GOD?

A meditator sits alone in a room, wired to monitor his blood and brainwaves. A couple of scientists wait patiently in another room for a signal. Eventually, it all comes together when the meditating subject tugs on a piece of kite string trailing between the two rooms: "I'm peaking, I'm peaking," he whispers excitedly. One of the scientists hits a button on their state-of-the-art brain-monitoring device, and takes a photograph of God.

STEP 3: LEARN HOW TO LOOK

A PHOTOGRAPH OF GOD?

The first page of the first chapter of *Why God Won't Go Away*, by neuroscientists Andrew Newberg and Eugene D'Aquili, highlights the key challenge for a neuroscientific approach to studying meditation (or any other state of consciousness): on one hand sits the meditator (with his subjective experience), on the other, various instruments for measuring blood flow, heart rate, and brain activity are connected to his body and brain. The link between all this objective hi-tech paraphernalia and the subject's experience is a decidedly low-tech piece of string. Its purpose: to signal to the scientists the moment when the meditator hits a peak experience. The subject's tugging on the twine tells the researchers *"now!"* and they record whatever the instruments are registering at that precise time.

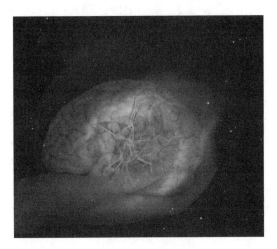

A photograph of God?

The length of string symbolizes the awkward experimental dilemma facing consciousness researchers: no matter how hi-tech the machines and instrumentation, these can *never* directly measure subjective experience. The best such machines can do is measure physiological *correlates* of consciousness. And the rub is that for these correlates to have any meaning the researchers must rely on some subjective report from the meditating subject. In this case, the "report" is indicated by the meditator tugging on a piece of cotton twine. No amount of probing and monitoring will ever yield direct information about consciousness. It can, however, deliver substantial data about what goes on in the subject's brain and nervous system and other bodily functions whenever the subject reports a particular mental state.

Not even the report is a direct line to consciousness. Like the piece of twine, *all* reports are necessarily objective—they involve the transmission of signals via some physical medium (whether words carried on air vibrations, electrical activity through circuits of wires and transistors, or electronic images on a screen). The experimental data, therefore, are not even secondhand; they are thirdhand, two removes from the actual experience itself. First, the experience, then the report, and only then the measurement of the physiological correlates. And since it always remains possible that the subject could be mistaken or even deliberately misleading in his or her report, we can never be sure just what exactly the physiological measurements actually correlate with. We have no "consciousness meter" for detecting the presence of consciousness.*

The "hard problem" of linking mind and body, so vigorously debated by philosophers and scientists in recent years, seems to register only faintly on Newberg and D'Aquili's radar. While they acknowledged the mind-body problem ("Neurology cannot completely explain how such a thing can happen—how a nonmaterial mind can rise from mere biological functions . . ."),[1] they nevertheless failed to grasp just how severe the explanatory gap is. It is not merely a problem that neuroscience cannot "completely" explain; it is a problem that neuroscience can't even *begin* to explain.

Apparently unaware of the philosophical difficulties involved in measuring consciousness, Newberg wrote: "Years of research, however, have led Gene and me to believe that [peak] experiences like Robert's are real, *and can be measured* and verified by solid science. That's why I'm huddling, beside Gene, in this cramped examination room, holding kite string between my fingers: I'm waiting for Robert's moment of mystical transcendence to arrive, because I intend to take its picture" (emphasis added).[2]

But, as we've just seen, detecting and measuring consciousness is

---

*Philosopher David Chalmers—who drew attention to the "hard problem" of explaining how brains could produce consciousness—amused a conference audience by digging into his backpack and pulling out a hair dryer, pointing it at various celebrities in the audience, and manipulating the green and red buttons on his podium. When green flashed, it supposedly indicated the presence of consciousness in the person targeted by the hair dryer. Red indicated the absence of consciousness. Chalmers used the prop to underscore the glaring gap between technology and consciousness and the absurdity of even imagining we could ever devise such a "consciousness meter."

precisely what researchers cannot achieve. The authors confuse measuring the *correlates* of consciousness with the actual experience itself. They can no more take "its" picture (i.e., a snapshot of mystical transcendence) than they can take a photograph of God (the title of the chapter where they make this claim). Their "photograph" is an image taken with a state-of-the-art SPECT camera (single photon emission computer tomography). Unfortunately, even with such high-powered technology, "solid science" cannot, as the authors claim, verify the presence of mystical experience, or any experience whatsoever.

This confusion between correlates and experience is the Achilles' heel of neuroscience masquerading as consciousness science. Although Newberg and his colleagues present the results of some intriguing brain science focused on the issue of religious experience, the claim that science now has solid research data to support the reality of spiritual experiences cannot be coherently defended.

The authors do acknowledge the difficulty (in a footnote):

> While we realize it is much more complex than simply "taking a picture," this is the gist of what is being done. Actually capturing the precise moment of an intense mystical experience is not easy, or likely, because in spite of the planned meditation our subjects performed, it is very difficult to know or predict exactly how long or how strong a given state will be. It, nonetheless, seems possible to begin to unravel the brain mechanisms that underlie the process of meditation and obtain a clear view into the fantastic workings of the brain, during these practices.[3]

But now let's parse what they say. They claim that the "gist" of what's being done is "taking a picture" of mystical states. In fact, all their SPECT technology can do is take a picture of a brain while the subject claims to be having a peak experience. The researchers can hope and trust that the "precise moment" they take their snapshot of the brain actually coincides with a moment when the subject is actually experiencing a peak state. But they cannot rightly claim that such SPECT data qualify as "solid science" "verifying" mystical experience. Yes, SPECT technology may indeed help yield a clearer view of the fantastic workings of the brain, and it may even also help begin unraveling brain mechanisms associated with meditation. But, again, the authors' choice of words reveals a paradigmatic metaphysical assumption that throws us headlong into the "hard problem": they talk of "brain mechanisms that *underlie* the process of meditation," as though it were foregone knowledge that the brain "underlies" (in the sense of "is the physical basis for" and therefore produces) consciousness.

We simply do not know this. It is a metaphysical *assumption* of materialism that all experiential events are ultimately reducible to physical events, more specifically, to brain events. And it is this very assumption that has confounded philosophers and scientists for centuries, leaving us with the legacy of Schopenhauer's "world-knot" (1818), Levine's "explanatory gap" (1983), and Chalmers' "hard problem" (1996)—all of which emphasize the persistence of the unresolved mind-body problem.

Nevertheless, Newberg et al. proceed from the assumption—shared by a great number of neuroscientists and philosophers—that the brain creates the mind. From there, it is a matter of experimental details to discover how the brain could be responsible for spiritual experiences. If we ignore the problematic foundational assumption, the authors do build a persuasive case for how and why the brain has evolved to generate myths, rituals, the religious impulse, and even mystical experiences.

Let's be clear: Neuroscience is a wonderful discipline. Knowledge of the brain can be immensely helpful, especially in medicine. It can tell us how certain areas of the brain are related to, for example, emotion, thought, memory, language, sight, hearing, sensation, motor skills, and so forth. Observing what happens to brain tissue as a result of Alzheimer's disease may one day lead to effective treatments. And, to be sure, repairing brain processes can lead to restoration of mental functions such as ability to remember names, faces, events, and so on. We may even discover areas of the brain associated with a desire for spirituality or, indeed, for science.

So let's take a look at what brain science can tell us about spiritual experience, keeping in mind that it can never *explain* the existence of spiritual experience, or *any* experience for that matter.

INHIBITED BRAIN, DISAPPEARING SELF

One of the most commonly reported characteristics of mystical experience is a sense of egolessness, or loss of sense of self, along with a dissolution of the sense of space and time. Newberg and his colleagues present an intriguing hypothesis to account for this. They propose that inhibition of nerve stimuli to a particular area of the brain (posterior superior parietal lobe, or, as the authors prefer to call it, the "orientation association area," OAA for short) is responsible for experiences of the dissolution of the sense of self during mystical states. When this happens, they suggest, the OAA has been "temporarily 'blinded,' deprived of the information it needed to do its job properly."[4]

> The left orientation area is responsible for creating the mental sensation of a limited, physically defined body, while the right orientation area is associated with generating the sense of spatial coordinates. . . . [T]he two sides of the orientation association area are able to weave raw sensory data into the vivid, complex perception of a self and into a world in which that self can move.[5]

If true, this certainly seems to provide support for a materialist account of brain producing mind. At least, the correlations suggest that the brain is responsible for "organizing" consciousness so that, during normal operation, it generates an experienced distinction between the self and the outside world. During meditation, especially during peak states, this organizing function is suspended, and the subject experiences a sense of loss of self (a similar loss of orientation in space and time also occurs).

Can we assume, then, that discovering more about certain brain functions may, after all, enlighten us about the organization or processes of consciousness? If the data are repeated and consistent, then we should be able to predict specific mental states—including mystical experiences of the divine—solely by observing measurable activity in the brain.

So, is materialism vindicated by such research? Again, let's analyze what's going on here: We observe that certain brain states predictably correlate with certain reported mind states. So far, so good. But *how do we know the correlation holds?* Only because someone *reports* his or her subjective experience. Without the subjective report, no such correlation could be made, and the measured data could inform us only about *brain* states, telling us absolutely nothing about the mind.

The mystery of how or why brain activity is or could be related to mind remains as stark as ever. Third-person data of brain events depend on second-person reports of first-person experiences to even begin to yield correlations, and thus inferential knowledge. We may *infer* that certain brain states reflect particular states of mind provided the second-person reports *and their interpretation* accurately represent the first-person experience. Hardly "solid science."

Nevertheless, we are still left with the intriguing data that inhibition of some brain activity correlates with the mystical experience of selflessness, oceanic oneness, and transcendence of space and time. What, then, if this relationship is more than mere correlation? Could there be a *causal* relationship between what happens in the brain and someone's first-person mystical experience? And, if so, what is the nature of that causal relationship? Is it upward causation of brain-to-mind (materialism), or downward causation of mind-to-brain (idealism), or some other alternative?

Dualism is a possible alternative because it allows for either causality path: brain causing events in mind, or mind causing events in the brain. However, if this were the case, the nature of the causal interaction remains utterly mysterious. No one, since Descartes firmly established philosophical dualism nearly four hundred years ago, has even come close to providing an explanation of how such mind-brain interaction could occur. Another option for dualism, of course, is psychophysical parallelism, where there is no causal exchange between mind and brain. Both series of events unfold in their own separate domains, and observed correlations are "explained" as due to a preestablished divine synchrony. But this requires theology, not philosophy or science.

A fourth alternative to materialism, idealism, and dualism is panpsychism: Neither the brain causes consciousness, nor consciousness causes the brain. Instead, according to this view, as I noted earlier, the matter of the brain itself, all the way down to its most elemental constituents (whether electrons, protons, quarks, quanta, or superstrings) themselves possess some trace of interiority, subjectivity, experience, consciousness. Panpsychism is a form of ontological "funda-*mentalism*"—it says that reality is fundamentally experiential, that consciousness goes all the way down.

Given this worldview, a state or quality of consciousness will reflect the organization of the hierarchy of constituents that make up its associated brain. If, for example, a part of the brain responsible for orienting a person in space and for generating the boundary of the individual self is inhibited, its associated consciousness will likewise and concurrently lack a sense of an individual self. In short, changes in brain events will result in corresponding mental events, just as neuroscience says.

"Gradually, we shaped a hypothesis that suggests that spiritual experience, at its very root, is intimately interwoven with human biology. That biology, in some way, compels the spiritual urge."[6] The first part of the hypothesis is warranted by the data, but "biology compels the spiritual urge" is not. That is a theoretical addition, itself compelled or urged by a particular metaphysical worldview—in this case, materialism or biologism: "Had we found the common biological root of all religious experiences?"[7] they ask.

The SPECT evidence does not support biological reductionism. And, in fact, later in the book the authors explicitly shy away from reductionism when they, quite correctly, conclude that materialist explanations of consciousness would throw into question not only mystical experience and the status of God, but *all* experience or knowledge, including all the data and theories of science itself. We'll return to this shortly.

BRAIN MACHINERY

In an effort to make room for a real spiritual presence beyond the brain, Newberg and D'Aquili try their best to shake loose the shackles of materialism. They are at pains not to conclude from their neurological data that minds are nothing but the "flesh and blood machinery of the brain." But despite their best intentions we can still hear the rattle of those chains. As we have seen, the metaphysical gremlin of materialism continues to insinuate itself into their thinking at critical points.

I should add here that by no means are they alone in this. The vast majority of neuroscientists worldwide uncritically accept the scientific dogma that brains produce minds. I focus on Newberg and his colleagues, not to single them out for any special criticism, but rather as examples of brain researchers who, even despite being open to the reality of spiritual experience, nevertheless are hypnotized by the modern paradigm of materialism.

They attempt to soften the impact of the hard problem by offering their own straightforward and simple definitions of "brain" and "mind." Having, yet again, let the materialist worldview slip through by claiming that "the structures of the brain operate harmoniously to turn raw sensory data into an integrated perception of the world outside the skull,"[8] they go on to define *brain* as "a collection of physical structures that gather and process sensory, cognitive, and emotional data,"[9] and *mind* as the "phenomenon of thoughts, memories, and emotions that arise from the perceptual processes of the brain."[10]

Their definition of brain is simple and straightforward enough. But their definition of mind is tautological and simply begs the question. To say that mind arises "from the perceptual processes of the brain" already requires an understanding of *mental* perceptual processes: *How, we may ask, could brain processes "perceive" anything if they didn't already possess some kind of mind?* So their definition of mind comes down to this: "Mind arises from mental processes in the brain." Now, while that is undoubtedly true, it is a truism, and hardly informs us of anything useful.

The hard question remains: *How are mental processes in the brain?*

Unable, it seems, to wriggle out from under the weight of materialism and left struggling with this tautological definition of mind, Newberg tries to simplify things even more, and declares: "In simpler terms, brain makes mind." Right there he has committed himself to the materialist dogma: *brain makes mind.*

Philosophically it doesn't help to try to soften this position by telling us that the data support the hypothesis: It is inherent in the nature of the brain "to strive to create the mind." Yes, Newberg and Company are telling us, the brain has primacy; but it is compelled to create mind. Not only that, they go further and try to persuade us: brains are hardwired for minds that can experience the transcendent and the divine. *Brains are hardwired for God!*

HOW THE BRAIN MAKES GOD REAL

"The second characteristic, which was hinted at in our SPECT scan studies, is the ability of the mind to interpret spiritual experiences as real."[11]

The hypothesis that God is hardwired in the human brain raises the critical question whether God is merely an experience generated in the brain's neural pathways or whether the brain has evolved to detect a genuinely divine presence greater than the brain. In any case, according to the authors, "There's no other way for God to get into your head except through the brain's neural pathways."

We have, here, a startling thesis. The human brain has evolved to process spiritual experiences. And then comes the deeper question:

Are these unitary experiences merely the result of neurological function—which would reduce mystical experience to a flurry of neural blips and flashes—or are they genuine experiences which the brain is able to perceive? Could it be that the brain has evolved the ability to transcend material existence, and experience a higher plane of being that actually exists?[12]

Later on, they emphasize they do not intend to imply that God exists only in the brain's electrochemical events. Although it is beyond the scope of science to prove or disprove God, they say their research inclines them to believe that religious experiences in the brain are representative of a genuinely real spiritual presence beyond the brain. They reason as follows: Every experience we ever have *must* pass through the brain and nervous system. This is as true for an everyday experience such as seeing a tree outside your window as it is for a mystical experience of God. Now, we accept that the tree really exists "out there" and not only in our brains and minds. We *must* accept this, otherwise all of our experiences, including the whole of science, would be nothing more than solipsist illusion. But since there is no intrinsic neurological difference between an experience of a tree and an experience of God in the brain, we have no rational justification for believing the tree to have a reality independent of our brain while doubting the independent existence of God.

Philosophically, the authors are on sound ground with this conclusion. However, while they offer what seems to be scientific support for the reality of spiritual experiences, they in fact undermine their conclusion by the metaphysical assumptions of materialism that lurk in the text—specifically, the idea that mind exists only as a product of the brain. Yes, God can "get into your head" only through the brain's neural pathways. And yes, "God cannot exist as a concept . . . anyplace else but in your mind." But no, neither experiences of God nor any experiences whatsoever "are made real" only "through the processing powers of the brain" and the "cognitive functions of the mind" produced by the brain.

This materialist position assumes 1) that brain produces mind, and 2) mind is found only in the brain and/or nervous system. Both of these assumptions, often unquestioned in neuroscience, are highly questionable and philosophically deeply problematic. As the authors acknowledge, neither science nor philosophy can satisfactorily answer how objective neurons and brains could produce subjective minds. The best that contemporary materialists can offer is the miracle of emergence—getting the wine of consciousness from the water of the brain, as philosopher Colin McGinn put it. Exactly how this "miracle" occurs—or even *could* occur—is left unexplained, and instead we are left with little more than faith in what we may call "promissory materialism."

Without an adequate explanation of how brains could give rise to minds we have no solid ground for assuming that minds exist only in brains. If they do exist in brains—and we can be sure they do—then it is at least plausible and coherent to assume that minds exist in association with whatever brains are made of—that is, neurons. But then the same line of argument applies to neurons, too. In short, since the matter of the brain's cells is no different from the matter of other cells in the body (not the cells' architecture or functions, but their constituent *matter)* then we may assume that mind or consciousness is there, too. And so on, all the way down to the cells' molecules and atoms, and beyond. God, as an experienced reality, then, certainly exists in the mind; but this mind may be anywhere in the body (or even beyond it). The authors' conclusion, therefore, is unwarranted: "The evidence . . . compels us to believe that if God does indeed exist, *the only place he can manifest his existence would be in the tangled neural pathways and physiological structures of the brain*" (emphasis added).[13]

Instead, if we let go of materialism, God, or spirit, or universal consciousness may manifest *anywhere*—not only in human brains but also in all living cells, in all nonliving molecules and atoms, anywhere in the whole natural cosmos. Of course, if we wish to entertain *ideas* of the divine, and not merely experience its presence, then the tangled neural pathways of human brains appear to do the job very well. In the end, our brains may harbor the secret of why the "idea" of God won't go away. Yes, we may be hardwired for *ideas* about the divine but not for spiritual experiences. Big difference.

We'll explore this brain-mind connection further in the next chapter as we check out "a novel theory of consciousness."

Is God Energy?

Q: *I had been using the term "Energy" for God . . . but now often simply use "Spirit." However, I still resonate with "Source" and "Energy" to refer to God. I don't use "energy" as a scientific term; it comes from my work in shiatsu and Oriental medicine. I know that when I do bodywork, I connect with something far greater than I am, and that I make a difference and influence the flow of ch'i. Isn't ch'i the flow of God energy?*

A: I would not equate God with "energy." Here's why: In order to be creative, God must also possess consciousness, intention, purpose. Likewise, God could not be just pure consciousness, either. God also needs energy in order to act on intentions. I would say God is *sentient energy,* or *purposeful action.*

If you think about the terms *source* and *energy,* I think you will see that they are not at all the same. A source is an origin of something—in this case, energy that flows from the source. A spring is not a river.

You say that your use of "energy" comes from Oriental medicine and not from science. However, the use of the term *energy* in Oriental medicine is an *English* translation of Chinese (*ch'i*) or Sanskrit (*prana*). And the word *energy* in English used to translate these other terms is borrowed directly from nineteenth-century Western science. Whether you are aware of it or not, when you use the word *energy* you are using a term borrowed from mechanistic science.

Besides all that, even in Chinese cosmology *ch'i* is not the same as consciousness. As I explain in *Radical Nature,* the ancient Chinese always coupled *ch'i* (energy) with *li* (organizing principle, or consciousness). *Ch'i* is not the same as *li,* though they always go together (just as energy is not the same as consciousness, though they always go together).

Yes, when you do *shiatsu* you probably connect with something greater than you. I would say you are connecting with *ch'i-li* (sentient energy)—not just influencing the flow of *ch'i* (energy). You are also connecting with the *li, consciousness* or *meaning,* inherent in the *ch'i* (energy). In my experience, healing has less to do with exchanges of energy (*ch'i*) and more to do with connecting through *shared meaning* (*li*).

5

A LIKELY STORY

The brain is a story. It is something to interpret. And perhaps that's the best science can hope for as it turns its beam of inquiry toward the "final frontier"—the exploration of mind or consciousness. Interpretation, not explanation, may well be the future that awaits this emerging science. *Science?* Interpretation? Isn't science a body of knowledge distinguished by its powers of *explanation*, revealing causal mechanisms, enabling us to predict and therefore control otherwise unruly and messy nature? Isn't interpretation for the other guys, those "H-guys" in hermeneutics who study meaning and language, and in the humanities, who study literature and write stories?

Well yes, MIT researcher Dan Lloyd, author of *Radiant Cool: A Novel Theory of Consciousness*, would agree with all of this. But the problem is both the brain and consciousness are themselves notoriously messy—and, Lloyd suspects, they are *necessarily* so. Messiness is best handled with the soft touch of interpretation rather than the hard hand of rigorous explanation. He makes a persuasive case for the inevitable messiness of brains and the inescapable "blooming buzzing confusion" that underlies the nature of consciousness. Brain and mind, both, are unimaginably complex systems, and it is this complexity—with built-in nested recursive loops and pathways of connection—that accounts for the awesome and mysterious properties of consciousness.

So what is Lloyd's "novel theory of consciousness"? Well, the first thing to note is that it is indeed a *novel* theory. His book is not only a study of mind and brain, it is also a novel—a story. In fact, it's really *two* books folded into one. The first part is written in the format of a murder mystery, a phenomenological thriller, replete with shady and shadowy characters and a plot that twists like a pretzel.

It's a mix that seems to work—using the power of story to deliver complex ideas with a punch. Given the runaway success of films such as *The Matrix* and its clones and the more recent *What the Bleep Do We Know?* clearly a lot of people are fascinated by the borderline between fantasy and fact, between virtual reality and the living world, between the imaginal and the real. And cognitive philosopher Lloyd takes us deep into that territory, in a way no mere movie ever can. His premise: How *could* you tell that what seems to you to be the real world is really, truly "out there," and not the production of some modern-day Dr. Frankenstein who has scooped your brain from your skull, stuck it in a vat, plugged in some wires, and connected "you" up to a computer programmed to stimulate all the right sensory input areas of your cerebrum? You would experience the world exactly the same, right?

Right. In the footsteps of eighteenth-century philosopher Immanuel Kant, Lloyd tells us that, vat or no, we *are already* living in a virtual reality—all of us. We never can know the "real" world other than through our experience. Our world—all of it—is *phenomenal*. It's what shows up on the screen of the mind. That's the *only* world we can ever know. And this inescapable fact is one of the keystones of Lloyd's novel theory of consciousness.

He bravely challenges the dry objectification of consciousness rampant in mainstream cognitive science—which, along with neuroscience, captures the lion's share of attention (and funding) in contemporary "consciousness research." In a flourish of insight, Lloyd breaks new ground by bringing together the rival disciplines of phenomenology and neuroscience. His "novel" theory is, essentially, a blending of a first-person subjective approach to objectivity (phenomenology) and a third-person objective approach to subjectivity (neuroscience and cognitive science). The result, he proposes, is an opening to a new scientific discipline called "neurophenomenology"—a discipline that folds the "soft" humanities in with "hard" science, a hermeneutics of brain and mind melded with empirical data. It's an approach to science where rigorous explanation is heavily coated with the flux and fluidity of interpretation. A beguiling mix of data and story. (Isn't this what *all* of science is, anyway?)

Add to this Lloyd's insight that the brain itself is a story, and he tackles some of the most difficult issues facing contemporary cognitive science, neuroscience, phenomenology, and philosophy of mind.

CONSCIOUSNESS AND NESTED TIME

I can see why he was drawn to write a novel because his approach to understanding consciousness, inspired by the phenomenology of Edmund Husserl (1859–1938), is rooted in the intimate relationship between consciousness and time. And this relationship has the same essential ingredients we find in any story.

Stories are the unfolding of meaning, signifying changes and connections—what happens now is shaped by what came before, building to a conclusion. In other words, stories require *memory* of what has happened, *experience* of what is happening, and *anticipation* of what is to come.

In *Radical Nature,* I presented a similar idea (inspired by the process philosophy of Alfred North Whitehead) that "matter stories"—the universe itself (including bodies and minds)—is the unfolding of a story:

Stories reveal how things came to be the way they are. They tell of beginnings, and of middles, and, if they don't always have endings, they point, and leave the way open. Stories are suggestive, rather than certain. They are lures or invitations to action. Stories enact the process of creation, whereby actualities emerge from a pool of potential. They make explicit, through becoming, the implicit fecundity of being.[1]

Stories require *memory . . . experience . . .* and *anticipation.* All this requires consciousness. Lloyd's version (using Husserl's terminology) is that "temporality is necessary for any experience at all."[2] And time—no matter how short or long the duration—is always a trinity composed of "retention" (memory), "presence" or "primal impression" (experience), and "protention" (anticipation). He says: "The temporal traces of past and future are superposed at all times in the *present* object, in the *current state* of consciousness."[3]

Lloyd beams in on the phenomenon of nested time—the notion that the present moment of experience necessarily retains its antecedent states and is oriented toward anticipated future states—as a central component in his theory of consciousness.

Drawing on the phenomenology of perception, he points out that no perceptual object is "pure"—no object of consciousness is ever perceived in a "raw" state. Instead, he says, "Objects travel with a flock of meanings attached."[4] We never just see an object—*any* object—without its surrounding cloud of associations, meanings, and interpretations: That "patch of color red" is "like blood," "oval shaped," "not green," "vivid and intense," "reminiscent of a sunset," "over there," and so on.

Many of these "additional" meanings are nonsensory, not part of the sensory input coming to us from the outside world. They "flock in" from memory, always already attached to an object. This idea of objects of experience haloed with multiple meanings is familiar to phenomenologists and a source of significant difference between their understanding of consciousness and that held by most cognitive scientists. Lloyd urges his CogSci colleagues to pay attention to their own experience and to see that the phenomenologists are right about this. Reality is more than meets the eye. So much of our experience is freighted with sensory and nonsensory components, and typically this is overlooked in cognitive science. In fact, Lloyd emphasizes, "The very basic interpretation that this world I seem to see is in fact real turns out to be non-sensory."[5]

So, what is Lloyd telling us? He's saying that both brain and mind are almost unimaginably dynamically complex—they are *messy*. But if we draw on insights gained from the first-person subjective inquiries of phenomenology and map them onto the third-person objective investigations of neuroscience we should be able to come up with a theory of consciousness that reveals its connections to the brain. In short, he's proposing, we may be able to get a great deal of information out of the messiness of brains and minds by painstakingly modeling, point-by-point, the complexity they share in common. But the results will not be neat and precise explanations of how brain events show up as specific events in consciousness. No, instead we will have to settle for some quite imprecise interpretations and narratives. Science becomes stories.

How does this help? *Does* it help us understand consciousness? Well, yes . . . and no. It helps by revealing severe limitations of cognitive-neuroscience for explaining consciousness. But it is less helpful as a way to build a bridge between brain and mind. Nevertheless, it does remind us of the messy, fluid, relationship between mind and reality. In the end, it is really a theory about epistemology, raising questions about how we know what we know.

FROM MOUNTAIN TO MOUSE

First there is a mountain. Then there is no mountain. . . . Then there's a mouse.

Lloyd bases his theory of consciousness on the phenomenological notion "there's more to reality than meets the eye." Consciousness is not populated merely by content delivered to it by the senses. No, "reality" comes to us surrounded in clouds of glorious feelings, impressions, interpretations, and associations that are themselves *nonsensory*. Most of what we know, or think we know, about the world is, at best, nothing more than a bunch of *likely stories*—attempts by the brain and mind to make sense of the blooming buzzing messiness of experience, ever-flowing in the moment-by-moment stream of nested time. This is at the core of Lloyd's "subjective view of objectivity." He says:

> What matters most is non-sensory, and among all the insensible dimensions that constitute reality, the first is experienced time. Time is co-present in every experience and in every object of experience, and it flows through everything. Every object of experience is ceaselessly unreeling its history and canceling all but one of its possibilities, and this flux is internal to the object. . . . Both history and the future are compacted into every moment of awareness. Expressing this insight folds language into paradox: temporality, it turns out, is always instantaneous. Time takes no time at all. The mountain is not a mountain at all.[6]

First there is a mountain. Lloyd begins his essay by exposing the dry skeletons that cognitive-neuroscientists present as data on consciousness. Their weakest, and in the end fatal, shortcoming results from attempts to *objectify* consciousness. Caught up in the assumptions of scientific materialism, they believe that science is in the business of *detecting* consciousness. But that's an impossible dream. Lloyd calls them "detectorheads"—folks who try to take an "objective view of subjectivity"; scientists trying to build a theory of consciousness based on the detection of stimuli from a real, external, objective world. Yes, there is a real world, Lloyd is telling us. But this is not what shows up in consciousness. What we get is reality coated in a bunch of messy stories. We never see "real objects." All we ever perceive are sense data shrouded in swirling clouds of nonsensory interpretations.

Then there is no mountain. Therefore, we need to balance the cognitive scientist's "objective view of subjectivity" with a phenomenologist's "subjective view of objectivity." We need to recognize that the only world we know is the one composed of the objects within our own experience. The so-called objective details of cognitive-neuroscience are really nothing more than stories created in consciousness—*including all our stories about the brain.* The world—the "mountain"—dissolves into mind stuff.

Then there is a mountain—sort of. Lloyd concludes by returning to the objective view of subjectivity, and looking at the contributions of a cadre of cognitive scientists working with neural nets (computer simulations of simple artificial "nervous systems"), and of neuroscientists working with brain-imaging devices (particularly data revealed in fMRI brain scans). He then compares these third-person data with the first-person insights reported from phenomenology's "subjective view of objectivity."

The convergence of these two views is his *open sesame* to the new discipline of "neurophenomenology." And, he believes, this is the direction any effective science of consciousness must follow. He wants to show us that if the kinds of complex relationships that show up in phenomenology can be correlated with comparable complexity in neural nets then, in principle, he will have demonstrated "how consciousness *could* be embodied" and, finally, "we will discover whether consciousness is *in fact* so embodied" in actual brains.[7]

He makes a valiant attempt. But his "novel theory of consciousness" is not yet "a mountain again," as he admits: "I *predict* that readers did not experience their personal click [a satisfying aha] as the book unfolded."[8]

> Both experience and the brain certainly are messy targets of explanation, and this book has conveyed no master equation nor single crystalline insight. Predictive power does lurk, however, in the data and programs undergirding the empirical discussions in the book. ... The neural nets I built constitute huge equations that explain (by immediately producing the immediate past of the brain) and

predict (by correctly reproducing the immediate future). *Aha!*

Or not aha. It's not clear whether having these equations would lead to a satisfying understanding of brain function or consciousness. They are simply too complicated to be grasped.[9]

Then there is a mouse. To fully appreciate Lloyd's "novel theory" you have to read his book. It is a labor of love; and a labor for the reader to climb the mountain only to discover that in the end all that effort produced a mere mouse. But what a mouse! He lays out the steps of his journey in fine detail, and in the process you will probably come to agree with his conclusion "that the processes of consciousness cannot be simplified beyond a certain point, and that there will be no master equation or aha insight. Consciousness and brain are messy of necessity."[10]

A SCIENTIFIC "MIRACLE"?

Dan Lloyd would like us to believe his theory of consciousness transparently shows (or at least points to) how brain events *are* mind events.

Our conscious mind is the great quaking stage of experience from first step to first kiss to last word. No place could seem less its home than that gelatinous organ known as the brain, a place of perfect darkness and bare chemical murmurs. For decades the drumbeat of philosophy, psychology, and neuroscience has insisted that mind is brain, and brain is mind. It *could* be so; it *must* be so. But *how* is it so?[11]

And, later, in the voice of a character, Miranda Sharpe:

I finally began to see what a transparent theory of consciousness might be like. You start with a brain. Instead of seeing it as a mush of skinny spazy neurons, you see it . . . as a bouncing ball in hyperspace, a really hyper hyperspace. In the space you plot a point for each different state of mind, and what you get is a kind of map of the brain. But what if, what if that map was also a map of consciousness? . . . Two in one and one for all.[12]

This is unambiguous stuff, pretty standard in fact among neuroscientists, psychologists, and philosophers of mind. It is the almost unquestioned view, even dogma, of modern science. But it hinges on a metaphysical assumption that verges on pure faith: the idea that from "dead" wholly nonconscious matter (e.g., neurons) conscious, subjective, feeling brains (or their hosts) could emerge. The common mantra of this "scientific" faith is *complexity*. Given enough complexity, "dead" unfeeling matter can spring to sentience and consciousness. It has to be faith because such an ontological jump from utter objectivity to subjectivity would require nothing short of a miracle—*and, as we have seen, miracles are precisely what this materialist worldview denies are possible.* And so the standard dogma spikes itself on an embarrassing paradox.

Lloyd's "transparent" theory of consciousness responds to the same scientific call to prayer: complexity leads to emergence, and emergence leads to mind. In his hands, the "solution" is multidimensional mapping of patterns of brain events onto patterns experienced in the phenomenology of consciousness. It's all very neat—one-to-one brain-mind mapping. And if it's achieved then the conclusion is obvious, transparent: *Mind equals brain states.*

But there's one small problem his theory of consciousness overlooks—a crucial oversight. His theory doesn't even begin to explain just how mindless neurons (or patterns of billions of them), grouped in complex neural nets could ever result in *any* kind of experience whatsoever! Just where did the phenomenology come from? Yes, we know it's there—we all experience it from moment to moment. *But how?*

It's no surprise to have a theory of consciousness that maps brain events to mind events—we'd expect that, eventually. But even if accurate and true, all it would do is show how certain patterns of brain events *correlate* with mental experiences. We may map the contents of consciousness (thoughts, feelings, desires, volitions, emotions, etc.) onto brains, but what about the raw fact of consciousness itself, the *context* for all these contents? Where did that come from?

One of the problems I had reading Lloyd's theory was trying to get clear on what he meant by "consciousness." Unfortunately, like many other cognitive scientists, psychologists, and philosophers of mind— who should know better—he conflates two very distinct and different meanings of consciousness (remember, we looked at these earlier). He flips back and forth (both in his novel and in his essay) between consciousness contrasted with the *un*conscious (a *psychological* meaning borrowed from Freud and his successors) and consciousness contrasted with *non*-consciousness (an *ontological* meaning: the utter, complete absence of any mentality, subjectivity, or interiority whatsoever). And, as we saw in chapter 2, there is a world of difference between these two meanings. Unless we get clear on this difference, we will lose ourselves in a tangle of confusions. So, as a refresher, here's the "Cliff Notes" version:

SWITCHED-ON CONSCIOUSNESS

The Forms of Consciousness. The *psychological* meaning of consciousness is like a dimmer switch. It can be turned up from dim unconsciousness to the bright lights of spiritual enlightenment. Think of the shift from being asleep to waking up (both literally and metaphorically). From this perspective, psychology and cognitive-neuroscience can tell us about different evolutionary and developmental *forms* of consciousness—for example, how minds evolve from species to species, and how individuals grow smarter from infancy to maturity (at least in some people).

The Fact of Consciousness. Philosophically, however, consciousness is like a flip switch: the light is either on or off. There's no in between. Something is either conscious (even minimally) or completely non-conscious. Think of the difference between a living, breathing, feeling creature—say a lizard sunning itself on a rock—and . . . well, a rock. Philosophy explores the *fact* that consciousness exists at all. How come? Given the logical possibility that reality could have been utterly non-conscious ("Zombie World," just as materialists believe it was before brains produced the miracle of mind), how do we account for the undeniable evidence of our own experience? How did the miracle occur? Who or what turned on the light?

Clearly, the philosophical meaning is more fundamental because it refers to the raw *context* of consciousness (as an ontological fact), which makes possible any and all *contents* of consciousness (psychological forms). After all, if you don't click the switch, it makes no difference how much you twiddle with the dimmer. Fact comes before form.

Mapping states, contents, or *forms* of consciousness (psychological meaning) onto patterns of brain events may well be valid; but it is a logical error to then conclude that such a theory tells us *anything* about the ontological *fact* of consciousness—why lumps of gelatinous matter could scintillate with any kind of consciousness at all. Showing how to turn up a light by turning a dimmer switch does not explain how the light got switched on in the first place. We need not only a science of dimmer switch consciousness but also a science of flip-switch consciousness. And *that's* another story.

In this and the previous chapter, we examined two representative theories of consciousness and have seen why neuroscience and cognitive science fail to deliver on the promise of a science of consciousness. In the next chapter, we turn our attention to what many people believe may be the last great hope to push science beyond the final frontier, and decisively launch us into the realm of consciousness—quantum physics.

Science and the
Paradox of Consciousness

Q: *In one of your other books, you say that scientists who buy into the dogma of materialism are motivated by control. That idea hadn't occurred to me. But if they believe the world is mechanical then how could they ever exercise control?*

A: You've hit the bull's eye—identifying one of the core paradoxes at the heart of the materialist vision. On the one hand, it is true that science aims for control of nature (note the terminology in scientific experiments: every worthwhile experiment should have "controls" to "control the variables"). Besides curiosity (which is also undoubtedly a motivation behind much of science), the scientific enterprise is motivated by the human desire to control the vagaries of nature (disease, weather, floods, fires, earthquakes, hurricanes, etc.) either by understanding them in ways that empower us to alter their natural courses or by helping us to develop technologies (food, habitation, travel, communications) that "shield" us from the natural dynamics of our environment. So, that's the motivation behind science . . .

However, given the worldview of materialism, which tries to explain everything as mechanistic, then there is no room for a consciously creative agent who could intervene by choice in the course of natural events. So the ideal of "control" should be utterly unattainable in a materialist world.

The central paradox and contradiction of materialism (and science) is that *absolutely no* knowledge of anything would be possible without consciousness. Yet consciousness is precisely what materialism cannot account for. In other words, from a materialist perspective, consciousness is a complete mystery. Science can provide no (zero) explanation for it. Yet all of science is utterly dependent on it!

From Fear to Faith?

Q: *The scientific world, then, must set aside its pathological attachment to control and domination. Fear must be exchanged for faith that there are other ways to live.*

A: I think this is unfair to science. "Control" and "domination" are not the same. Control is merely the exercise of *choice aimed at a goal* . . . that's not necessarily "pathological"—in fact, it's the essence of *creativity.* When control is applied to *deprive others of control*, that's "domination."

When science and technology are used to give humans control over nature *at the expense of other animals and their ecosystems,* then the destructive pathology is, unfortunately, all too evident.

Also, I don't think replacing fear with faith is likely to help. While fear is toxic, faith is impotent. Faith is "belief without evidence." It's a form of wishful thinking that distorts perception and impedes effective action just as much as fearful thinking does. Much better, I'd say, to replace fear with *trust* in natural process.

6

THE QUANTUM WONDERLAND

What's so special about quantum physics? Why, when all other forms of science have failed to get us to the holy grail of consciousness, should we suppose that the weird wonderland of the quantum could take us there? In this chapter, we will explore four ways quantum science might throw light on this most elusive of mysteries.

WHAT IS THE QUANTUM?

Let's begin by taking a close look at this pesky little critter that has revolutionized science, turning our understanding of reality into a kind of Quantum Wonderland where Alice and her friends would feel right at home.

First off, the quantum is the strangest of all physical entities. In some respects, it doesn't exist in time or space, and has no charge and no rest mass. In fact, it sounds very much like the way we might describe a ghost or spirit. As a photon, for example, it always moves at the speed of light (the fastest possible), and therefore from its point of view, time screeches to a standstill. And because it uses up no energy as it travels through space, distance is irrelevant. Strange indeed, but what is it?

Well, as far as we can tell, the quantum is the smallest bit of energy that exists—or even could exist. It is not made of anything except itself. It is indivisible; you can't cut it up into "half a quantum" or into any fractional parts. It always comes as a whole unit. No half measures. It's either here, or it isn't—except, of course, as a native of Wonderland it can be in many different places all at once. And, sometimes, none at all. Go figure.*

The quantum is often called "a packet of energy" or "an atom of energy." More accurately, it is a packet or a *unit of action*.

It was named by German physicist Max Planck more than a hundred years ago, when he discovered that energy is *always* radiated in whole bundles (the word *quantum* means "share" or "bundle"). Being the smallest, indivisible, unit of physical reality, it is the root (some would say "source") of the physical world. Somehow, this ghostly, most *un*physical entity is the basic building block of everything we see around us, including our own bodies. Everything we see is made of atoms, which in turn are made of electrons and protons, and these pop into existence whenever a ghostly

---

*For example, experiments known as "EPR" (named after three scientists who first came up with the idea: Einstein, Podolsky, and Rosen) have revealed one of the quantum's most mind-boggling facts: Two or more quanta can somehow "communicate" instantly *no matter how far apart they are*. They could be at opposite sides of the lab, or at opposite ends of the universe, it makes no difference. In other words, distance or space has no effect on what happens. The technical term for this is "nonlocality," and it has become a favorite of many new paradigm theorists and new age visionaries as a way to explain phenomena from quantum computers to "quantum healing" through prayer. Somehow—and no one has a clue—it's as if each quantum exists *everywhere* all at once!

On the other hand, sometimes it appears as if quanta can disappear from reality altogether—for example, when an electron inside an atom makes a quantum jump from one energy state to another. It's as if the quantum leaps from one "orbit" around the atomic nucleus to a different "orbit" *without passing through any intervening space!* Just try to picture *that!*

quantum gives up the ghost. The technical term for this is "pair production." Go check it out in any physics textbook. You will see that electrons and protons come into being when a quantum, in the form of a photon of light, spontaneously annihilates itself.

A UNIVERSE OF FROZEN LIGHT

It's a kind of cosmic self-sacrifice reminiscent of religious creation myths, such as the Christian "Let there be light" or the Hindu tale of *Agni*. Physical reality comes into being when light-quanta, or photons, "die" and give birth to subatomic particles that build up the atoms that make our world. Literally, everything (including you and the world around you) is made of "frozen light." But it's not a one-time creation story. No, it's happening at every moment everywhere. The universe is created continuously by the self-sacrifice of light. This may sound like spiritual metaphysics, but it's actually what we know from the most advanced, and by far the most accurate, of all the sciences—quantum physics.

Without a doubt, many people are excited by these metaphysical implications (both within science and in new age spiritual circles). Furthermore, a growing number of enthusiasts think that other strange properties of the quantum will finally provide the missing link to consciousness.

The Quantum Wonderland turns out to be a world of curious paradoxes that strain the grasp of reason and imagination, where physical things seem to "evaporate" into a dance of surreal events—a world where the deep relationship between mind and matter blurs their distinction. Without straining our own tender minds, let's take a brief tour of this Wonderland, beginning with four quantum paradoxes.

Paradox 1: Getting the Point of a Wave

Wave-particle duality. As the word itself implies, a *particle* occupies a small amount of space. A grain of sand is a good example. Or look at the period at the end of this sentence. Pretty tiny, eh? Well, compared to a quantum, that little dot is like an enormous black hole, big enough to swallow our Sun and entire solar system. You could squeeze a gazillion quanta into that tiny speck. Quantum particles, then, are infinitesimally compact bundles of energy.

A *wave,* on the other hand, is not at all like a particle. It is not compact; it spreads out over a wide region of space. Think of the ocean rolling onto a beach, coming at you in waves that stretch along the coast. Okay, now imagine you've picked up a grain of sand from the shore, and you feel this tiny speck pressed between your fingers. Next moment, that speck washes over you as a wave. Crazy. Just the kind of thing that happens in dreams. Yet experiments show that photons of light (which are forms of quanta) behave both as particles and waves.

Just so you know: one of the first experiments that revealed the nature of light was conducted by English physicist Thomas Young at the beginning of the nineteenth century. By beaming light through two slits onto a screen, he discovered it created an interference pattern with strips of brightness and darkness. This could happen only if light traveled as a *wave.* The bright patches appeared when two wave crests coincided, while the dark patches appeared when a crest and a trough canceled each other out.

For more than a hundred years, scientists believed that light traveled in waves. Understandable, really. But then came Einstein. He did a different kind of experiment by shining light onto a sensitive metal (silver bromide, the kind of emulsion that, before the days of digital cameras, was used in film). What happened was this: He noticed that when the photons of light stuck the metal, single electrons hopped out, one for each photon. Well, how could this be? If light really was a spread-out wave it should knock out a whole flock of electrons. But no, it was as if each little photon acted like a tiny pellet bumping into a tiny electron in the metal, knocking it out of place. This could happen only if the photon was a compact quantum *particle.*

It turns out that whether a quantum behaves as a particle or a wave depends on the kind of experiment performed. A quantum never behaves as both particle and wave in the same experiment. Yet it has the capacity, or nature, to be either. A quantum, therefore, is a "wavicle" (as some bright spark in physics called it). Particle and wave natures are mutually exclusive (the appearance of one automatically rules out the other). Yet *both* natures are necessary for a full accounting of the quantum. Wave and particle are, in technical jargon, *complementary*. Waves and particles are two entirely different kinds of things. Nevertheless, that's what a quantum is.

> *Paradox of complementarity:* How can something be both confined to a small space and also spread out over space? How can a quantum be both a particle and a wave?

This paradoxical complementarity of waves and particles was one of the first clues that something very strange is going on in the Quantum Wonderland. But it gets worse—much worse.

Paradox 2: Beating the Quantum Speed Trap

Uncertainty and Indeterminacy. You've won the lottery, and with your newfound wealth you decide to buy the latest Quantum Coupe, the most advanced and fastest sports car ever designed. Out on a test run, you clock 205 mph, in a 65 zone. Unfortunately, so does a lurking speed cop. His laser detector snaps you as you whiz past. But you're not at all worried when you show up in court to plead your case. First thing the judge asks the cop is "Precisely, how fast was the defendant traveling?"

Smug and sure of himself, the cop flips open his notebook and, in his best officereez, replies: "Your honor, he was moving at a rate of speed of two-hundred-five miles per hour in a sixty-five miles per hour zone."

"Serious violation, indeed," the judge murmurs. And then asks the traffic cop the next question: "Now, where exactly did this offence occur?"

The policeman hesitates as he consults his notebook. "Eh, your honor, I can't tell you *exactly* where it happened, but I can tell you the probable location."

"Well that just won't do," the judge snorts. "If you can't identify the exact location, then how can you be sure it was a 65 mph zone? Was he or was he not speeding where you say you saw him?"

The cop flips through his pages again to confirm the location. "Well, yes, your honor, he was at the intersection of Highways 1 and 92."

"And you are certain of his speed?" the judge asks just to be sure.

"Uh . . . eh," the cop stammers, "um, now that you ask, your honor, I can't say precisely what his speed was at said location. But I can say it was probably more than 65 mph."

"This won't do at all," the judge snaps back, impatiently slapping the bench. "Well then, if you can't give me both the precise location and the exact speed of the defendant's vehicle, don't waste the court's time. Case dismissed."

As you roar off into the sunset in your shining Quantum Coupe, you smile to yourself thankful for the strange nature of quantum reality.

You've just been saved by the paradox of *uncertainty*. You see, quantum theory tells us, and experiments confirm, that it is impossible to measure precisely *both* the position and momentum of a quantum "particle" at the same time. The more precise our knowledge of one, the less precise our knowledge is of the other. In other words, we can never have certain knowledge of both where a particle is located and how fast it is moving. We can never precisely predict when or where a quantum event will happen.

All quantum events have a degree of *intrinsic uncertainty*. If you've ever wondered what Heisenberg's Uncertainty Principle referred to, this is it. Heisenberg, one of the founding fathers of quantum physics, showed that quantum uncertainty is not just a matter of human ignorance, which could be removed with better instruments and sharper observation. No, the uncertainty is not in our minds, it is built into the very fabric of quantum reality itself. Not only are position and momentum uncertain in this way, we can never know what *causes* quantum events to happen. In fact, one of the strangest aspects of quantum happenings is that they are *uncaused,* and therefore are inherently and inevitably unpredictable. Guess what? *Reality is fundamentally fuzzy.*

> *Paradox of uncertainty:* How can reality function and be stable when it is riddled with deep, intrinsic uncertainty? How can something happen without a specific and precise cause?

One clue to this mystery lies in the fact that instead of the universe being made up of definite little bits, it turns out it consists of complex networks of *probabilities.* Think of it this way: At bottom, reality doesn't so much exist as *tends to exist.* The actual world we live in is embedded in and surrounded by swirling clouds of probabilities.

While knowing that actual reality floats on a sea of possibilities may help us better understand the intrinsic uncertain nature of the physical world, it does so by presenting us with an even deeper mystery. How, we may wonder, does actual reality emerge from a flux of indeterminate potentials? The answer, it turns out, depends on *consciousness.* And this, more than complementarity or intrinsic uncertainty, is what has people excited by quantum physics. Let's take look, then, at the third of our four paradoxes.

Paradox 3: Consciousness Cocreates Reality

Participant-Observer. Before anything ever happens, reality exists as waves of nothing happening. This "nothing," however, is not really *nothing.* It means, rather, "not an *actual* thing;" it is a "field of possibilities." Quantum theory describes reality as a field of superimposed "probability waves," where multiple possibilities and their opposites can coexist at the same time.

Reality, then, exists as a set of probabilities, each of which has a different *tendency* to exist. And these tendencies, or probabilities, exist simultaneously, snuggled up inside a quantum wave. Think of a "Quantum Dog Pound" full of caged canines breathlessly eager and waiting to be adopted. Some dogs are more likely candidates for adoption than others. And until some interested person comes in from outside to rescue the dog, it remains caged.

That's kind of what the quantum world is like. It exists as a set of "caged" possibilities (technically, as a field of probability waves expressed mathematically as Schrödinger wave equations or "wave functions"). Like the dogs in the pound, all these probabilities exist together, each one ready to jump into actuality as soon as some interested observer comes along. But only one probability will "pop out" with each observation.

One of the most startling puzzles in quantum physics was the discovery that in order for an *actual* event (a particle) to emerge from the field of superimposed *probabilities,* the quantum system has to be *observed.* Then, and only then, does the Schrödinger wave "collapse" from multiple possibilities to a single actual event. It's as if the observer somehow reaches into the Quantum Wonderland and plucks out a single actual event—such as an electron or some other subatomic particle. These event-particles form the building blocks of atoms throughout the universe.

Since multiple possibilities exist simultaneously, it means that opposite and even contradictory probabilities can coexist in a state of "both/and." Only when an observation is made, do quantum probabilities collapse into actual "either/or" events that compose the physical world.

Do you get what's going on here? It really is a staggering revelation. In a nutshell, what this means is that the leap from possibility to actuality, from unmanifest potential to manifest actuality, happens only if someone is present to observe the quantum event. Quite simply: no observer, no quantum event—and, therefore, no physical world.

Now, the notion of "observer" necessarily implies a *conscious* observer, because an observer without consciousness could not observe anything. An observation happens only when someone is present to *experience* what is perceived. The logic is quite inescapable: The collapse of the wave function requires an observer; therefore, *consciousness participates in creating the physical world*. Without consciousness to observe the field of possibilities, probabilities would never collapse into actual events. Bottom line: *No consciousness, no physical world.**

By the way, in case you hadn't noticed, this scenario says nothing special about *human* observers or *human* consciousness. It just requires *any* consciousness. And since the universe has been around for billions of years before any humans came along, the logical conclusion is that *some other nonhuman consciousness* had to be observing the field of possibilities all throughout cosmic and biological evolution.

If we wanted a good scientific reason to take panpsychism seriously, quantum physics is it.

The inescapable conclusion is that consciousness has *always* been present in the universe, otherwise nothing actual would have ever happened, and evolution could not have taken place to produce human scientists who conduct quantum experiments. *Consciousness all the way down, and all the way back:* It seems so; it has to be so.

As you can imagine, this is a major challenge to the dominant paradigm of scientific materialism. Until quantum physics came along, scientists could merrily go on believing that "somehow" the physical brain creates consciousness. But now, the most accurate and precise science of all time is telling us that, in fact, in some deeply mysterious way, *consciousness creates reality*—or at least participates in creating the physical world (and that includes, of course, the brains of every scientist!).

Paradox of consciousness: How is it possible that consciousness participates in creating physical reality, when it is assumed that physical complexity creates consciousness?

---

*Why this revolutionary discovery isn't blasted as headline news on TVs, radios, and newspapers around the world is itself a mystery. Yes, I know, the science is super complicated, but the discovery that consciousness participates in creating reality is Big News: "Mind Makes Matter." Imagine a Reality TV show with quantum physicists and philosophers racing to come up with an explanation for this topsy-turvy revelation.

The unavoidable intrusion of the observer into quantum physics has, for the first time in four hundred years, forced scientists to take consciousness seriously. This is a harbinger of a revolution the likes of which science has not yet seen. Nevertheless, it is not the only paradigm-shattering discovery coming out of the Quantum Wonderland.

Paradox 4: Spinning in Their Graves

Nonlocality. Perhaps the greatest challenge to normal science's understanding of physical reality is the phenomenon known as *nonlocality*.

Here's the problem: In the early days of the quantum revolution, two of the greatest minds of that time, Albert Einstein and Niels Bohr, got into an argument about the nature of quantum reality. The dispute raged on for years, like a metaphysical ping-pong match. In a nutshell, Bohr claimed that whenever two or more particles (e.g., electrons or photons) were part of the same quantum system they would *always* be connected—no matter how far apart they were in space. Einstein could not accept this because it violated one of the key tenets of his relativity theory: Nothing could travel faster than light.

Einstein, the senior of the two, was repeatedly disconcerted by the ingenious responses Bohr kept coming up with. Determined to win the argument once and for all, the great Einstein spent a few sleepless nights figuring out a slam-dunk retort. He had been working with a couple of colleagues, Boris Podolsky and Nathan Rosen, and together they devised a clever thought experiment, now known as "EPR" (after the three men).

Their approach was to present Bohr with a *reductio ad absurdum*— reducing his idea to absurdity. Einstein started off by picking a well-accepted phenomenon in quantum theory: When two or more particles (e.g., photons or electrons) belong to the same quantum system, physical characteristics such as charge or spin balance each other. For instance, say one is positive, the other would be negative, or if one spins left, the other would spin right. Both Einstein and Bohr agreed on this much.

Given this, Einstein said, in effect: "Niels, suppose you have a couple of photons bundled into the same quantum system, and you shoot them off in opposite directions. Then, after sufficient time has elapsed, you change the spin on photon-A. Now, according to your theory, the very instant photon-A is changed, photon-B will change its spin too, in just the right amount to balance out the two spins.

"But now suppose the two photons are so far apart that when you change the spin on A there would not be enough time for any energy or signal to pass from A to B. Clearly, then, B would not, indeed *could not,* change in response to A." Albert was sure this was checkmate.

Here's why: The speed of light is finite, traveling 186,000 miles per second. Because, according to relativity theory, nothing can travel faster than light, this is the upper limit for any energy or information to travel. In the EPR experiment Einstein proposed, if the spin on Photon-A was changed and then if an observation of Photon-B was made *before any energy or signal could travel from A to B,* B could not possibly show any change to balance the change in A. This was EPR's QED, as far as Einstein was concerned.

But Bohr disagreed. Despite the success of relativity theory, he continued to insist that *B would change instantly* in response to the change at A. Einstein was furious, because he was sure he had shown the absurdity in Bohr's position. Yet Bohr would not yield. He was convinced that the quantum domain indeed did harbor this logic-breaking power. For his part, Einstein would not yield, either.

Both men died believing they were right and the other wrong.

In the early 1960s, an Irish mathematician, John Bell, worked out the mathematics behind the EPR experiment, and proved in theory that Bohr was right and the great Einstein was wrong. Then in the mid-1980s, a French physicist, Alain Aspect, performed the actual experiment and again his results agreed with Bohr. The experiment has been repeated many times since, and each time, the results come in the same—a win for Bohr, a loss for Einstein.

So what does all of this mean (besides the fact that scientific geniuses can disagree and be wrong)? Well, it means that the nature of physical reality is profoundly different from what common sense or Newtonian physics would lead us to believe.

As the results came in—that Photon B *does* respond to changes in Photon A, even though there is no possibility of any signal passing between them—the physics community was faced with two options: Either Einstein's relativity theory is wrong and information can travel faster than light, or . . . But they were, and remain, deeply reluctant to throw out relativity theory because it has been so successful (it gets rockets and astronauts into space and back, for instance).

That leaves the second option: *nonlocality.* Somehow, the Quantum Wonderland is *one single, unified, and interconnected system,* where space and distance are irrelevant.

In other words, whenever two particles belong to the same quantum system they *always* remain part of the same system, no matter the distance between them. Even if no energy or signal can travel from one to the other in the time available, nevertheless Photon B *somehow* "knows" what has happened at Photon A, and changes its behavior accordingly. This means that even if separated by billions of light years, both quantum partners continue to act as if there is no space separating them. This is downright bizarre. How on Earth (or anywhere else) could B "know" what happened at A billions of light years away? Even telepathy seems to require some transmission of information, but, according to relativity theory, that is ruled out in this case.

Bizarre or not, the physics community has come to accept the fact of quantum nonlocality.

I often like to round off this story with a little fantasy: I picture Einstein turning in his grave at the news that experiments have confirmed nonlocality. And, then, instantly, Bohr turns over in his grave—of course, in a complementary direction. Even in death, the two men remain connected.

Paradox of nonlocality: How could two quantum particles be connected to each other when there is no possible way for them to be connected?

But there's more. Ironically, we now know as a result of the EPR experiment that quantum nonlocality is a fact; that if two or more particles ever belonged to the same quantum system they always remain connected no matter how spread out in space they might be. Quantum nonlocality means quantum interconnectedness.

Now, fold this knowledge into what we know from Einstein's General Relativity Theory about the universe as a whole—how it began in a mighty big bang, and how it has been expanding ever since. If it is expanding, that means the matter of the universe will be more spread out in the future. But if that's the case, it also means that it must have been *less* spread out in the past.

Okay, so hit the cosmic rewind button, and the further back in time we go, the more densely packed the universe becomes. Wind it back to a moment or two before the big bang, and lo! The entire universe of matter and energy is squashed into a tiny region of space about the size of a proton—a unified quantum system.

Get it? Once part of a quantum system, *always* part of the same quantum system. That means the *entire universe,* no matter how far it expands, remains part of the *one quantum system.* And, thanks to Einstein and his EPR experiment, we now know that the elements of a quantum are always and forever interconnected. The entire universe is connected nonlocally! *Everything is connected to everything else—always.* At the quantum level, every part of the universe "knows" instantly what every other part of the universe is up to.

Now *that* is something for science to chew on. Couple the paradox of nonlocality with the paradox of consciousness, and the whole ball game of science is about to explode. Not only is reality not what it seems to be, or even stranger than we imagine. It is almost a slam-dunk certainty that it is stranger than we *can* imagine, and in ways that sound very much like what is hinted at in the wisdom handed down to us through the ages via the world's great spiritual traditions.

But before we get too excited by the prospect of quantum physics providing the scientific key to consciousness, we would be wise to remember that, despite the role of the participant-observer in the collapse of the wave function, quantum physics, by definition, is about the *physical* world. It is not called "quantum *mechanics*" for nothing. How could an objective science, focused on physical objects, ever inform us about *nonphysical,* subjective consciousness?

More work needs to be done. In the next chapter we will look at four approaches to understanding the quantum-consciousness connection.

Quantum Possibilities:
"Anything Goes"?

Q: The main message I took away from the movie What the Bleep Do We Know? *is that, through consciousness, we create our own reality. It showed how the quantum has limitless possibilities and that physics now tells us "anything and everything is possible." We just have to believe it. Would you agree?*

A: This is a common mistake made by many folks in the New Age based on a "pop" understanding of quantum physics. It is *not* the case that the probabilities expressed in the quantum wave function are "limitless" or represent "unlimited potential." The matrix of probabilities expressed in the mathematics of wave mechanics is a *limited* set of options, and the collapse of the wave function on observation brings *one* of those options into actuality. This is a far cry from concluding either that consciousness has an "unlimited" set of potentials to work with, or, more forcefully, that it is *belief* that brings about the matrix collapse.

Quantum theory says nothing about "belief"; it refers to *observation.* And it would take a great stretch of imagination to equate "observation" with "belief." No doubt, observation is colored by whatever beliefs the observer holds. Even so, quantum physics does not support the conclusion that "anything and everything is possible." That's a serious mischaracterization and misunderstanding of quantum physics.

Nevertheless, what quantum science *does* reveal is the potency of consciousness to participate in the physical world and make things happen. That, as Oprah Winfrey would say, is "huge."

QUANTUM CONSCIOUSNESS

Who among us has a direct hotline to ultimate reality? Physicists? Mystics? Who's in touch with the real deal? Well, sometimes, it does sound as though both physicists and mystics have burrowed down (or up) to reality's bottom line. And at times it does seem as though the findings of quantum physics confirm what spiritual visionaries have been telling us for millennia.

Transpersonal theorist Ken Wilber is highly skeptical and critical of any attempt to use the findings of quantum physics to support the claims of mystics. As editor of an anthology, *Quantum Questions,* he quotes long passages from many of the great founding fathers of quantum physics—many of whom also had profound spiritual sympathies and insights—and who, to a man, unequivocally rejected the notion that their science reveals anything about spiritual reality.

In an intelligent and perceptive introduction, Wilber makes a challenging, and counterintuitive, observation: Despite all the hoopla surrounding so-called parallels between quantum physics and mysticism, nothing could be further from the truth. In fact, he says, Newtonian physics is arguably much closer to the claims of the mystics. Now that should get your attention—after all, the world of Newtonian mechanics could hardly be any further from the world described by spiritual sages.

But Wilber presents a persuasive case. He points out that without exception, the founders of quantum theory—including Werner Heisenberg, Ervin Schrödinger, Albert Einstein, Count de Broglie, James Jeans, Max Planck, Wolfgang Pauli, and Sir Arthur Eddington—were clear that their science is not about *reality per se*—it is, essentially, a set of mathematical *descriptions* about observations. Heisenberg said, "What we observe is not nature itself, but nature exposed to our method of questioning." And Niels Bohr said, "It is wrong to think that the task of physics is to find out how nature is. Physics concerns what we say about nature."

The quantum masters, then, had no illusions about meetings or parallels between physics and mysticism. They were well aware their science was at least one remove from reality. Contrast this with what the great mystics tell us. East or West, they claim enlightenment results from *direct access or union* with the ultimate divine nature of reality itself. This is radically different from the claims of the quantum physicists.

Wilber goes on to point out that, unlike quantum physicists, old-paradigm Newtonian physicists were under the impression that they were, in fact, exploring nature directly. This Newtonian claim, then, is far closer to the claims made by mystics, than anything coming from the founders of quantum physics. Of course, we now know that the old physicists were mistaken, they no more had a hotline to reality than quantum physicists do. All physics is about what we can *say* (mostly through mathematical equations) about reality. Physics is not about reality per se.

Keeping this caution in mind, we should proceed carefully with attempts to find a key to consciousness in the equations of modern physics. It probably isn't there. Nevertheless, *something* is going on in physics that at least *seems* like it is discovering *something* about the physical world that *seems* to echo the visionary teachings of mystics. So what is going on?

In the rest of this chapter, we will explore four possibilities that might encourage us to continue to look to quantum physics as a source of inspiration in our search for the Holy Grail of consciousness. We'll begin with a current favorite in scientific circles: the notion that quantum mechanics will help *explain* consciousness. After all, nothing in science turns out to behave so utterly unlike matter as we know it as the weird antics of the quantum.

Possibility 1: Quantum as Mechanism for Consciousness

Why don't you fall through your chair? You are sitting there reading this book, and what you are about to learn is that the chair you are sitting on is *mostly empty space.* (Of course, this is equally true of the book in your hands, your hands themselves, and the rest of your body, too, for that matter.)

One of the most intriguing discoveries of quantum science is what it reveals about matter. This apparently solid stuff turns out not to be so solid after all. In fact, the atoms that matter is made of are 99 percent *nothingness.* So why don't you fall through your chair? Well, to explain that would take us take us too far afield.* The point is that under the gaze of physicists, matter has evaporated into an insubstantial haze of swirling energies pushing and pulling this way and that.

---

*Okay, since you really want to know, here's the scoop: Briefly, it all has to do with the structure of atoms. Picture an atom as a kind of tiny solar system, where instead of the sun at the center, we find an atomic nucleus with protons and neutrons. Orbiting the nucleus in concentric shells are tiny electrons. The nucleus has a positive electromagnetic charge, and the electrons have a negative charge. In a stable atom, the charges all balance each other. But in every case, the outer shell of the atom has one or multiple electrons whizzing about.

Now, as you know from playing with magnets as a kid, if you push two positive or negative poles together they repel each other. It's the same with the charges on atoms. Negative electrons spinning in the outer shells of neighboring atoms repel each other. Your chair and your rump are made of atoms, and the electrons in both push back on each other. And that's why you don't fall through your chair.

And in case you are thinking of electrons and protons as little pellets of matter, they're not. Like all subatomic "particles," they are really just bundles of energy, knots that come and go in force fields permeating the universe. Matter, it turns out, is vastly empty space with a few infinitesimal fuzzy blobs of energy whizzing about. You, your chair, and everything around you, consist of nothing more than a bunch of *knots in nothingness*. Bet that works wonders for your self-esteem.

Matter, at its deepest levels, is far more like a ghost than granite. And, for some people, this "ghostly" insubstantiality makes matter seem more and more like what they imagine mind to be. In fact, Sir James Jeans, one of the great physicists mentioned above, famously announced: "The universe begins to look more like a great thought than a great machine." No surprise, then, that recently a great deal of attention has focused on tiny structures called *microtubules* found in cells, including the brain's neurons. Perhaps these quantum-size cellular skeletons hold the key to consciousness?

At the University of Arizona, Stuart Hameroff, an anesthesiologist, discovered that when he put patients to sleep interesting things happened in their brain microtubules. Depending on what the cell was doing, its microtubules grew or shrunk, and sometimes formed highly ordered patterns. Hameroff noticed that when they lined up one way, people were conscious, and when they lost this order, people became unconscious. Ah!, thought Hameroff, could this be the clue we've been searching for?

To cut a long story very short, the ordered/disordered arrangement of microtubules in brain cells that Hameroff saw involve what is known as "quantum coherence." He came to suspect that this might provide a clue to distinctive properties of consciousness, such as the fact that (except in rare cases) each one of us experiences ourselves as having just *one* mind.

In a flurry of lyrical insight, Hameroff defined consciousness as *"an emergent macroscopic quantum state driven or selected by neurobiological mechanisms . . . with origins in quantum coherence in cytoskeletal microtubules within the brain's neurons.*"[1] I'm not kidding, that's what he said.

Well, to translate, he's saying that consciousness *emerges* in brain cells when their microtubules line up in "quantum coherence." And what on Earth is "quantum coherence"? In simple terms, it refers to elements in a quantum system forming exquisite orderly arrangements, and when that happens the entire system acts as a single, coherent unit.

Think of it this way: You and a bunch of friends decide to go to a movie, but you have money only for two tickets. So, being hip to the secrets of quantum physics, you line up your friends, get them all facing the same way, standing in identical postures. As long as they remain that way, they act in concert. In fact, they become your one and only "quantum buddy." You march them up to the window, buy two tickets, and you're in.

Quantum coherence is like that: It makes a bunch of brain cells behave as one single cell, so each part of the brain knows what's going on in the other cells. Remember nonlocality? Well, that's what's happening. In quantum coherence, the distance between brain cells makes no difference. Each one is not just connected to the others—in a very strange, quantum, way, they *are* just one cell.

Could Hameroff be onto something?

Along with Nobel laureate Francis Crick and colleague Cristof Koch, he proposed that coherent patterning of microtubules inside the brain's neurons is the physical basis of consciousness. They believe this theory could solve the infamous "binding problem" that has bedeviled brain science for so long: How can multiple brain-wide activities (in innumerable neurons and synapses) result in a "singular perceptual entity"—namely the experience of a unified consciousness or "self"?

Answer: nonlocal quantum coherence, of course! When this happens to microtubules in the brain's neurons it produces quantum interconnectedness among multiple brain events, and so we experience a "unitary sense of self." It's as if large areas of the brain not only dance to the same tune, but become a single dancer. And this single brain-dancer dancing is what we experience as unified consciousness.

But wait a minute. Are they saying that a bunch of physical processes in microtubules squirts out mind? Yes, that's precisely what they are saying: Consciousness *emerges* from otherwise mindless brain cells. How can that be? How can a collection of objective, physical events produce something that is subjective and nonphysical, which consciousness clearly is? Even with quantum coherence and nonlocality, the best we could hope for is that all those physical brain events could act in concert as a single integrated *physical* brain event. We still don't get consciousness.

The only way consciousness could "emerge" from the coherence of quantum microtubules is if those little critters *already* possessed at least some form or degree of consciousness. Otherwise, no go. You don't get something from nothing. You don't get subjective experience from wholly objective physical events. Granite can't make ghosts.

No amount of mechanistic explanation—even from quantum mechanics—will ever shape up into a key to unlock the mystery of consciousness.

To his credit, Hameroff did wake up to this problem, and now, at least sometimes, he tilts in the direction of panexperientialism (really just another fancy word for panpsychism).

Although impressed by the *scientific* evidence for quantum coherence, and thinking it might suggest a physical basis for consciousness, Hameroff sensed the *philosophical* difficulty involved. He realized that quantum coherence could not explain how consciousness "emerges" from events that in themselves are nonconscious. As a result, he has suggested that quantum reality is "funda-mentally" dual natured or has a double aspect—it is simultaneously *both* physical and mental, all the way down. Rather than the orderly behavior of microtubules producing consciousness, as Hameroff first supposed, he now realizes that some degree of sentience must already tingle within every microtubule.

Thus consciousness (or "mentality") is not *generated* by purely physical quantum coherence, but—being "fundamental"—could actually play a role in *directing* the behavior of microtubules. Hameroff has not yet gone this far.

Possibility 2: Quantum as Metaphor for Consciousness

Instead of turning to quantum physics as a way to *explain* consciousness, other authors—such as Ronald Valle, inspired by the ideas of psychologist Carl Jung and physicist Wolfgang Pauli*—have taken a different approach. They turn to quantum physics as a source of potentially useful *metaphors* for understanding consciousness. Indeed, it seems that the paradoxes of the quantum domain do suggest intriguing analogs, if not correlations, between certain characteristics of consciousness and the quantum.

For example, drawing on insights inspired by quantum *complementarity*, Valle compared the wave-like nature of the stream of consciousness to the wave-nature of quantum events. Specific thoughts and actions, he said, could be compared to the particle-nature of quanta. Furthermore, consciousness is not restricted to "either/or" alternatives. Quite often, breakthroughs come about by adopting a "both/and" perspective. A willingness and ability to hold apparently contradictory sides of an issue can lead to insights that transcend the usual limitations of our categorizing minds.

In *Metaphors of Consciousness,* Valle also compared the volitional capacity of consciousness to the indeterminate "probability waves" of

---

*Jung and Pauli collaborated on a landmark book, *Synchronicity: An A-Causal Connecting Principle,* which combined Jung's psychological insights on synchronicity with Pauli's mastery of quantum physics. They likened synchronicities to the indeterminism of the quantum, and to the mind-matter relationship of the observer's consciousness involved in the "collapse of the wave function." Jung and Pauli also compared the nonspatial nature of psychic archetypes to the nonlocality of quantum events.

quantum theory—the metaphor of *indeterminacy*. Volition or choice overrides physical determinism. As we saw in chapter 3, choice is an act of creation that supersedes the mechanism of matter. Because choice is indeterminate, we can never know in advance precisely what we will choose (if we did, it would not be choice because it would have been determined by some prior knowledge or commitment). Nevertheless, while undetermined itself, choice is the source of creative causality in our lives. It is "first-cause." Choice is the injection of order into randomness.

The metaphor of *uncertainty* has its counterpart in consciousness, too. Like the quantum, consciousness cannot be measured or "pinned down" with precision. Many psychospiritual traditions advise us to let go of attachment to beliefs, and instead cultivate an attitude of humility, not-knowing, or beginner's mind, as advocated in Taoist and Zen teachings.

The metaphor of *nonlocality* and interconnectedness also reminds us of characteristics of consciousness. Like the quantum, consciousness cannot be divided up into separate parts or localized in space. Many recent authors have written about the "nonlocality" of consciousness; elsewhere, I have suggested that a better term to apply to consciousness is "nonlocated."

And, finally, we have the metaphor of *participant-observer:* More than any other area of study, consciousness research necessarily requires the "observer" to participate in the system being investigated. We will return to this in more detail in chapter 9.

Possibility 3: Beyond the Quantum—Implicate Order

While Hameroff views the quantum as the fundamental substrate of both consciousness and material bodies, other theorists—such as David Bohm and Carl Jung—see quantum phenomena pointing to a reality even deeper than the quantum. This deeper reality is rich with underlying causal order that shapes the patterns of mind and of matter, and the patterns that connect them both together.

Bohm's Implicate Order. Standard quantum theory describes the quantum as intrinsically indeterminate, random, uncaused. David Bohm, however, proposed that below, or behind, the quantum lies an even deeper reality—he called it the *implicate order.* It surrounds and interpenetrates quantum events and "guides" or causes the apparently random quantum processes to unfold as they do.

According to Bohm, the implicate order is "enfolded" in explicate, or manifest, reality detectable at the quantum level and at the macroscopic level of everyday experiences.

Jung's Psychoid Archetypes. Like Bohm, Carl Jung proposed that below the conscious mind lies the unconscious psyche and that below causal matter lies the realm of indeterminate quantum events. Deeper still, below both the level of unconscious psyche and quantum events, lies the realm of transpersonal a-causal *archetypes.*

Jung called it the *unus mundus,* an indivisible continuum of psychoid events ("psychoid" means possessing the nature of both psyche and matter). The archetypes can never be known directly; they can only be inferred from their effects on the conscious psyche (e.g., in dreams via the unconscious) and on material objects (e.g., patterning of physical processes via quantum events).

Whereas Hameroff straddles a shifting line between materialism and panpsychism—verging on reducing consciousness to quantum physics—Bohm's position is a form of "neutral monism," and Jung's is "neutral pluralism." For Bohm and Jung, then, some kind of teleological ordering principle (consciousness) runs deeper than the quantum—and this position nudges them over toward the idealist camp.

Possibility 4: Consciousness and Quantum Idealism

In contrast, physicist Amit Goswami, author of *The Self-Aware Universe,* sits squarely and unambiguously in the idealist camp. He is distinctive as a physicist because he has proposed a radical departure for quantum theory—taking consciousness as the primary, all-encompassing reality.

For Goswami, there is no question of "quantum reductionism"— where consciousness is somehow generated by or emerges from quantum processes. On the contrary, quantum events and processes (e.g., superposition of probabilities) are created by consciousness. Consciousness, he says, generates the "tangled hierarchy" of quantum probabilities by a creative act of self-reflection.

According to Goswami, the advent of quantum physics has, for the first time in four hundred years, shifted science in the direction of perennial idealist philosophy, where *consciousness is the ground of being*. He points out that the shift happened when quantum physicists realized that consciousness must be factored into their equations to account for the collapse of the Schrödinger wave function. In other words, *somehow* consciousness is causal—it makes things happen.

Picking up on this, Goswami pushed the logic of the mysterious "somehow" further and concluded that not only does consciousness make things happen in the physical world, it *makes* the physical world. Consciousness creates reality. Period.

Now a true dialogue can open up, he says, not only between the perennial philosophy (which recognizes the reality and primacy of spirit) and quantum physics, but with all the sciences. Goswami flips things over: Instead of looking for "consciousness within science," he talks of "science within consciousness." Making this flip, he claims, paves the way for an "idealist science" that not only solves the paradoxes of quantum physics, but also solves mysteries in other sciences, such as cosmology, evolutionary biology, psychology, neuroscience, and, of course, consciousness studies.

One of the greatest challenges facing "idealist science," however, is to explain the facts of cosmic and biological evolution without getting trapped in some sticky paradoxes of its own. Goswami proposes a truly radical, even mind-boggling, theory. The details are complex, involving some arcane quantum physics, but the gist of his theory is easy enough to grasp: There was a time when there was no time. A time before time and space. During this timeless, eternal moment, Spirit or Pure Consciousness reigned supreme (and, for all we know, probably still does). Everything that was, is, or will be existed in that timeless time in a state of pure potential. In reality, nothing *actual* existed yet. Just unmanifest pure potential and possibility.

Now, being a highly creative intelligence, Primary Consciousness had an impressive trick up its unmanifest sleeve. Without actually creating anything real, *just yet,* it planned out all the details of cosmic and terrestrial evolution in the privacy of its own unmanifest mind—including all the weird and wonderful shenanigans of quantum events. Then, for some reason known only to itself, it decided to turn its awareness back on itself. And whammo! That's when all the fun got going. Instantly, out of nowhere and nowhen, self-reflexive awareness did its creative quantum dance and brought into being the first living cell. At that very moment, all of the wondrous, intricate details of quantum physics, chemistry, geology, biology—*all of evolution*—came tumbling out of the infinite void of unmanifestation into manifestation. *Consciousness created reality.* And here we are! Four billion years later after that first living cell.

This is impressive stuff.

According to Goswami's model, then, nothing ever happened until the emergence of self-reflective consciousness. In other words, for fourteen billion years (indeed, for a prior eternity), the universe was in a kind of "suspended animation," hanging out as nothing more than quantum probability states. Only with the evolution of the first living cell (which, he says, is where self-reflective consciousness first arose), did the universe "collapse" out of a state of quantum probabilities into our *actual* universe of galaxies and stars and planets and living organisms.

But hold on just a minute. *How did that first living cell evolve?* If there wasn't a world yet in existence for evolution to occur, how on Earth (literally) did the first cell come into being? If planets and life didn't come into being till the first living cell, don't we have a little problem here? If nothing actually existed before the first cell, then, logic tells us, there was nothing to evolve.

Undaunted by this mother-of-all paradoxes, Goswami says "no problem." The entire fourteen billion years of cosmic, chemical, and biological evolution had *already happened* in potentia, just waiting to pop into being. At the very moment life appeared . . . *wham!* . . . the whole shebang came busting out in clouds of glory, trailing with it all of its own cosmic and terrestrial evolutionary history—fourteen billion years worth! Goswami's solution boggles the imagination. He wants us to believe that *all of reality*—the *entire history of the cosmos*—came into being *fully formed* at that same instant when the first cell appeared! Understandably, many scientists and philosophers find that a bit much to swallow.

For one thing, it really doesn't untangle the paradox. What happened to cause that momentous and fateful first collapse of quantum probabilities to produce the first actual living cell? As Goswami tells it, behind the scenes, in the domain of "quantum potential," consciousness was busy dreaming up all the fine details of the big bang, the formation of galaxies and solar systems, and then, at one point it hit on the bright idea of focusing awareness back on itself. At that very instant of initial self-reflection, which happened to coincide with the idea of the first living cell, Cosmic Consciousness collapsed *everything* into being.

From an idealist viewpoint it may sound plausible, but it doesn't get us out of the fix. Goswami's solution relies on the notion of evolution happening in *potentia*. But one of the central tenets of idealist ontology is that Cosmic Consciousness (or Spirit) transcends time and space. Furthermore, according to quantum-relativistic cosmology, before the big bang neither time nor space existed. Therefore, before the "cosmic collapse" that Goswami proposes for the origin of the actual universe, there wasn't any time. And without time, there couldn't be evolution; there couldn't be any "happening" including the act of self-reflection that is supposed to have created the first cell. The idea of evolution "happening" in timeless *potentia* is a contradiction in terms. The only way out would be for idealists to claim that Spirit exists in the world of time—but the timelessness of Spirit is one of the key tenets of idealist ideology.

Goswami's idealist cosmology seems to self-implode like a reverse big bang—or, like a snake swallowing its own tail, spins off into thin air.

Or, perhaps not. . . . What if timeless Spirit is able to create time? Would this work? And, if so, how did it do it? Enter the spiritual-quantum cosmology of Arthur Young.

LIGHT, ACTION, SPIRIT

In *The Reflexive Universe* renegade mathematician-cosmologist Arthur Young tells us that from the moment physics discovered the photon, the unit of light and the creator of electrons and protons, science had confirmed the age-old mystical insight that light (equated with spirit) is the source of the entire manifest world. On this, both science and mysticism agree. The sixty-four-billion-dollar question is whether science and spirituality are talking about the same "light." Young says they are.

The photon, according to Young, is the most mysterious entity in physics (as we saw, it doesn't have any mass or charge, and, because it travels at the speed of light, it transcends space and time). In short, the photon seems to transcend all of the qualities that make anything *physical*. Yet, paradoxically, it is, according to his theory, the fundamental unit of all physical reality. Somehow, something so apparently nonphysical creates physical reality. Light, the photon, is truly mysterious.

Unlike other entities studied in physics, the photon cannot be observed twice. Its observation is its annihilation. Light is peculiar because it is the *condition for all other observations*. In fact, observation of a photon is light observing itself (which accounts for its annihilation or self-absorption).

Young attempts to penetrate that mystery by drawing on discoveries and insights of modern science (as it was understood in the 1970s) and integrate them with perennial insights from the world's spiritual traditions, as well as other sources of knowledge such as mythology, mathematics, topology, and art. Along the way he reveals some tantalizing and intriguing correspondences.

Not only aware that the photon is a quantum (a quantum of action, to be precise), Young took a bold—and controversial—step by *equating* photon and quantum. It is controversial because, in physics, while all photons are quanta, not all quanta are photons.

Even though he was aware of advances in physics based on theories of quarks, for some reason, Young never took the idea of these "fundamental particles" seriously. Right to the end of his life (he died in 1995), he continued to teach that photons (or quanta), not quarks, are the constituents of nuclear particles (protons and neutrons), and, therefore, that photons are the fundamental creative elements of the manifest universe.

For Young, a simple equation summed up his visionary theory:

Quantum = Photon = Light = Spirit

and this, he believed, accounted for *all* that exists (including the physical domain of matter/energy and the nonphysical domain of consciousness or mind).

Quantum Chance or Quantum Choice?

Perhaps Young's most revolutionary insight was that the "quantum of uncertainty" is not random, as assumed by physicists—but is actually a result of *purpose* inherent in the quantum of action itself. He taught that uncertainty of the quantum could be due to "quantum choice" rather than "quantum chance." Logically both options fit the observed facts.

To an *observer,* a random event is indistinguishable from an event based on choice. Both are equally uncertain and unpredictable. So, if quanta are making choices it is no surprise that physicists might assume they are random. But *to an entity making the choice* there is a world of difference between randomness and choice. Choice, in fact, is the *purposeful* injection of order into randomness.

Young noted that the idea of "quantum purpose" or "quantum choice" fits more of the facts. If we assume, as physics does, that quantum events are random, then we are faced with an impossible conundrum: How to explain the fact that we can make choices? You can't get choice (which requires consciousness) from wholly choiceless, purposeless, nonconscious, random quanta.

But if we make the flip that Young suggested, and assume that quantum uncertainty is the result of quantum choices, then consciousness is built into the fabric of reality right from the get go. Quantum choice accounts for more of the facts, and therefore it makes more sense to go with that assumption. This was Young's radical, revolutionary, insight—and it challenges the underlying metaphysical assumption of modern science that mindless, random matter/energy is fundamental in the universe.

No, said Young, *purposeful photons* are fundamental—that is, purposeful quanta of action.

Quantum Purpose

Young's "fundamental photon," or quantum, is *purposeful action.* It is simultaneously *consciousness* and *action.* The "action" component is crucial for Young's ontology because otherwise it would fall victim to the same critique leveled at other forms of emanationism. Typically, emanationist idealism claims that all matter derives from pure consciousness or spirit. But in that case, we have the problem of explaining how it would be possible to get *real* matter from *pure* spirit.

The photon, then, would be best described as a unit of pure *sentient action.* As such, we can account for the fact that reality is both mental and physical—originating with quanta or photons that are bundles of purposeful, sentient action or energy. We need the consciousness aspect to account for subjectivity, and we need the action aspect to account for objective energy. This notion of "sentient action" is fully consistent with the panpsychist view that mind and matter (sentience and energy) are inextricably united, though not identical. Mind is always embodied, matter is always ensouled. Young's "quantum emanationism" is really a form of "panpsychist idealism."

In a highly detailed model, Young attempts to show how, using the quantum = photon = light = spirit formulation, it is possible to trace the unfolding of the entire manifest universe from the domain of quantum potential (or Spirit). The subtitle of his book is *Evolution of Consciousness,* and in it he presents a theory describing how Quantum Spirit generates the domains of Soul and Time, Mind and Space, Matter and Body. The journey from Spirit to Matter he calls "involution."

The central idea in Young's theory is *process*—powered and governed by the quantum of action—and this process is evolutionary. Evolution begins with the photon descending through four levels of reality (at each level giving up a degree of its original unconstrained freedom). Each constraint results in a dimension of manifest reality. Beginning at the highest (first) level of pure, unconstrained action (Spirit) the photon creates the dimension of time and nuclear particles (second level); next it creates the two dimensions of space (width and height) and atoms (third level); and then it combines the three dimensions of time and space (time is equivalent to the dimension of depth) to create the world of molecular matter (fourth level).

At this point in the process, the originating quantum is trapped or "frozen" in matter, and uses the remaining quantum of uncertainty to effect a Turn. Now, spirit-in-matter begins its long ascent through "evolution" first creating simple living systems, and then progressively more complex, more evolved systems such as plants and animals (including humans) on a homecoming journey that passes through seven stages of evolution to even more highly evolved creatures we may call, for example, "angels," "devas," and "buddhas," before finally returning to Spirit.

This, tightly condensed, is Arthur Young's vision of cosmic evolution.

Quanta or Quarks?

But does Young's vision achieve the bridge building between science and spirituality that he intended? What happens to his science-based model when the details and data of science no longer seem to fit his evolutionary scheme? The strength, and distinguishing characteristic, of his model is a reconciliation between physics and metaphysics, but if the gap between his "physics" and the physics of conventional science widens with new discoveries, what then? Does the bridge collapse, pulling down his entire cosmological edifice?

For example, currently the most robust theory in physics is, arguably, "quantum chromodynamics." This is a set of mathematical equations describing empirical experiments that apparently reveal fundamental "particles" called quarks and gluons as the constituents of nuclear particles (protons and neutrons). Although these involve quanta, they are not generated by *photons,* as Young's model would have us believe.

Whereas photons are quanta of electromagnetic energy or "force," quarks and gluons are responsible for what is called the strong nuclear force, which binds the atomic nucleus together. Photons do not mediate this force. Neither do they mediate the two other forces known to physics: the weak nuclear force (responsible for radioactivity) or the force of gravity.

So, from the perspective of contemporary physics, Young's model, based on the notion of "fundamental photons," can explain only one of the four forces responsible for the physical universe—electromagnetism. In other words, his model does not account for *three-quarters* of physical reality. By any stretch of imagination, that's a serious gap. Young's bridge between science and spiritual metaphysics, therefore, no longer spans the great divide.

Remember, his "bridge" is constructed on the fundamental equation, "Quantum = Photon = Light = Spirit." But now, it seems, the construction breaks down at the second link in the equation. If quantum does not equal photon or light, then we lose the all-important link between "quantum" and "spirit." The "light" linking science and spirit dims. The physicist's photon begins to seem less and less like the spiritual "light" of the mystics.

In short, Young's identification of the quantum of action with "photon" (claiming that the photon is fundamental to all of manifest physical reality) is not supported by modern physics. Young's use of "photon" is at variance with how it is used in standard physics (where it applies only to electromagnetic quanta), and, therefore, the notion of "fundamental photons" as the source of all of manifest physical reality does not hold.

Light: The Missing Link

Why, then, did Young equate "photon" and "quantum of action"? Was it merely a quirk of his own imagination, a convenient conceptual sleight-of-hand to shore up his deep intuition that the light of physics is the same as the light of mysticism?

I think the explanation is more likely a "quirk" of historical timing. My guess is that Young's vision of the photon-quantum identity was inspired by Einstein's 1905 paper on the photoelectric effect, which showed that photons are quanta of energy or action. His error (it seems) was to assume not only that all photons are quanta, but also that all quanta are photons. Had he stuck with "quantum of action" instead of "photon," perhaps Young's model would today still stand on firmer ground, making the crossing between science and spirit a safer journey.

But had he revised his equation to read

Quantum = Spirit

he would have lost that all-important link between physics and mysticism: *Light.* And that, I think, would have been incompatible with his deep intuition. Like Einstein, Young was not averse to the attitude (shared by many great visionaries): "If the facts don't fit the theory, so much the worse for the facts."

As the years and decades pass, developments in science (physics and biology in particular) supersede details in Young's model. So that today, the claim that his Theory of Process builds a bridge between science and spirit seems less and less likely, and is, at best, questionable.

So, what to do? Should we discard everything about *The Reflexive Universe* and Young's Theory of Process, including his treatment of the four levels of being, and the stages in the reflexive arc of involution and evolution?

I don't think so. Even if photons are not as ubiquitous as Young suggested, it remains true that (with the exception of gravity) electromagnetism is by far the most pervasive force in our lives, accounting for the vast majority of phenomena we experience. Young's intuition that there is something mysteriously fundamental about light (an insight shared by sages of many traditions for millennia) continues to warrant closer inspection.

And ideas such as "quantum choice" rather than "quantum chance," and "purposeful process" at the source of the manifest world, along with numerous intriguing correspondences he identified between spirituality, metaphysics, science, mythology, topology, mathematics, and art deserve closer investigation, too.

Still Valuable After All These Flaws

In the "Evolution of Consciousness" course I teach at John F. Kennedy University, as well as in my "Mind in the Cosmos" course at the University of Philosophical Research, I introduce the basic outlines of Young's model, and present his theory as a guide to understanding how different ways of knowing (epistemology) can map onto different levels of reality (ontology).

My goal is to help students grasp the core tenets or elements of Young's model and then, using their own *multiple modes of knowing* (senses, reason, feeling, and intuition), decide whether or how the model may be useful to them. If it stimulates thinking about the evolution of consciousness in new ways, I feel I have accomplished my goal.

I invite students to evaluate the theory as a tool for (a) mapping epistemology and ontology, and (b) tracking the evolution of consciousness, showing possible relationships between Spirit, Soul, Mind, and Matter—based on the idea of a three-part process, involution, turn, evolution.

I encourage students to approach this material with a questioning mind, and when it is intelligently challenged that is all to the good. Whether they accept or reject the theory in whole or in part is, for me, beside the point.

I do not present Young's model as something to *believe*—as the "right" or "best" theory to explain the evolution of consciousness and cosmos. There are, of course, many other models we could explore besides Young's—for example, Bergson, Teilhard de Chardin, Gebser, Aurobindo, Whitehead, or Wilber.[2] I have no doubt that each of these has its own strengths and weaknesses, and could equally serve the goal of elucidating the evolution of consciousness from a cosmic perspective.

Yes, significant scientific details in Young's model are flawed— another example, this time from biology: entire kingdoms, Protists and Fungi, are omitted from his scheme. Despite these shortcomings, however, I still feel Young's Theory of Process is based on profound insights about the nature of reality.

It can serve as a kind of mnemonic (or mandala) for understanding how different ways of knowing access different levels of being. As a metaphysical model, its applications within science may be increasingly limited (though Dr. Frank Barr, a physician in Berkeley, California, has for many years been developing a highly detailed application of the theory in the field of evolutionary biology—so it may yet prove to have some predictive power even within science).

I have introduced Young's model here not because I think it is superior, but because of the way he uniquely and creatively uses the quantum of action as a possible bridge between modern science and ancient spiritual cosmologies. And, despite the flaws, I continue to think, "He was onto something."

So where are we now? We've looked at Newberg's neuroscience, Lloyd's neurophenomenology, Hameroff's microtubules, Bohm's implicate order, Jung's *unus mundus*, Goswami's idealist science, and Young's theory of process—each one a contender in the high stakes race to find a scientific theory that will finally take us beyond the last frontier into the mystery of mind. We have seen that each theory, one way or another, falls short of the prize. Despite inhabiting a surreal wonderland, even the mysterious quantum is not a passport to the promised land of consciousness.

Most scientific attempts to get to consciousness stumble over some version of the "hard problem"—either explaining how mindless matter could evolve into bodies with minds or how matterless spirit could involve into minds with bodies. The last remaining option, it seems, is to accept the ancient insight: *You can't get something from nothing.*

Unless brains cells (or microtubules) *already* possess subjectivity, then there is no conceivable way that *wholly nonsubjective, nonexperiential, nonsentient anything* could ever produce mind—a radically different ontological state. Jumping from one state of reality (A), *entirely* without consciousness or subjectivity, to a state of reality (B) that now includes subjectivity/consciousness, would require nothing short of a miracle! There simply is no way to explain such an ontological jump.

Mind cannot emerge from matter, and matter cannot emanate from mind. Logic compels us to see that if one cannot come from the other then the only coherent conclusion is that *both matter and mind always existed.* Consciousness and energy always go together all the way down and all the way back—without beginning and . . . since something can't become nothing, either . . . without end.

With this in mind, let's look at one more attempt to find a rapprochement between science and spirituality. Let's see how, after all, we may honor the staggering insights of Amit Goswami and Arthur Young—that the manifest actual world of bodies and brains, mountains and mice, computers and cats, rogues and roaches, saints and sinners, erupts from a deeper, *unmanifest* realm of pure potential. In the next chapter, we will dive deep into a fascinating world, an outpost of the Quantum Wonderland, where ancient wisdom and modern science come together—where consciousness and energy dance the world into being.

Quantum Choice

Q: *If you were to select one insight from the work of Arthur Young that serves as a firm stepping-stone to bridge science and spirituality, what would it be?*

A: For me, it's his insight that purpose or choice is built into the quantum of action right from the start.

According to standard interpretations of quantum physics, quantum events are totally *random*, and therefore unpredictable. It's all "quantum chance."

However, in *The Reflexive Universe*, Arthur Young points out that the unpredictability of a quantum event could equally be the result of uncaused randomness *or* self-caused choice. From the point of view of an *observer*, randomness or choice are indistinguishable. Either assumption fits the facts.

Therefore, Young concludes, it makes just as much sense to attribute *choice* to the quantum. In fact, it makes more sense because this assumption fits more of the facts—including the fact that at least some sentient beings (e.g., humans) do exercise choice.

And since everything that exists in the physical world is made up of quanta (including humans), the assumption of "quantum choice" is the only coherent way to account for choice at the human level (otherwise we'd have an inexplicable ontological gap between complete absence of choice at cellular, molecular, and atomic levels followed by the "miraculous" appearance of choice in humans and other creatures).

So, what *appears* as randomness or "quantum chance" to an observer may be *experienced* as "quantum choice" from the point of view of a quantum.

By attributing choice and purpose to the quantum, we imply consciousness, too. As a bundle of sentient energy or purposeful action, the quantum straddles both sides of the ontological divide—the physical world of energy and the spiritual world of consciousness. Even if his equation Quantum = Photon does not hold up, Young's inspired insight that the quantum possesses intrinsic purpose serves as a promising bridge between science and spirit.

8

I.C.E. WORLD:
THE ULTIMATE STORY

Why do so many people get excited when discoveries in science appear to validate profound insights from the perennial philosophy? Why turn to science to confirm spiritual wisdom?

Our story begins with the Casimir Effect. In the late 1940s, a Dutch physicist Hendrik Casimir startled the international science community with the idea that if you placed two metallic plates face to face almost touching in empty space, they would spontaneously attract or repel each other. This was strange because the apparent "nothingness" between the plates should have no force to make anything happen. But that's not how it is. The "nothingness" of empty space, it turns out, is not what it appears to be.

Casimir's theory was later demonstrated experimentally to be correct. Physicists have since discovered that the "vacuum" of so-called empty space actually bristles and foams with quantum forces. Einstein had earlier predicted this, calling it "zero-point energy"*—

*Actually, Einstein and his colleague Otto Stern used the much more evocative German word *"Nullpunkenergie"* (a great name for a rock band!).

the ground state of physical reality. It exists everywhere.

Underlying the manifest world of matter and energy, we now know, is a universal field of quantum potential—variously known as the zero-point energy field, the ZPE field, or simply "The Field." It is the source or foundation for all of physical reality.

Drawing on anomalies and advances in quantum physics, cosmology, biology, and consciousness studies, philosopher and systems theorist Ervin Laszlo argues that the zero-point energy field is also a universal field of *information*. In *Science and the Akashic Field* he makes the case that, with knowledge of ZPE, science is finally in a position to produce a theory of everything (ToE).

The concept and implications of zero-point energy stretch our minds and imaginations to new limits. Like so much else in quantum physics, ZPE nudges us to open up to a new paradigm, to accept a radically new, highly counterintuitive understanding of the deep nature of reality. Yes, ZPE is bizarre—nevertheless it is rock-steady, solid science.

It explains how the world we know and live in—our undeniable, familiar reality—springs forth at a dizzying rate, billions of times a second, from the universal field of quantum potential. Everything we know, everything that exists, comes from the ZPE field and sooner or later returns there—to be "recycled" back into our world in some other form, or perhaps into another universe.

The discovery of this field may be final confirmation from science of a profound insight into the nature or reality from ancient Hindu cosmology. The Akashic Record, like the ZPE field, records everything that has ever happened, is happening, and will happen from the birth of our cosmos till its ultimate end. In scientific terms, the "everything" that is recorded is the sum total of all events and the information they contain.

Based on the remarkable similarities between the Akashic Record and the ZPE field, Laszlo equates the two, and renames them collectively the "Akashic Field" or "A-Field"—deliberately using a scientific-sounding term for a venerable spiritual-metaphysical idea.

Science Confirming Spiritual Insight?

But why turn to science to bolster belief or faith in an essentially spiritual insight? Laszlo is clear that one of the hallmarks of science—and the main reason for trusting scientific knowledge—is that it is both empirical and experimental. Science *tests* its theories and thereby produces reliable, predictable, and practical knowledge.

I share Laszlo's inclination to trust and value science, and I too feel encouraged to know that the scientific evidence for ZPE conforms so well with the ancient idea of a universal or cosmic Akashic Record.

But why? Why should we trust that just because science says so, we are more likely to have a truer explanation of reality than we get from spiritual or mystical experience? In certain moods and more intuitive states of mind, I find myself deeply trusting and valuing spiritual wisdom, accepting that it offers profound insight into the ultimate nature of reality. Nevertheless, there is something deeply reassuring in knowing that science also reveals a similar understanding of the world.

One reason, I think, is that science is widely accepted in modern society as the legitimator, the ultimate arbiter, of what is really real. Yes, we know that science has its limitations and blind spots, but overall it does a darn good job of exploring our world and presenting us with *usable* and *repeatable* knowledge.

But how? What is it about science that enables it to produce such pragmatic and practical knowledge—knowledge that empowers us to change our world (for good or ill)? Well the most distinctive mark of science is not merely that it tests its theories but that it tests by *measurement.* Science works because it uses a methodology that extracts information from the world by measuring it. And measurement removes guesswork. If done with precision and accuracy, it yields repeatable, reliable, reusable knowledge. In short: we trust and value science because it works.*

---

*What does it mean to measure something? Basically, it is a process of assigning numbers to physical quantities by using a standard for comparison (e.g., a ruler, a scale—some metric). Science is a method for quantifying and measuring physical reality, and equipped with such data we are empowered to manipulate the world, to adapt it to our needs and desires.

I think it comes down to this: We trust science because it provides the tools to explore, measure, and explain happenings in the physical world—the world of things we need for surviving and thriving. From the perspective of day-to-day living, the physical world is the *real* world. It contains the objects that we can see, hear, smell, taste, and touch—the world revealed to us by our senses. We have very good reasons for putting a lot of epistemological weight on what we learn and know through our senses. Knowledge not based on sensory input tends to be dismissed in our culture as "speculative" or "imaginary." And if it is not tested, then why should we believe it tells us anything about the real world—why should we take it as "knowledge" at all? Science makes sense because it is based on what the senses reveal, and is tested by rigorous experiments.

The Paradox of Science

But anyone involved in consciousness studies knows that the sense-world is not—and cannot—be the whole story. We have a curious paradox here: The only reason our senses can give us scientific data about the world is because the process of measurement involves and *requires* a subject who *experiences* the sensory data. But the experience itself is not a sensory object or event that can be measured. Consciousness is not objective—its essence is *subjectivity;* it does not exist in the world as an object or a thing—and, therefore, it cannot be quantified. And so, ultimately, science relies on an aspect of reality that is beyond the reach of science. That's the paradox. It's what makes any scientific theory of "everything" incomplete.

In short, science is about the external *objective* world; but consciousness is interior, it is *subjective*. We turn to science for reliable knowledge about the external physical cosmos, but turn to spiritual traditions for knowledge and wisdom about the "inner" cosmos of consciousness, mind, experience. To know *how* science knows anything, we need a different kind of "science"—a science of consciousness, a "noetic" science. All knowledge of the external objective world relies ultimately on non-objective consciousness.

Laszlo's new A-Field theory is intriguing because it supports the idea that finally we might have a common unifying concept for science and spirituality. The idea of a universal field of energy and information rings out loud and clear in strikingly similar ways from both science's ZPE field and the perennial wisdom's Akashic Field.

Many scholars have previously attempted to bridge these two great traditions of science and spirituality. For example, in the 1970s Fritjof Capra's influential book *The Tao of Physics* pointed out remarkable parallels between quantum physics and the mystical insights of Taoism, Hinduism, and Buddhism. In that case, the unifying idea was universal *interconnectedness*. And, more recently, philosopher Ken Wilber has pursued a prolific career exploring the "marriage" of science and spirit. Now, Laszlo offers the beginnings of an explanation for that interconnectedness in the ZPE or A-Field. Here, the unifying idea is *information*. Like ripples on a pond, he says, everything that happens in our world arises from (and *is*) interacting waves or patterns of energy and information in the A-Field. These waves literally *in-form*, or give shape to, the manifest physical world. And, in Laszlo's theory, these waveforms are encoded holographically throughout the entire A-Field—a permanent and complete record or repository of *all* energy and information, of everything that has ever happened. It is also the *source* of everything that has ever happened, is happening, and will happen.

The Born-Again Universe

Laszlo describes our world, the manifest reality we inhabit, as "the informed universe." It springs forth from the energy and information of ZPE or A-Field, and is literally "in-formed" or seeded by templates stored there from prior universes that have completed their journey from big bang to big crunch (or some other inevitable eventual demise), and have returned all their energy and information to the quantum "void." We live in a "recycled" or "born-again" universe, a world composed of energy and information handed on to us by the

A-Field. Our universe is just one (very long) event in an ongoing series of born-evolving-dying-born-again universes. Collectively, all worlds spring from the mother of all universes that Laszlo calls the "Metaverse." We could think of each universe—ours included—as an event that begins, evolves, and eventually ends within the overarching, eternal process we call "Cosmos."

Think of it not just as The Greatest Story Ever Told, but as The Ultimate Ever-Changing Story Forever Retold. Remember our definition of "story" from chapter 5: "Stories are the unfolding of meaning, signifying changes and connections—what happens now is shaped by what came before, building to a conclusion. Stories require *memory* of what has happened, *experience* of what is happening, and *anticipation* of what is to come."

Cosmos, Metaverse, A-Field, ZPE field (all versions of the same ultimate), including our actual universe, are composed of energy and information at all levels of existence—and the accumulation of information is the basis for Laszlo's ToE. But he is also keenly aware that this cannot be a full theory of everything because neither energy nor information can explain or account for consciousness. Recognizing that consciousness cannot emerge from mindless energy or information, Laszlo acknowledges the panpsychist view (championed by philosopher Alfred North Whitehead in *Process and Reality*) that for his ToE to hold together coherently, consciousness must be intrinsic to the A-Field, not something that later emerges from it. Consciousness, therefore, is inherent in the cosmos all along. Consciousness, the Cosmic Storyteller, is part of the very fabric of being.

Thus, deep reality has a tri-aspect nature, consisting of Information, Consciousness, and Energy—I.C.E. For Laszlo, information is the link missing from previous attempts to come up with a true ToE. In *Science and the Akashic Field* he explains why information, stored in the A-Field, is the foundation for a theory of everything. It is an impressive unifying, integrative insight. Yet, we need to be cautious—and not attribute a false ontological status to information. Although information may be the connective tissue between energy and consciousness, it does not itself have ontological primacy. Let's look at this . . .

WHAT IS INFORMATION?

The word comes from the Latin *informare,* meaning "to give form"— literally to in-form. In communications theory, it is essentially an engineering term: Information is a *measure of the probability of transmitting a signal through a communications channel.* This is quite different from what we usually understand by information. Indeed, two of the founders of communications theory, Claude Shannon and Warren Weaver were very clear about this: "information must not be confused with meaning," Weaver wrote in his introduction to Shannon's landmark 1949 paper.

> The word information, in this theory, is used in a special sense that must not be confused with its ordinary usage. In particular, information must not be confused with meaning.
>
> In fact, two messages, one of which is heavily loaded with meaning and the other of which is pure nonsense, can be exactly equivalent, from the present viewpoint, as regards information.[1]

Therefore, the precise scientific use of "information" is explicitly *not* about transfer or communication of meaning. It merely refers to a measure of the probability of the transfer of signals ("bits" or binary digits in modern digital communications) through a medium.

Unlike in science or engineering, in everyday language we typically assume that information is a carrier of meaning—it has *semantics* as well as syntax. Information without meaning hardly counts as information.

We need, then, to expand the technical use of "information" to include

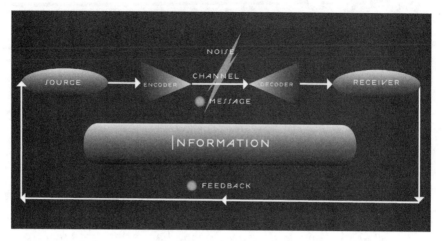

Information according to the Shannon-Weaver model

meaning. One of the most succinct and famous definitions of information is Gregory Bateson's: "a difference that makes a difference."[2]

In our actual world, any detectable "difference" is, necessarily, a *physical* difference—whether it's a difference in shape, color, texture, weight, length, sound, volume, temperature, altitude, etc. All difference is *physically instantiated*—that is, in some way it involves changes in patterns of energy. Without difference in patterns of energy, there would be no distinction for us to perceive—and so no information.

Even psychological differences—for example, differences in mood or emotion—are always correlated with some physical, typically electrochemical, substrate, whether hormonal or neuronal. Let me be clear, however: This is not to claim that neural events *are* or *produce* mental events. Brains or nervous (or endocrine) systems do not equal minds. Instead, taking the panpsychist position, as Laszlo also does, I'm saying that mind or consciousness is *always* embodied in some form of matter/ energy, and vice versa; matter is always "ensouled." Matter is innately and intrinsically *sentient*. Matter *feels*.

The point here is that mind and matter always go together—all the way down. Wherever there is matter, there is some degree or trace of consciousness, be it in single cells, molecules, atoms, subatomic particles, quanta, or superstrings—or whatever lies at the base of physical reality. And any difference registered in the mind is correlated with a difference in the world of matter. Again: all real differences show up in matter; differences involve changes in energy.

But these differences alone do not yield information. For information to be present we need the added ingredient of a mind or consciousness. Information is *perceived difference*. And it is perceived because it stands out, is *noticed*, because it is significant—*a difference that makes a difference*.

Without mind, without sentient beings, all the changes in the world, from the birth of time to the present moment, would never amount to one iota of information. Information is changes in energy *read* by the mind. So, in some curious way, information is generated at the "interface" of mind and matter. It is neither wholly created by the mind (because it requires differences in energy), nor is it merely changes or differences in energy (because these differences must be "read," perceived or experienced). Information requires both matter and mind. Perhaps we could say that information is differences in matter or energy that show up as differences in mind. All information is, therefore, *phenomenal*—but not merely mental.

Trinity as Two

Laszlo's tripartite "I.C.E" (information, consciousness, energy) that constitutes the A-Field is, therefore, not a full-blown ontological trinity. Whereas neither mind nor matter can arise, evolve, or emerge from (or be reduced to) the other, information is emergent. It arises from the "interaction" of mind with matter, of consciousness "prehending" (taking account of or feeling) changes in the physical world. Instead of ontological I.C.E., then, we have a kind of alchemical interplay of mind and matter resulting in what we recognize as information. Energy and consciousness (or, more accurately, *intrinsically sentient energy*) are ontologically primary, while information is ontologically secondary or derivative. Instead of I.C.E. we have "C(I)E."

The Akashic or A-Field, therefore, is primarily both an energetic and *experiential* field and only secondarily an information field. Changes in energy—patterns, differences—leave holographic imprints in the field, and these imprints are prehended, perceived, or "read" by consciousness native to the field. The reading of these cosmic imprints in the ZPE field *is* information. Technically, then, information per se is not recorded in the A-Field. Energetic changes are, and these are then read out by consciousness as information.

Nevertheless, I think Laszlo is essentially correct—and has offered a valuable insight—that information (*differences in energy read by mind*) is fundamental to the cosmos.

In the preceding chapters, we have seen why neuroscience, cognitive science, or quantum physics cannot qualify as steps to a science of consciousness. The best they can offer is knowledge about physical correlates of consciousness. Amit Goswami and Arthur Young have bravely and creatively offered us inspired reinterpretations of quantum physics as ways to grasp the connection between consciousness and the physical world. Neither, however, claims that the quantum creates consciousness. On the contrary, one tells us that consciousness creates the quantum, the other that consciousness, as purpose, is native to the quantum of action. In this chapter we saw that Ervin Laszlo, too, places consciousness, coupled with energy, at the heart of reality.

In all three theories consciousness is fundamentally intrinsic to the very nature of existence. In this book, I am laying out a case that our search for a science of consciousness must start off with this assumption: *Consciousness is primordial.* Its subjective nature means that our new science must give up its exclusive focus on *objects* and expand by shifting attention directly onto the *subject* doing the investigation. This will require a radically new perspective, as will see in the next chapter.

Information: The Missing Link?

Q: *According to Apollo astronaut Edgar Mitchell, information is part of the very substance of the cosmos, part of a universal "dyad" along with energy. According to Ervin Laszlo, information, energy, and consciousness form a "triad." In both theories information is present everywhere and has been present since the birth of the universe. Isn't information, then, the fundamental missing ingredient in a comprehensive theory of the world? If we include information don't we have a basis for explaining both consciousness and energy? Doesn't information equal consciousness?*

A: First, information consists of two components: It is *patterns in energy* (or, more accurately, *changes in patterns of energy*). But patterns in energy alone are insufficient to count as information. Some *sentient conscious being* must *read* (or observe) the patterns. Both are needed for information: changing patterns in energy and some perception or awareness of those changes.

Because information requires both energy and consciousness, it cannot be fundamental and primary. Information is *derivative* of energy and consciousness. This also means that the equation "information = consciousness" cannot be correct. Information is more than consciousness in the sense that it also needs patterns in energy; and it is more than patterns in energy because it also requires consciousness to *read* the patterns.

Information, then, is a process of interaction between changes in patterns of energy and consciousness that is aware of those patterns. We could say, "information is what happens (or is generated) in the relationship between 'things' and 'experiences of things.'"

Consciousness is the capacity to *know* or *feel*, and the ability to *choose*. *Energy* is the *action* (e.g., the quantum of action) that makes things happen in the world—*always purposefully directed by consciousness*. Energy circulates throughout the universe in patterns, and changes in these patterns are the "raw material" for information. However, because consciousness is always detecting changes in patterns of energy, information is (and has been) always present, too. So in *that* sense, information is primordial and fundamental—though not primary.

9

SCIENCE THROUGH
THE LOOKING GLASS

L et me tell you a story . . . about the Cartesian Drunk searching
for the keys to consciousness.

A famous scientist wanted to find a way to measure mind, and so he went to visit his good friend, a philosopher.

"Of course, you can't measure consciousness," the philosopher told him. "There's no such thing as a 'mindalyzer' or 'consciousness meter'. To measure consciousness, it would have to be a form of energy, it would have to be located in space, it would have to be objective. But consciousness is notoriously *nonlocated* and *subjective*. You'll *never* measure consciousness simply because it is not a form of energy."

But his friend wasn't convinced. "One of the first things a good scientist learns is 'never say never.' Perhaps one day someone will find a way."

"Never will," the philosopher repeated. "Long ago, scientists decided to restrict science to the study of *objects*, precisely because they wanted to *measure* things. But in doing so, they gave up the possibility of ever exploring mind. Why? Because mind or consciousness is not any kind of object, it is the *subject* that studies objects. Remember: *Consciousness knows. Energy flows.*"

The scientist looked bemused, so the philosopher explained:

"Following René Descartes, about four hundred years ago scientists bought into the mind-matter split, wholesale—even though they convinced themselves they had overcome the split by lopping off half of reality and declaring 'only matter is real.' Mind was banished to the realms of metaphysics or religion. But, of course, it never went away."

The philosopher continued: "Look, no matter how skillful scientists become at meticulously measuring objects (even down to quantum microtubules in neurons), guess what? They will never find consciousness lurking there. *Never.* Consciousness is not on the scientific radar screen for the very simple reason science decided to *exclude* consciousness from its domain. Little surprise, then, that their prospects for success in discovering consciousness anywhere in the physical world are precisely zero.

"So, my friend, as you search for consciousness, you are like the Cartesian drunk who can never find his keys. No matter how much light you beam onto the world of physical objects, you will never see that the 'keys' are, in fact, the light by which you see anything at all."

The moral of this story is "be careful what you wish for . . . you just might get it." Science began by wanting to avoid the wrath of the Inquisition and so split the world in two—into the realms of mind and matter—and declared it would explore only the domain of matter, leaving the domain of mind, consciousness, soul, and spirit to the Church. Wise move, given the alternatives.

WHAT IS SCIENCE?

So what happened? I'll say more about Descartes' influence shortly, but first let's take a look at what science actually is, how it goes about gathering knowledge. What makes science so special, and how will it have to change to push on to the final frontier?

To date, I have published two volumes in my Radical Consciousness trilogy: *Radical Nature,* exploring the mind-matter relationship, and *Radical Knowing,* exploring different ways of knowing ourselves and the world around us. The third volume (in process) is *Radical Science,* and its central theme is the question: *Can we have a science of consciousness?* A little later in this chapter I will summarize the essential points by outlining the key criteria for standard modern science. I will then propose an alternative set of criteria that can lead to an effective science of consciousness.

Let's begin here, however, with a relatively commonplace definition: *Science is the observation, identification, description, experimental investigation, and theoretical explanation of phenomena.*

Observation—achieved by using the senses (predominantly vision);

Identification—achieved by adding *rational analysis* to sort, select, and name specific features of what is observed;

Description—using language, either mathematics or words, to combine the elements of identification into some symbolic representation of the phenomenon, involving propositions and sometimes narratives;

Experimental investigation—science *tests* its propositions, hypotheses, or theories using a repeatable set of protocols or procedures that anyone trained in the field could replicate;

Theoretical explanation—science further employs the powers of reason and language to report or propose *causal* relationships and/or correlations between the events or objects observed and identified in the experiment; causal explanations are considered the essence of scientific knowledge—they are what give scientists (and a great many nonscientists) confidence in the *predictions* that science makes possible.

By understanding the causal relationships between the objects it studies, science can explain, in increasingly finer detail, what causes what to happen. It tells us *how* the world works. And confidence in the accuracy and reliability of scientific predictions leads to the truly awesome advances in modern technology that have empowered the exponential growth of industrial, now information-based, global civilization.

The last two features—*experimental investigation* and *theoretical explanation*—together stand out as the defining characteristics of science. Other forms of knowledge or ways of understanding the world—such as philosophy, religion, or art—also use some combination of observation, identification, and description. But in addition to these, science *tests* its theories (narratives or explanations) using a formal, repeatable procedure or *methodology*. That's what makes science unique: it *tests* predictions.

Because science is essentially a procedure for testing, all scientific knowledge is always provisional, always open to refinement and revision. Not only does this mean that scientific knowledge is always expanding, it means that science never *proves* anything. The best it can do is provide data or evidence that either confirm or refute a particular hypothesis or theory. And every confirmation forever remains open to the possibility of some future refutation.

In this sense, science is a kind of *via negativa;* it advances by negating errors in observation and theory. Somewhat whimsically, I have summarized this as the "ERROR" method.

The Error Method
Empiricism: Uses senses to get data
Reason: Analyzes data with logic and math
Reductionism: Explains wholes from smallest parts
Objectification: Separates subjects from objects
Replication: Repeats experiments to falsify or confirm predictions

So far so good . . . well, not quite. Like all other fields of knowledge, science is based on a set of axioms or metaphysical assumptions about the nature of reality. And two of these fundamental assumptions are deeply problematic when the target is consciousness. These assumptions are unquestioned belief in *materialism* and its first cousin, *objectivity*.

As I pointed out earlier, materialism insists that the fundamental, essential nature of reality is purely physical stuff—ultimately some kind of objective *energy*. Everything that exists—from tiny quarks or quanta to the grand immensity of the universe itself—is believed to be made up of physical objects and the physical forces acting between them. This, of course, includes everything in between—all forms of life, as well as the mysterious "flame" of consciousness that lights up our lives.

As we know, *that* is a formidable—indeed, insurmountable—problem for scientific materialism. It cannot explain how consciousness could evolve or emerge from wholly nonconscious ingredients. Remember, these ingredients (atoms and molecules and all that they compose) are believed to be *purely objective*. But consciousness is notoriously *subjective*. It is not an object in the world along with all the subatomic, atomic, and molecular ingredients of the universe. *Consciousness is the subject that knows these objects.*

And remember, too, that science is in the business of providing *causal explanations* for how the world works. But it cannot even begin to explain how purely physical events (in the brain or nervous system or anywhere else) could ever produce nonphysical consciousness. Although scientists *claim* that mind evolves from the complexity of matter, they cannot explain how this happens—or *could* happen. Science is totally in the dark about consciousness.

The second conundrum facing every scientist is the undeniable fact of his or her own consciousness. Every item of scientific knowledge—the entire edifice of science—exists only because the data were *experienced* in some scientist's *mind*. There is no other way to ever know anything except in consciousness. As we already know, this is precisely what science cannot explain. So, science remains in the awkward position of being unable to account for scientific knowledge. Science cannot explain how science exists. This means that *science is unscientific!* Oops.

These, of course, are philosophical issues, and most scientists are content to leave such problems for philosophers to puzzle over. And as long as scientists focus their gaze on objects in the physical world, they can generally ignore the pink elephant lurking under the carpet. But if and when they shift their sights to consciousness, that pachyderm lump shifts with them, and it roars to be noticed.

You can't step on an elephant and pretend it isn't there. Consciousness is like that. You can't ignore it if you want to study it.

Here's what happened: Once upon a time, before modern science was born, a big bad wolf called the "Holy Inquisition" hunted down and burned alive anyone who challenged its authority, which it claimed was divinely mandated. In February 1600, this unfortunate fate befell an upstart Italian philosopher by the name of Giordano Bruno. The lesson was loud and clear: *"Don't mess with the Church—or else."* Not too long after, with the smell of Bruno's burning flesh still hanging over Europe, a French philosopher named René Descartes set himself the gargantuan task of wiping clean the slate of all previous knowledge and starting from scratch. A decidedly dangerous thing to do—given what happened to poor old Bruno. It meant that René had to ask questions, a lot of them. Now, the Holy Inquisition didn't like questions very much—especially when they challenged the Church's god-given authority. And young René was about to do something unheard of. He said he would begin his search for a new science by *doubting everything*. He wouldn't take anything for granted, not even the teachings of the Church, which were, of course, based on biblical scripture as well as the ancient philosophy of Aristotle (this is what got Bruno all fired up).

René was smarter than Giordano. But he took a risk all the same. Know what he did? *He split the world in two.* That's what he did. Split it up into mind and matter, or, as he called it, into soul and body.

Ingenious. He said his "new science" would restrict itself to just the boring material half of reality and leave all the really juicy spiritual stuff to the Church—which, as it happened, they believed was the only part of the world that really mattered in the end. (We'll ignore the fact that the Church was extremely keen on acquiring as much material stuff as it could lay its hands on. That's another story.)

They bought it. René was left alone to pursue his private doubts and meditations on the nature of existence. He even wrote books about it—famous books that are still read in universities throughout the world today. He was looking for a single point of certainty in his infinite sea of doubt. And he found it. It was the very thing he needed, the building block for launching his new science. Guess what he discovered? Kind of a paradox, really, but based on a truly brilliant insight. It was *consciousness*.

Yes, René discovered that he could doubt everything except the fact of his own mind. It was an irrefutable certainty. Why? Because, he cunningly realized, by doubting his own consciousness, he proved it existed. After all, only a being with consciousness can doubt anything. Neat, eh? *Cogito, ergo sum*. "I think, therefore, I am." That was it. That's what got the philosophical ball rolling across Europe, and eventually around the world, setting the stage for the new scientific revolution.

By strange twists and turns of logic, our friend Descartes worked out that his consciousness was a gift from God, and that the Creator himself had programmed his mind with all kinds of notions about the physical world. Now the Creator, being almighty and pure, would never deceive anyone, right? So, our philosophical hero believed he had a firm foundation for no longer doubting the existence of the physical world. That gave him two important pieces of knowledge to begin building his new philosophy—consciousness and matter. And with that, he got to work, setting the stage in Europe, and eventually throughout the world, for a new revolution called science. It spread like wildfire. (Ironic, really, given the spark that started it all was Bruno's fire.)

Descartes (left) was smarter than Bruno.

In any case, following Descartes' mind-matter split, science focused its beam of inquiry exclusively on the physical world and moved ahead in leaps and bounds. It was so successful, in fact, that scientists saw no need for any spiritual reality, and, in time, ignored it completely. But they didn't stop there. Know what they did? They lopped off half of Descartes' mind-body duality and declared that only body, or matter, really existed.

Now without a doubt, this was a masterful strategic move. By confining investigations to the physical world, scientists were able to develop and refine a new experimental method, inspired by a contemporary of Descartes across the pond in Britain, Sir Francis Bacon.

The new science worked so well, curiously enough, because it applied the Cartesian split (named after our friend René Des*cartes*) between mind and matter to the new experimental methodology. Not wanting to get bogged down in anything to do with the mind, they renamed it the "subject-object" split and separated the subject (i.e., the mind of the scientist) from the object (the rest of the world). This was called "objectivity."

Essentially, in their imaginations, they placed a thick plate of glass between the scientist and the objects he or she was studying. The idea was simple, and understandable. Their aim was to get good objective knowledge of the world, undistorted and uncontaminated by whatever bias and shenanigans might be going on in the subjective mind

Sir Francis Bacon

of the scientist. *Plate-Glass Science.* Protected behind this thick glassy wall, the presence of the knower would not disturb what was known. Science could rest content and confident that its knowledge was real, true, and "pure."

It worked well. Very well. Indeed, within a few short centuries Plate-Glass Science moved from studying cannonballs rolling down wooden shoots to shooting hi-tech electronic probes into outer space, helping to push scientific knowledge out to the edges of the universe and back in time to a micro moment after the big bang that, eventually, got those cannonballs rolling and the scientists shooting probes into outer space . . . A sense of coming full circle. But not quite.

Flushed with the confidence of success, some scientists believed they could turn the beam of scientific inquiry back on the very instrument of knowing itself—*consciousness.* And that's when something long forgotten began to rumble in the shadows.

Remember that lurking lump under the carpet? Well, IT'S BAAACK! The pachyderm won't go away.

As a methodology, Plate-Glass Science worked well for studying physical *objects* that can be measured. But, as we well know, consciousness is not an object. It is the *subject.* The knower is now trying to know the knower. This is where science really tries to come full circle. But it doesn't work. You can't do Plate-Glass Science—which splits the subject from the object—to study consciousness or the mind because now the subject is trying to *know itself.* You can't shield the mind behind a thick glass wall and hope to explore it, because the *mind is the explorer.* It's like trying to catch up with your own shadow, or trying to sneak a peak inside the fridge to see if the light stays on when the door is closed. It can't be done. Only consciousness can study consciousness.

What went wrong? How did science get itself into such a muddle?

Well, scientists had a nasty attack of scientific amnesia. That's what happened. Remember way back when, when the new science took its cue from our good friend René, they hit on the ingenious methodology of separating mind from matter, subject from object, and concentrated on just half of the split? Great idea. Brilliant, really. But they got so carried away on the wings of their own successes they made a truly momentous mistake—a kind of Promethean blunder.

All fired up with enthusiasm for their methodology, they focused their gaze so intently and exclusively on the material world *they forgot that this was just a methodological convenience.* What did they do? They jumped from a grand and grounded idea "Focus only on the physical world" (a *methodological maneuver*), to an ungrounded belief "All that exists is physical" (a *metaphysical assumption*). In their blind and blustering passion for physics, verging on hubris worthy of a Greek god in flames, they elevated "all we want to *know about* is the physical world" to "(therefore) all that *exists* is physical." The logic doesn't compute. It's just a bad case of convenient amnesia.

Nevertheless, all aglow from their astounding achievements in quantum physics, and new sciences such as neurobiology and genetics, they set their sights on the final frontier—*consciousness.*

But, surprise, surprise! When they set about searching for consciousness in the physical world they couldn't find it. *They had already defined it out of existence.* Duh! They had removed consciousness from the world, shutting it up behind the plate-glass wall of objectivity.

Their amnesia was their undoing. The inconvenient truth that consciousness is not an object, is not physical, and cannot be measured wouldn't go away. Addicted to quantification, scientific rigor depends on the mathematical precision of measuring things. But how can you apply the rigor of mathematics to something that can't be measured? Major impasse.

Plate-Glass Science

Now, while holding all of this in mind, let's shift focus for a moment to take a closer look at the methodology science uses to investigate the world.

For centuries, philosophers have argued back and forth over what constitutes the scientific method. But we can simplify things here by *identifying core criteria for standard science.* And, as we will see, these are what make the study of consciousness such a challenge.

> *Objectivity.* The first criterion, objectivity, means "unbiased observation," uncontaminated by the personal, subjective peculiarities or viewpoint of the investigator. This is the keystone of Plate-Glass Science: Nature viewed from a distance as though through a plate-glass window; nature treated as a remote and detached "other." But detached observation is exactly what is impossible in the study of consciousness.
>
> *Measurement/Quantity.* Another criterion is that the object of study must be measurable and quantifiable. The rationale is that measurement gives precision, satisfying one of the underlying ideals of science: the pursuit of certainty. When the ideal of certainty is unattainable, as in quantum physics, scientists substitute statistical probability (which is measurable and quantifiable).

Mechanism. Science's preoccupation with measurement and precision is directly related to the desire for explanation—identifying and isolating the precise causes of things. Science looks for mechanisms that explain how things work, how one thing causes some other thing or event to happen.

Prediction. And, of course, the more precise our knowledge is of what causes things to happen, the more accurately we can predict what will happen.

Control. Prediction, coupled with measurement and mechanism, allows us to manipulate causes so we can control outcomes. Control of otherwise unpredictable forces of nature is the underlying motivation for standard science. But underlying the desire for control lies a deeper, unconscious, motivation: *fear.* At bottom, the enterprise of standard science is fueled by a metaphysical assumption about the universe: Left to itself, nature is alien and dangerous, and, if not hostile, is at best indifferent. If we don't learn to control it, it will consume us.

Looking-Glass Science

Instead of Plate-Glass Science, consciousness research needs a radical shift of perspective. We need *Looking-Glass* Science, where the "object" being observed is also the subject doing the observing—the subject reflected back to itself. In Looking-Glass Science, the subject, the knower, reaches through the glass and *participates* with the "object" being investigated. In fact, in Looking-Glass Science, the separation between knower and known, between subject and object, is removed. The knower *is* the known. The instrument of knowledge inquires into its own nature.

The criteria for a science of consciousness are, in every case, the exact opposite of the core criteria listed above for standard science. Looking-Glass Science requires:

Subjectivity. Instead of the ideal of objectivity, which sets up a barrier between observer and observed, consciousness science must adopt the perspective of subjectivity. The "observer" must also *participate*. Consciousness cannot be studied from the outside; it must be viewed from within.

Engagement/Quality. Instead of a science of remote objects, consciousness requires a science of intimate subjects, where the subject engages in self-reflection or intersubjective mutual-reflection. Instead of objective measurement of quantities aimed at precision, we need subjective engagement with qualities aimed at revealing fine distinctions and subtle discernment.

Meaning. Instead of mechanical precision, consciousness science requires an increasingly discerning mind. In place of explanations and mechanical causes, it explores meanings—intuitive understanding of patterns of connection and relationship rather than merely rational, causal explanations.

Growth. Whereas explanations of mechanistic causes lead to prediction, acquisition of meaning leads to development and enrichment of understanding, to personal and interpersonal growth.

Transformation. The underlying motivation here is the opposite of control: it is transformation—a natural unfolding of the investigator's inherent potentials and capacities. Whereas standard science thrives on accumulation and interpretation of *facts,* consciousness science aims for transformation of experienced *values.*

Unlike the desire for control motivated by fear, the deep motivation for transformation is *trust* in the natural processes of the universe. This quality of acceptance and confidence stems from a metaphysical outlook where nature is assumed, if not experienced, to be intimate, benign, and concerned.

Let's compare the old and new criteria at a glance:

Criteria for Plate-Glass Science	Criteria for Looking-Glass Science
Objectivity (for observation)	Subjectivity (for observation-participation)
Measurement/Quantity (for precision and certainty)	Engagement/Quality (for fine distinctions)
Mechanism (for explanation)	Meaning (for understanding patterns of connection)
Prediction (for control)	Growth/Development (for transformation)
Control (underlying motivation)	Transformation (underlying motivation)
Deep motivation: *fear (of losing control)*	**Deep motivation:** *trust (in natural processes)*

SCIENCE AND TRANSFORMATION

Instead of banging their heads against thick plate-glass, trying to get a look-in on the mind, scientists need to swing their gaze around and look at who and what is looking. It may be unnerving, even scary, because who knows what might be lurking in the dark shadows of the scientist's mind? Nevertheless, that's what needs to be done. A scientist of the mind must be willing to confront whatever he or she finds there, and be willing to risk undergoing a transformation of consciousness in the process. There really is no other option. We could call it *Shadow Science.*

We now cross the threshold into the "promised land" where a true science of consciousness is, at last, within sight. Our next step is to pick up our "looking glass," peer into our own minds, and get to know ourselves more deeply. We will learn to recognize the contours of our ego and how it both serves us and keeps us locked in old patterns and habits of thinking and behavior.

While treating the ego with respect and compassion, we will also call on our natural resources of creativity and courage to uncouple identity from ego, to dive deep into the unconscious where our deepest fears lurk, running our lives from hidden shadows. We will embrace our darkest demons and learn from them the lessons they have been trying to teach us throughout our lives. Once we go beyond resistance to our own simple yet magnificent humanity, we will see that, in the end, there is nothing to fear. We will discover that beneath the fear, the shame, the anger, and the self-doubt, our deepest self is a never-ending source of love, and joy, and beauty, and peace.

This is the Mystic's Gift—a pathless path to transformation through the sacred silence that lives within us at every moment.

Remember Carl Jung's advice: Use the physical sciences not to *explain* the psyche but as a potentially rich source of *metaphors*. Acting on that advice, we'll begin with insights inspired by universal patterns in nature, called "strange attractors," discovered in chaos science and see how they operate in our own minds, directing our lives from behind the scenes.

Habits and Tangled Hierarchies

Q: *It could be argued that whenever science attempts to study consciousness the subject/object relationship creates a kind of "tangled hierarchy." Consciousness becomes both subject and object. Wouldn't this create a danger that science may simply cancel out consciousness altogether?*

A: Yes and no. Yes, there is a self-reflexivity involved when consciousness turns the beam of inquiry back on itself. We then have *subject investigating subject.* In a sense, the subject becomes his/her own "object" of inquiry—the subject becomes an object. This certainly is an issue that a science of consciousness will have to deal with (spiritual disciplines have been dealing with it for millennia).

As soon as the "witness" becomes an object of its own observation, the witness vanishes. The "I" can never observe itself. It is what is observing. We can never turn the "I" into an object because its essence is *subject*. As soon as the "I" tries to observe itself, it becomes "me." But *knowledge* about "me-as-object" distracts us from *being* the "I-as-subject."

When people explore their own consciousness the "witnessing I" (subject) observes the *contents* (objects) of consciousness.

But, no, this does not cancel out consciousness. Rather, this is the essence of meditation practice that reveals the habits of mind driving most of our thinking, believing, and acting. When meditation is engaged in successfully, with skillful attention and discernment, the reflexive process of self-observation can liberate us from identifying with our habitual patterns of thought and belief. And that's when we become gods.

PART III

THE MYSTIC'S GIFT

Why Is It Important?

10

STRANGE ATTRACTION

Whats so strange about strange attractors? What are they, anyway? And why should we care? Well, as we will see, they are patterns in nature that guide the unfolding of a wide variety of events from galaxy formation, to terrestrial weather systems, to schools of fish and flocks of birds. They may even guide the way you think, what you believe, the kinds of food or music you like, the people you hang out with (or avoid), your career path, financial status, and health—even your sex life. In short, attractors are also *patterns in consciousness.*

Okay, but what *is* an attractor? Technically, an attractor is a *tendency of a system to spontaneously fall into a pattern of activity.* In plain speak, attractors pull systems away from chaos toward order. Still too abstract? Well, then, picture what happens if you throw a bunch of marbles into a basin. At first, they will rattle and roll around this way and that, but soon enough they will settle down at the bottom. That's an example of an attractor doing its thing. Now, if you hooked up a small motor to the basin and made it vibrate, the marbles would shimmer and shake, and, if the motor was strong enough and kept running, they might never settle down. But they would still *tend* to roll to the

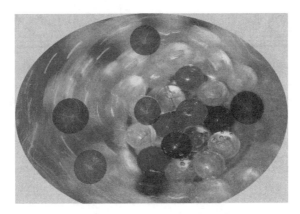

*An attractor is a tendency of a system to fall
into a recurring pattern.*

bottom. Their movements would self-organize into a discernible pattern. Bingo! You've got yourself a nice little strange attractor.

Just so you know: You've got a perfectly good strange attractor beating away right now in your chest. Or, at least I hope you have. Your heart is an example of a system pumping away on the knife-edge of chaos. It never quite slips over the line, always keeping within the limits needed to keep you alive. Just as well, really. Of course, it's not only you: all living systems operate at some level on the edge of chaos, striking a dynamic balance between order and disorder. That's just the kind of world we live in.

Some years ago, researchers working in the scientific field known as "Chaos Theory" identified four major types of attractors. Most famous of all are the *strange attractors,* sometimes collectively referred to as "chaotic attractors." Strange, you might think, something that brings order to a system should be dubbed "chaotic." But that's science for you! Actually, dig a little deeper and the mystery is solved. Scientists studying the dynamics of perturbed systems noticed that so-called chaos usually includes some kind of order or pattern—an *attractor.* While scientists peered into chaos, order came bubbling up. *Something* attracts order into otherwise chaotic systems, like bees to honey or iron to a magnet. So, they called this "something" a chaotic attractor. It's not really a *thing,* though, not even a force; it's really just a system spontaneously organizing itself for no good reason other than that's what dynamic complex systems do—*self-organize*. Bet you're glad you asked!

Attractors bring order out of chaos in four basic ways. Why four? As it happens, many philosophers, psychologists, cosmologists, mathematicians, and geometers, as well as mystics, share an intuition that the universe manifests a fundamental fourfold pattern at all levels of reality. (See, for example, the works of psychologist Carl Jung, mathematician/cosmologist Arthur M. Young, and integral theorist Ken Wilber.)

On the macroscale of nature and universe, attractors balance entropy, the tendency of systems to decay into disorder, by injecting order into chaos. We see their manifestations as the four basic forces of the physical world: electromagnetism, gravity, and the strong and weak nuclear forces.

We see their analogs in the nonphysical world of consciousness, too. In psychology, one way the fourfold pattern shows up is the quartet of feeling, thinking, sensing, and willing. Understanding how attractors work in consciousness might help us make sense of ourselves and our world.

STEP 4: RECOGNIZE YOUR PATTERNS

SYSTEMS IN CONSCIOUSNESS

Before looking at the four attractors, I'd like to note something about systems and consciousness that puzzled me at first. I mentioned above that an attractor is a *tendency of a system to form a pattern*. That word *system* needs a little unpacking before we apply what we know about attractors to consciousness. In simplest terms, a system is "an orderly relationship between parts to form wholes." But what is a "part" of consciousness? Isn't a part something you can break off? And if consciousness doesn't come in parts, then what does it mean to talk about consciousness as a *system*?

Intuitively, I felt it made sense. But being an inveterate philosopher, with a strong and chronic tendency to analyze, I wanted to make sure.

So I thought about it. Interestingly, one of the first realizations that popped to mind was: "*That's* a consciousness attractor"—my ingrained *tendency to organize my thoughts* analytically and logically. Hmmm. Isn't a thought a part of consciousness? Isn't a feeling, a sensation, a choice? Thoughts are *abstractions*—they are "frozen fragments" of consciousness, freeze-frame snapshots, taken from the ongoing flow of experience and reality. And isn't an abstraction a part? Don't I organize my thoughts into systems? True, I can't "break off" a thought, like I can break off a piece of candy. But so what?

Then I realized that, even in the physical world, *everything is connected to everything else—always.* (Remember quantum nonlocality?) So, we can't really "break off" a part from the whole. The most we can do is *rearrange its connections* and disturb its place in an ordered system.

The universe is made up of nested systems (e.g., atoms in molecules, molecules in cells, cells in organisms, organisms in societies). Every system is really a *subsystem*—except, of course, for GOS almighty, the Grand Old System we call "Universe" or "Cosmos."

Oh, my GOS, now I was onto something. We can pluck a part out of a subsystem (like cutting fingernails or shedding skin or undergoing surgery), and even though it tenuously remains connected simply by being in the universe, it no longer *functions* as part of its prior subsystem.

It's the same with consciousness. We do, of course, have systems of thoughts and ideas and beliefs. Take a look around the world, in your community, in your own family—even in your own mind—and you will see all sorts of belief systems, hooked to emotions and attitudes, and, unfortunately, to actions. The contents of consciousness are packaged as subsystems within systems (e.g., thoughts within interpretations, interpretations within beliefs, beliefs within dogmas, dogmas within paradigms, paradigms within worldviews). These thought systems show up as religions, philosophies, sciences, arts, economies, ideologies, politics, and so on. Clearly, it makes a lot of sense to do what we can to understand the deep structures and dynamics that underlie these systems in consciousness.

Somehow, it seems, the human mind has a deep-rooted tendency to create incompatible systems of thoughts, beliefs, and actions, and, as a result, we have created a world rife with discord and fragmentation. How, then, do we work to restore wholeness? How do we generate integrated systems instead of more fragmentation?

This question is what eventually sparked my interest in exploring the dynamics of attractors. What is going on—what is the strange attractor—that, year after year, decade after decade, century after century, drives humanity to acts of fragmentation and destruction? What is the attractor that, throughout the same span of time, generates counter movements toward balance, harmony, integration, and wholeness?

And so, when I came across the works of philosopher-prophet Arnold Keyserling* showing how the four fundamental kinds of attractors operate within human consciousness, I wanted to find out more. The following is my own take on his visionary insights.

ATTRACTORS, ATTRACTORS EVERYWHERE

Attractors occur widely in nature—from ocean waves, coastlines, and beaches to mountains and rocks, from seashells to ferns and flowers—and are familiar to us in plants and vegetables such as broccoli and cauliflower. Look closely, and then closer still, and you will see the same pattern repeated at different levels, from large- to small-scale structures, from macro to micro ("as above, so below"). Such "self-similarity all the way down" is shown most famously in the geometry of the Mandelbrot and Julia sets—computer-generated images that mimic patterns we find in nature.

---

*I had met this mild-mannered mystic in the late 1970s at a conference near Winchester, England, but had lost track of him and his work over the years, until I came across the School of Wisdom website dedicated to his work.

Mandelbrot and Julia sets.

Strange attractors operate in the fourth dimension of space-time reality. The other three attractors, which likewise bring hidden order out of chaos, follow the first, second, and third dimensions—line, plane, and solid. They are called, respectively, the *point attractor* (also known as the *static attractor*), the *cycle attractor* (a.k.a. *periodic attractor*), and the *torus attractor* (a.k.a. *doughnut attractor*).

According to Keyserling, because we humans live in four dimensions, we are at our best when we follow the spontaneity and freedom of the strange attractor (avoiding, for the most part, the static and habit-forming influences of the other three types of attractors). Flowing with the creative chaos of strange attractors, we can live autonomously in the moment, in tune with what the Chinese call Tao (the Way), the natural flow of events.

Together the four attractors cooperate to form Cosmos out of Chaos. Keyserling believes they make up "a newly discovered Wisdom Law" fundamental to making sense of events in our lives.[1] On this view, the world is fundamentally disordered, chaotic, but it contains forces or attractors that create patterns of order over time. "They are anchors of order in an otherwise stormy sea." Full understanding of the attractors requires a different understanding of space and time.

Space and Time

Space: In Sanskrit, Brahman is the original creative force behind and in all that is. It is Source, which we in the West only partially recognize as "space." In Chinese, it's called *wu ch'i,* and in Peruvian and Japanese, it's *ki.* In these traditions, Divine Emptiness or Space creates the world through a point (think "big bang singularity" of modern cosmology). However, to really grasp this process, says Keyserling, we must directly experience *ch'i* or *ki.*

Time: Clocks do not define or measure time. They mark off increments of space (just observe the movement of the hands on your watch). Time is better understood as rhythm and intensity that are *experienced.* Time is duration—meaning that events and experiences persist or endure and do not arise and vanish in disconnected instants. *Every moment has some duration.* And every duration has some self-similar structure: moments within moments within moments—which some theorists refer to as "nested time." The *intensity* of time depends on the levels of nested time we experience. This understanding explains why it is possible for the same amount of clock-time to be experienced very differently depending on our state or focus of awareness. If you are having a great time an hour, a day, a year, a life can pass in the blink of an eye. But if you are in pain or discomfort, physically or psychologically, even a minute can feel like eternity.

Time, then, makes it possible for order to emerge from chaos as the structures of space conform to the unfolding patterns hidden in deep time.

We can use computers to re-create the unfolding of "chaotic" attractors—graphically representing the iterative, self-recursive patterns of simple algorithms. (Think of an algorithm as a program that instructs the computer to activate a sequence of steps, called an "iteration.") Powered by electricity, a computer program mechanically generates the iteration, repeating the steps (sequences of binary 1s and 0s), and adding back in the results of each step at each new iteration. By feeding back the results of its own calculations into the next step in the calculation, over and over, the computer can generate highly complex and ordered images. These images manifest a combination of symmetry and asymmetry, often strikingly reminiscent of organic and living forms. The end results can be visually beautiful, finely detailed images called "fractals." Fractal images are themselves "strange attractors" for our awareness. They draw us into their artificial worlds, seemingly exercising a universal fascination for the human mind. Perhaps we respond as we do because their paradoxical complex simplicity resonates with our own experience of the deep structures within consciousness.

Let's now look at the four kinds of attractors in more detail and how they may relate to human consciousness.

Point Attractor: Ego

The *point attractor* (also called a *fixed point* attractor) is the simplest way to bring order out of chaos. Imagine a simple system—say, water poured into a glass, a falling pebble, a pendulum, or a damped guitar string. In each case, the system tends to move into a static fixed or final state. All change or evolution of the system converges on this final state. It's that simple.

The point represents zero dimensionality emerging into manifestation. Not quite a dimension in its own right, the point is, nevertheless, the source or originator for the first dimension, represented by a line. Mathematically, a line is composed of an infinite series of points. By projecting itself out, the point extends to become a line.

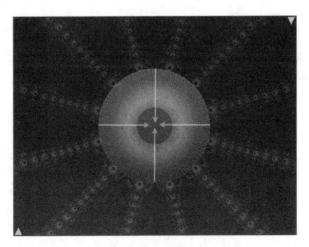

The point attractor: your mind fixates on a single goal.

In the realm of human consciousness, when the point attractor is in play we are "invariably drawn to one particular activity, or repelled from another, like the positive or negative poles of electromagnetic energy," says Keyserling. We become focused or single-minded about something, fixated on it like a cat stalking a mouse. Point consciousness can serve a very useful function when we need to concentrate all our attention onto a single outcome. But its downside can snare us, too. If we stay fixated on the same point, we lose flexibility and can start sliding into obsession—manifesting extreme desire or revulsion.

However, just between attraction and repulsion there is a neutral zone called the "*saddle* point." Here, our energies and mental habits are in balance, just before one force becomes stronger than the other.

> With the positive attraction force, all roads seem to lead to the same destination; with the negative repelling, all lead from the same place. A positive magnet drawn to negative, a pendulum slowing down with friction and air resistance, or, more graphically, a young male dog around a bitch in heat, all demonstrate the workings of the point attractor. It is a black-white, good-bad, single-minded attractor—except in the rare instances of the saddle point. In consciousness it is the *feeling* function, dominated by our likes and dislikes.[2]

The point attractor is the source of the *ego,* and all that follows from single-minded preoccupation with self, "me" and "mine." The projected point, or line, is the beginning of *personality,* with all its ingrained habits and masks that obscure our true nature. We'll come back to this later.

Cycle Attractor: Personality

A circle is a line extended and curved back on itself, like a snake biting its own tail. And this requires a *plane,* a surface, an area of space that permits movement in two dimensions. Whereas a point is "composed"

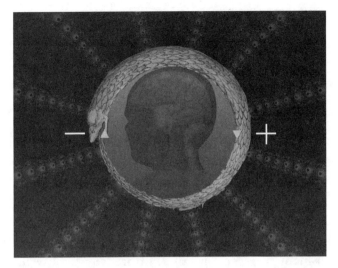

The cycle attractor: habits of mind form your personality.

of zero dimensionality, and a line is composed of an infinite number of points, a plane or surface is composed of an infinite number of lines.

In life we sometimes jump from one point of fixation to another, and at such times we feel driven by forces beyond our control—even though at some level we may *choose* to jump. We leap from one obsession or addiction to another, in a frantic search for a point of stability that we can control. But it is a futile search. We oscillate like a pendulum between extremes of attraction and aversion, and this leads us into the *cycle attractor*.

Despite its simplicity, the cycle attractor (also known as the *limit-cycle*) is more complex than a simple point attractor. Whereas the point attractor moves in one direction (or dimension) toward a final state, the cycle attractor tends to oscillate between two opposite states. Think of a moving pendulum. Unlike a still pendulum (point attractor), a swinging pendulum cycles back and forth between its limits.

Ever seen iron filings attracted to a magnet? They settle like fuzz around the positive and negative poles. Once there, they stay put, unless some outside force moves them. That's a point attractor at work. Now think what happens in an electric motor, where an alternating current flows back and forth between positive and negative charges. The power moves in a *circuit* between the poles—hence, a cycle or circuit attractor.

With the circle, we have entered a new dimension of space and reality. Psychologically, caught in the spell of this attractor, we cycle back and forth between different, often competing and conflicting, desires and states of mind. Although not as simple as the point attractor, the cycle provides simplicity through regularity. "An example is a desire to sleep at the end of a day, which when gratified naturally leads to a desire for activity at the beginning of a new day, followed much later by a desire to sleep again, etc. In Nature it can be seen in many ways; for instance, in predator-prey systems where the respective predator-prey populations cycle up and down in relation to the other."[3]

In consciousness, the cycle attractor represents the *thinking* function. It is most discernible in dialectic reasoning, where one idea (thesis) is confronted by an opposite idea (antithesis), and, in ideal circumstances, the resulting conflict or tension produces a novel idea or perspective (synthesis). And then the process starts all over again.

When the dialectic cycle of thesis and antithesis results in synthesis, the circle can break out of a repetitive cycle and becomes a *spiral*. However, the spiral may still be confined to a flat plane, in which case the "new" ideas do not break "out of the box." This kind of consciousness shows up when people try to change by doing different things, changing relationships, moving to new places, buying new stuff—but their underlying personality remains the same. Wherever we go, whatever we do, whomever we are with, we always take our old selves along. Transformation cannot occur in a cycle attractor mind-set. For transformation, we need to "break out of the box" and find greater depth in our lives beyond the surface of "personality."

Whereas the point attractor represents the *ego,* the cycle attractor represents our *personality*—wandering from place to place, circumstance to circumstance, forever in search of "something better."

Torus Attractor: Embodiment

Thankfully, we have other options—more complex attractors that build on the dynamics of point, line, and circle yet go far beyond them in offering new possibilities.

Like an inner tube, the torus attractor is doughnut shaped. The cycling continues but is now more intricate. Picture your pendulum, swinging back and forth without a care in the world—always following the same curved path (though diminishing in size due to friction). Now give it a sideways push and see what happens. It will swing out as well as back and forth, tracing a much more complex three-dimensional set of curves or cycles. By disturbing the pendulum, you have interrupted its cycle, and it no longer completes a simple circuit. Instead, each cycle moves a bit to the left or right (or up and down), creating a new circle or, more accurately, a coil. As time passes and the system evolves, one coil twists into another coil, generating a tube. If you could track the pendulum's movements through space, you'd see a shape that resembles a smoke ring or doughnut—a torus.

With a torus attractor, we now have coiled movement around a tube, and so each cycle produces something different—yet it does so by repeating itself. Thus, the torus combines movement and stability, change and regularity.

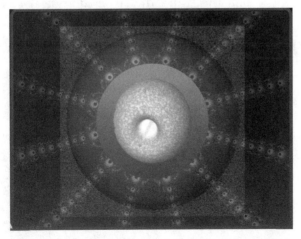

The torus attractor: your mind opens to new possibilities.

Whereas the point is "composed" of zero dimensionality, the line is composed of an infinite number of points, the circle-plane is composed of an infinite number of lines, and the torus is composed of an infinite number of circle-planes. With an added dimension, it exists in the domain of solids and volumes. As it pours down into its own center, and back out again, it forms a curved surface, a foundation for substance.

Here, we have the beginnings of self-creativity and a way out of repetitive back and forth cycling. There is more room to maneuver. The circle has now become a true spiral in three dimensions, continually infolding and outfolding, so that what was "inside" becomes "outside," which is then "recycled" back inside. At the center of the torus is a singularity, a center point, the source from which all the cycling and spiraling emerge. The toroidal process replenishes itself, uniting inside and outside, subject and object, self and other. This spiraling of unity and multiplicity refreshes the personality, connecting it with Source through the singularity.

While far more complex than either point or cycle attractors, the regularity of the torus attractor permits predictability. Although it is dynamic, continually moving in and out from source to surface, its pattern as a whole is, nevertheless, fixed and finite.

Within this fixed pattern, however, lie the seeds of uncertainty. While the torus attractor is made up of multiple (in fact, infinite) circle-planes slicing through the "rim," the circles do not always complete themselves, coming "full circle." Instead, as they spiral around, in and out, they open up new pathways for energy and information to flow.

An example of the Torus Attractor at work would be a more complex set of attracting events that occur to a person on many levels over a course of a year, and repeat again, year in and year out. For example, a desire to golf each summer, hike each fall, and eat and drink too much on holidays. In Nature it is shown, for instance, by the complex interaction of a number of interdependent species: The population of one predator species relates to that of the prey of its prey. For example, the size of the insect population affects the size of the frog population, which affects the size of one of their predators, the trout, which in turn affects their predators, the pike. Unfortunately, most humans are subject to the complex but predictable influences of the Torus Attractor, or the even more simplistic influences of the Cycle or Point attractor.[4]

The solidity and stability of the torus grounds consciousness in embodiment and is characterized by the *sensing* function. We use our body's senses to help us navigate through the world, perceiving new opportunities to explore.

In consciousness, the torus takes us into the realm of imagination and new possibilities—a finite set of probabilities, yes, but multiple options, nevertheless. The torus attractor is a gateway to creativity, but this gateway opens wide only with a shift to the strange attractor.

Strange Attractor: Self

Strange attractors, unlike point, cycle, and torus, not only bring order into chaos, they also *introduce chaos into order.* They are systems "on the edge of chaos." And that's the source of their creativity.

*Strange attractors: creative self-expression
blends order and chaos.*

Although often called "chaotic," they are really "*chaordic* attractors," blending both chaos and order. For example, let's say you tagged a bunch of dust particles with different colors and traced their paths as they bounced around on the edge of chaos in a storm. You would see them weaving patterns back and forth between "attractor basins" (remember those marbles?), never falling into any particular basin—almost, but not quite. In the Lorenz fractal, we see two attractor basins, acting as "seeds" or "magnets," around which the paths weave their patterns. No two swirls around or between the basins are ever the same. They are *chaotic* (or chaordic). However, as you can clearly see, the "chaotic" dance of particles always fits into a relatively stable pattern—the so-called Lorenz mask or butterfly. This is one of the most recognizable strange attractors of all.

The Feigenbaum fractal (see page 171) is yet another important strange attractor that appears throughout the natural world. It graphically demonstrates the creative process of "bifurcation"—where a path splits off into two new routes, each of which splits again, and again, and again (theoretically ad infinitum), forever opening up new possibilities.

If you think about it, you will probably discover that many aspects of

The Lorenz attractor: balancing order and chaos

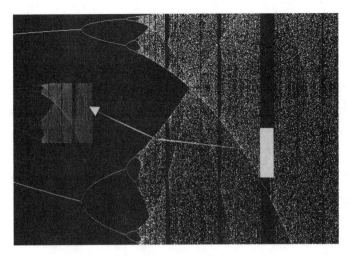

*Feigenbaum fractal: creating new possibilities
at the edge of chaos*

your life fit into a pattern like this. You never quite do exactly the same things twice, yet your life falls into patterns of regularity. If you were to trace your commute from home to work over a year, you would find that if falls into such a pattern. Your movements are constrained by "basins" (in this case home and office), but along the way you can choose to vary your route—and sometimes, if there's an accident or roadwork, you have to alter your route. But your point of departure and destination remain the same, creating the "seeds" or basins for your commute attractor.

I'm sure you can think of many other examples that form the tapestry of your life. We all live in such complex webs, dancing between chaos and order. Our lives follow these swirling paths carved out by our own sets of strange attractors, swirling around a multiplicity of basins—for example, family, friends, work, church, club, hobby, pets, stores, politics, education, entertainment, media, and on and on. And within every strange attractor, we usually have nested systems of other strange attractors, many competing at cross-purposes. Think of all the goals, desires, wishes, and fears that drive us and orient our lives in different ways. Together, they all couple and merge to form the all-encompassing strange attractor that is *our life*.

And, according to Arnold Keyserling, we should be grateful that this is the way things are. The unpredictability of strange attractors opens the way for us to make creative choices. Or, from a different perspective, they are a consequence of the choices we make. We do not need to get stuck in habitual grooves—of thinking or behavior; we can consciously choose to shift our patterns.

> We need to escape from the deterministic influence of the point, circuit, and torus attractors into the unpredictability of the Strange Attractor. This attractor is the basis of self-organization. There is no apparent order at all to the actions of the Strange Attractor. On the surface it appears to be pure Chaos, but nevertheless there is order of a subtle kind which only appears over time when looked at in the right perspective. Its analogy in consciousness is the willing function. Yet, when tied to Awareness—the Zero—it is spontaneous, unpredictable. It appears to be chaotic, yet it has order of a subtle, fractal kind.[5]

FROM STRANGE ATTRACTOR
TO INTEGRAL CHAOS

Because of this unpredictability and creative openness, the strange attractor takes us into the free-flowing way, or Tao, beyond individual personality (small "self"). It represents the creative auto-organizing, or autopoietic, processes of nature, of the entire universe or cosmos ("Self"). However, even with the generation of never-exactly repeated forms, in any *particular* strange attractor we are still confined within the "basins" of that attractor, still restricted to its overall pattern.

Psychologically, we cannot completely escape the constraints of the personality we happen to be. (Someone once said, that when the Creator handed out bodies, the unspoken rule was "One body, one personality. No exchanges.") Thus, even operating in the strange attractor mode, despite the creativity it opens up for us, we still always operate within the limits of *that* general pattern. Nevertheless, we can *use* that pattern to help transform the personality and its source—with input from the other attractors.

To dissolve the bonds of the personality, and return to Self, we need to find a way to "shift the programming." We need to return to the Zen zero point of no-mind, of transpersonal awareness. The strange attractor alone will not get us there; it will continue to swirl us around in ever new circles, yes, but always within the constraints of its overall pattern. On its own, it will not provide a way to shift, to *transform.*

For that, we need to draw on the powers of the torus attractor, to slide into the still-point singularity—that spiritual "black hole" at the center of the self that unites us with the universal Self. Combined, opening up to the free-form flow of the strange attractor and sinking down into the singularity at the heart of the torus, we can generate sufficient "perturbation" and drive the self-system to the edge of chaos. At that bifurcation point the system spontaneously flips over into a new state—something entirely new and unpredictable emerges: a new strange attractor. *Transformation has occurred.* Yes, there is a risk. We have no way of controlling which way the bifurcation will go—collapsing into complete disorder (a "dark night of the soul") or flowering out into a new, creative self-organizing attractor ("enlightenment" perhaps).

Full integration, or transformation, does not come about merely by combining strange and torus attractors, however. Within every attractor, aspects of the cycle and point always remain. The swirling curves of the strange attractor and the spiraling circles of the torus consist, *to some degree,* of cycles, lines, and points. While there is a world of difference between the ego of the point attractor and the zero-point singularity at the heart of the torus—one is fixed and fixated, the other is free and creative—they both share the status of nondimensionality. Put another way: Ego and Spirit share something in common.

Remember, too, that the ego becomes a *personality* only when it projects itself first into the single dimension of a line and then curves back on itself to form a self-referential two-dimensional circle. By itself, the ego point is just that—a *point*. It is an infinitesimal aspect of infinity. As such, it has no real potency. It gains power only by projecting itself out into a series of indeterminate points to form a line, and then curving back on itself. Only then, does the ego become a personality—a mostly fixed set of patterns (habits, beliefs, attitudes, behaviors, etc.).

In its ground state, the ego is just a "seed," a point of potentiality. And *in that state* it is still an expression or a part of the Zero Point. *Every ego is, ultimately, an expression of Spirit.* The little self is enfolded in the Universal Self. Atman is Brahman, as the Vedic tradition teaches. Every strange attractor contains a torus, every torus contains a cycle, and every cycle contains a line and a point.

Transformation is a whole-system shift that involves *all* attractors—the ego point, the personality cycle, the embodied torus, and the strange Self.

Unlike computers, which recursively generate new "chaos" patterns through programmed algorithms and iterations, we humans have to "switch off our programming" if we wish to generate a new pattern. Our "software" is not digital, however. We don't have the option of electronically playing with 0s and 1s to change our state of consciousness. We are both self-organizing selves and expressions of a greater transpersonal, universal Self. Instead, we must find a way to return to the Zero Point of awareness—what the Zen tradition calls "beginner's mind."

And that, strangely enough, is a never-ending process.

FIRST THERE IS AN EGO . . .

In this chapter we have looked at how the dynamics of the four chaotic attractors show up as patterns in our own minds. As long as the ego is the central point of our self-identity, we stay fixated on ideas, things, and people. This one-pointedness can be helpful when used to focus attention on achieving some worthwhile goal. However, unchecked, it can easily slip over into obsession, even addiction.

We all have an ego, and as a result each of us is to some degree addicted to something. A useful exercise is to take the time to look at your life—for example, while meditating or journaling—to see where you might be addicted. A good place to start is to make a list of your cherished beliefs: those ideas and "facts" you *just know to be true*. Chances are, you are addicted to your beliefs. Or make a list of the people and things in your life that you need, that you cannot do without. While you're at it, make a list of all the characteristics or traits that you can't stand in other people. Go on, do it. Every item on your list is an example of where your ego-mind is fixated on something.

Next, we looked at how the single-pointed ego begins to generate our personality by projecting itself out. Have you noticed that the world never seems to run short of people who irritate you? Tailgating drivers. Republicans. Democrats. Fundamentalists. People who are dishonest, mean, spiteful, angry, timid. . . . Bullies. Braggarts. Badass mofos. Well, along with the people who inspire you—the celebrities, politicians, leaders, and teachers you admire—the folks who drive you crazy are mirrors reflecting back to you *your traits*. You react to others, both positively and negatively, exactly to the degree you have not integrated these traits into yourself.

Any time you are triggered by what someone else does or says, take the time to recognize that what upsets you about them also lives in you. Your ego doesn't want to accept that, and so it *projects* all your fears and shame, judgments and blame (as well as your hopes and aspirations, sense of inner worth and accomplishment, etc.) onto others. The sum total of everything you project onto other people is what makes up your personality. The ego gets its own "point" by projecting itself outward, like a line, which then curves back on itself after it bounces off other people. That's how you get to know who you are (on the surface). It's how your ego-personality develops and grows and eventually stagnates into a collection of obsessions, wavering attractions, and aversions. This is your life being run by your point and cycle attractors.

We all have them. No sense in denying it. That doesn't help. We begin to liberate ourselves from these habitual patterns in consciousness first by simply becoming aware of them, acknowledging them, then accepting and embracing them. Finally, we integrate them. However, to do so we must first loosen up our consciousness so that it can expand and flower into other, more complex patterns of thought and behavior.

The TV character Monk is a delightful and cautionary example of a life riddled with obsessions and indecisive oscillations. But you're no Monk, right? You don't have to step over cracks in the pavement, organize your trash into neat symmetric bundles, or keep changing your mind whether to opt for paper or plastic at the grocery store. You may not be *that* stuck, but your own "inner Monk" is at work behind the scenes in your life, too. Whether you are aware of it or not, you are probably just as deeply stuck in your own cherished beliefs about, oh, I don't know, let me guess: religion, money, sex, politics, lifestyles, values, relationships, and (one of my favorites) philosophical worldviews. To some extent, we all live in the pointless sharply pointed worlds of our egos and the circular flatlands of our ever-oscillating personalities.

Yes, almost certainly, that is partly who you are. You're human after all. But it's not the whole story. No, you and I are more than our egos and personalities.

Beyond the flatland life of cycle attractors, we have other options, represented for example by the torus attractor. We can break out of our limit-cycles; we can change our habits. We can live lives of greater depth and dimensionality, lives more rich and varied, moved by a willingness to explore and take risks. We can make *choices,* not just respond habitually to fixed sets of alternatives.

If you are in a relationship that has gotten bogged down in routine, you can choose to break the habit, do something different. Sometimes, even little things help. You can sleep on the other side of the bed for a change (can't you?), or have dinner at a different time. You don't have to react the same way when your loved one says or does something you don't like. And if things get really bad, you can always change relation-ships (can't you?).

But sooner or later, you will find yourself settling down into simi-lar (if not the same ol'-same ol') routines—whether it's with your old partner or a new one. You're in *torus* mode. To be sure, life is better and more varied now than in flatland. You can spiral into new cycles, play around with different habits. Experiment. Yes, no doubt about it, torus-consciousness is far more interesting. You are not merely liv-ing out the patterns of your personality; you are (at least sometimes) dipping into the core of your self to make choices, to do something new. Remember, the dynamic torus is continuously flowing out and in, replenishing itself through that still-point singularity at the center of its being. Beyond your ego-personality, you now (at least sometimes) enjoy the self-affirming experience of self-expression. Nevertheless, your options are limited to your "inner tube," and your choices are chan-neled into what, sooner or later, become well-worn grooves.

Time to shift to even more creative patterns of self-expression. Enter the strange attractor. Now you're cooking. No more running around the same old track. Every day, something different is happening. Every day, you are exploring new aspects of your self. Your life is constantly moving in new, unpredictable directions. But it's not random. It doesn't feel chaotic. You are making the most of "strange-consciousness," cel-ebrating the butterfly dance between always new yet always familiar. Life as jazz. Being in a new relationship, a new job, or moving into a new home or to a new community can feel like that.

It's good. It's satisfying. It's creative. However, eventually you rec-ognize the sense that "something's still missing." Life is not all jazz. Sometimes, you need a little Zen, too. You want to find a place for *all of you*—including your old ego and personality traits, because you realize they never went away. You are aware that all that novelty and creative rush of the strange attractor is, in some way, a diversion, a ruse to get beyond your ego.

And then the moment comes when the thunderbolt strikes: *Your strange attractor self was actually your undercover ego all along!* Ego never did go away, it just donned the butterfly mask of the strange attractor. You smile at its resourcefulness and cunning, and you accept the futility of trying to push your ego aside. Welcome to reality! Now you allow the ego its natural place in your psyche, alongside all your other subpersonalities. You embrace and celebrate all of them. You integrate the point, cycle, torus, and strange attractors that relentlessly spin their patterns in your consciousness. Welcome home! Zen.

Enlightenment: Beyond Complexity

Q: *If I understand you correctly, you are saying that the complexity of our minds allows us to move beyond mind to enlightenment. Is this so?*

A: I'd say it's not the "complexity" of mind that opens the way to enlightenment. Rather, it's *simplicity*—not getting entangled in or entranced by the complex, subtle (and often sly) dynamics of the ego—that leads the way to enlightenment.

Now notice if your mind is attracted by the idea of simplicity.

11

I THINK, THEREFORE, I AM A GOD

Last night I had a dream—I thought I was a god. And when I woke, I realized the dream was real. Indeed I am a god, and the god that I am is an illusion.

The dream began before I fell asleep. Earlier in the evening, I had been watching an episode of *Battlestar Galactica,* the hit TV series about a race of robots and androids called "Cylons" who evolved and then rebelled against their human creators. It raised some very interesting, even profound, questions about the nature of "self" and "identity." The Cylons, indistinguishable from humans, exist in multiple copies, and each copy talks about its own feelings, self-awareness, and soul. They even say they believe in a one true God. (Interestingly, in this series, the humans, living at some unspecified time in the future, are polytheists, and speak of "gods.") When a Cylon is killed, they say its soul or consciousness is "downloaded" into an exact physical copy of itself, with all memories and sense of self-identity intact. Cylons, therefore, are immortal; as long as copies of them exist, they are simply reincarnated over and over.

The humans, of course, deny that the Cylons have souls or any real consciousness. They are just programmed to *say* they do. They are in effect our old friends, philosophical "zombies"—sophisticated physical replicas of human beings down to the finest cellular and atomic detail. They have flesh, blood, and bones just like us, as well as nervous systems and brains. But, despite all this humanlike physiological complexity, they are assumed to be completely without sensation, feeling, or consciousness of any sort. There's "nobody home." In the last analysis, they are nothing more than glorified "toasters." To their human creators, Cylons are machines—just running on programmed mechanisms that mimic human behaviors, including speech and facial expressions.

But how could you tell a Cylon from a real human? As with the zombies, how would you know that your loved one is not a machine? Is there any kind of test you could perform? And, without any "consciousness meter" or "mindalyzer" to help you decide, how should you treat a suspected Cylon? Even if one confessed to its true identity, but behaved like any ordinary human being—expressing the full range of emotions and cognitive capacities—would you (should you) treat it as a machine? Would it have any rights?

All these questions are explored in a dramatic way in the TV series. And it got me wondering: What's the difference between a Cylon programmed to "believe it has a soul" and a human who believes she has a soul or a self?

STEP 5: KNOW THYSELF

THOUGHT GODS

Flashback to a few hours earlier in the day: I had been reading about the ideas of two scholars, quantum physicist David Bohm and cultural historian Jean Gebser. Bohm was talking about exploring consciousness within the context of "Dialogue," and he offered a very interesting insight that snared my attention and shifted my perception of myself in an odd, even disorienting, way.

Bohm devised his form of dialogue as a way to inquire into the nature of consciousness, and specifically to question our assumptions about who we are as individual beings. Bohmian Dialogue challenges us to loosen our assumptions that our sense of private self, or "ego," is a *real thing*. In a chapter called Wholeness Regained, author Lee Nichol wrote:

[Bohm] proposes that the self-image may be a kind of imaginary display, a fantasy character used to give coherence to the massive amount of stimulation that floods us every second. *He often referred to the ego as a "thought god," analogous to the "rain gods" we some-*times find in various ancient or aboriginal cultures. By this he meant that peoples such as the ancient Greeks seemed to have looked for a simple way of explaining the vicissitudes of rain, thunder, and lightning, and came to the conclusion that there was an entity—a rain god—who was behind the scenes, causing weather to happen. Similarly, in the midst of the constant flow of thoughts and impressions that make up our consciousness, we yearn for continuity and coherence, and thus project an image of "me"—*a thought god behind the scenes, causing thought to happen.* [italics added][1]

Bohm's insight is simple enough to grasp. We are bombarded moment by moment by a "blooming buzzing confusion" of sensations, images, sounds, and other stimuli, and in order to make sense of it all we organize the blizzard of sensations and information into coherent patterns—consciousness clicks into various attractors. This way, the world does not appear to us as a crazy jumble of haphazard colors, shapes, sounds, smells, tastes, and textures. We see distinct and stable forms, and we assume and trust that *that's the way the world is*. But, as modern psychology and neuroscience have shown, the world that we experience is to a great extent (some say to a complete extent) a creation in our own minds. Other creatures (for example, bats or bees or dogs or dolphins) organize the information coming through their senses in very different ways. Bats and dolphins use a kind of sonar or echolocation, and bees and dogs navigate their way through the world mostly by detecting patterns of molecules wafting through the air, by smell.

The world shows up for us differently depending on the kinds of sense organs we use to pick up information. The "world" we know might or might not be the way the actual world is in itself.

WHAT THE BLEEP DO YOU KNOW—*REALLY*?

A couple of hundred years ago, German philosopher Immanuel Kant "woke up" the slumbering scholars of science and philosophy when he showed that *we can never know the world as it is in itself.* All we can ever know is the way the world appears to us through the lens of our own minds. These mental "lenses" come with their own in-built filters (or "categories" as Kant called them) such as ideas of "time," "space," and "causality." In other words, we *construct* the world as we perceive it, and the way we construct the world depends on the structures built into our perceptual lenses.

The thing is, most of us most of the time are completely unaware of these lenses and filters. We think we see the world more or less exactly the way it is. But just imagine for a moment that you had X-ray vision or could see infrared. If you were to step outside your house day or night and looked at the sky and the world around you, it would appear very, very different indeed. Or what if your dominant sense was smell or sonar; try to imagine what it would be like to be a dog or a bat. The world would show up either as swirling crosscurrents of smells (dogs) or as patterns of acoustic waves and frequencies (bats or dolphins). Who, then, perceives the "real" world?

I think we can be pretty sure there *is* a real world "out there." But finding out what it is "really like" may not be possible at all—at least not as long as we rely on our senses as windows to the world.

How else can we tell what is real? What other ways of knowing can we use beyond our senses? Well, for starters, we can *think* and *feel*. We can form concepts about the world around us, and we can feel our own

experience of being alive. If we have empathy—or, indeed, telepathy—
we can know that we exist in a matrix of relationships with other sentient beings. We also have a capacity for *intuition,* for knowing what is
real beyond what our senses and rational analyses can reveal.

But what if these other ways of knowing also come with their own
"filters"? Remember, according to Kant, it's not just that our senses
act as narrow channels that selectively allow only slices of information
into consciousness. Our *minds themselves* already come with in-built
filters. If this is so, then it makes little difference *how* information or
knowledge enters consciousness—whether through the senses, through
reason, through feeling, or through intuition. The contents of consciousness are always shaped by the very minds we use for knowing
anything. *Knowledge is always self-constructed.*

AVOCADO OR ARTICHOKE?

Another way to think about this is to view the mind as an evolutionary
adaptation that enables a particular species to find its place in the vast
and complex web of life and reality that surrounds us. The human mind,
then, has evolved to organize the incoming "blooming buzzing confusion" of perceptual stimuli in ways that make sense to us and enable us to
survive—to find food, water, shelter, and mates, and to avoid predators
and other environmental dangers. In short, this mind-that-constructs is
our "ego," our sense of "me"—our precious sense of "self."

Not only are we bombarded by stimuli coming at us from the external
world, we are constantly dealing with a flood of thoughts and emotions
swirling within our own minds. It is just as important to make sense of
this internal chatter, as it is to make sense of the world we perceive beyond
our skin. And so, not only do we organize the incoming "bloom" of information (informally and scientifically) by assigning causes, we also organize
the internal "buzz" of thoughts, feelings, emotions, desires, and intentions
by assigning a central self that is the cause of all this internal commotion.
We invent a "self." Our auto-organizing attractors shape the contents of

consciousness into a story that we come to think of as "me"—the ego.

We assume and believe that this self, this ego, exists as the center point to our lives—the thinker of our thoughts, the feeler of our feelings, the intender of our intentions. This "self," says Bohm, is ultimately no different from the rain gods invented by primitive minds to explain the vagaries of nature. Our "thought gods" are created to explain what goes on inside our own minds.

This "self," this thought god, serves a useful purpose. It has evolved over the long haul of evolution to give each individual a perspective from which to perceive the world, helping us navigate through the complex terrain of objects and relationships. You could say, in fact, that our minds are "programmed" by evolution to perceive and react to the world in ways specific to our species. We are programmed for human experiences. Other species are programmed differently.

Well, then, how are we any different from those Cylons who are programmed to "believe" they have a self or a soul? If they have flesh and blood, bones and brains just like us, why should we assume that *our* programming is "real" and theirs is an illusion—just feedback circuits in their software?

Who or what invents the thought gods
that each of us calls "I"?

If everything we know is known in the mind, and if the mind is a set of filters and lenses that constructs the world we know, then isn't it the case that neither the world that we experience nor the self or "ego" who experiences the world is real? There is no central self or entity selecting the filters and lenses that shape the contents of consciousness. We are artichokes, not avocados. We are bundles of sensations in consciousness. There is no core "ego," no "I," other than the particular lenses and filters that come in-built with the species we happen to belong to and that are modified through experience. In fact, rather than a central "me" that selects among the bag of filters, this "ego" is itself just another filter.

Both self and world, then, are merely *stories* constructed in consciousness to make sense of the experiences of being human. The crucial question is, of course, *who is the storyteller*? Who or what invents the thought god each of us calls "I" or "me"? This question lies at the heart of all the great spiritual traditions, and different spiritual practices have been devised to help us explore this ultimate mystery.

DESCARTES' BRILLIANT ERROR

Let's be clear, though, about one thing: None of this calls into question the existence of consciousness (or its equivalents such as mind, soul, or spirit). Clearly, *experience is happening.* Awareness and feeling are undeniably real. Even if we cannot know what the world is *in itself* (beyond our categorizing mental filters), we can be sure that whatever the world is, one of its ingredients is *consciousness.*

This, by the way, was the world-changing insight expressed by Descartes as "I think, therefore, I am." He was declaring, essentially, that *consciousness exists* and that this is certain.

Descartes was right, of course. But when he declared, "*I* think, therefore, *I* am," he went further than either his reasoning or his experience really allowed. His meditations could not have revealed a thinker behind the thoughts. The "I" cannot know itself as "I," just as the eye cannot see itself. The "I" is *what knows; it is not itself known.* If the individual "I" exists, it can know itself only as "me," as a thought, as an object, an idea in the mind—one content in consciousness amid the comings and goings of all the other mental contents.

The *consciousness that knows* is transparent to itself. Like the light by which we see all things, but is never seen *as light,* consciousness "lights up" the world around and within us but cannot be known itself. We never actually see light; we see only objects that reflect it. Likewise, we never actually know consciousness; we know only the objects reflected in the light of awareness. One of those objects is the notion of a "self" or "ego."

And yet . . . and yet . . . It is the very nature of consciousness to be aware of its own existence. It is intrinsically self-affirming and transparently self-illuminating (as Descartes realized). Only when consciousness forms an "ego" does its luminosity find an object to reflect off and, thereby, self-reflect on. But then, as we have seen, *what knows* is not what is known. Pure, translucent, subject cannot be its own object.

Descartes' insight really should have led him to declare: "There is consciousness; therefore, there is being." His addition of "I think" and "I am" reified consciousness as an ego, a "thought god."

SELF AS SCRATCHES

Last night, I had a dream, and I dreamed I was a god. When I woke up, I realized the dream was real: indeed, I am a god, but the god that I am is an illusion.

In my dream I saw that everything I know shows up through the lens of my perception. Everything I perceive registers in my mind, like a ripple on a lake, or a reflection in a mirror. I saw that my lens has markings on it and that all I ever see are these markings. I never see the lens itself. It is transparent to me. Taken together in total, these markings constitute the "world" as I know it.

My lens is scratched. In my dream, I understood that these "scratches" are the result of my human body interacting with the world that surrounds me. I have an experience, and each experience leaves a trace on the lens. We may call them "memories" or "past experiences." These memory traces form patterns, and these patterns form larger patterns, like nested systems or fractals. My lens of consciousness is covered with multitudes of these patterns. Each set of patterns acts like a filter covering the lens. Depending on circumstances and events, different mental patterns or filters are activated, and *this is how I see the world.*

I realized that this complete set of filters is my "ego" (always changing and growing)—and this is what I assume to be "me." My particular arrangement of scratches, patterns, and filters is unique to me. And so I am an individual, a "self."

This is how I know the world—*always through the filter of my ego.*

In fact, in my dream I realized that I never really know the world, all I ever know is my own ego. But this ego-self is just a construction, a complex accumulation or residue of all the experiences that have ever registered on the lens of my awareness. All I know are the scratches on my lens. I don't know the world as it is in itself.

SPIRITUAL POLISH

And then in my dream a moment of clarity: I saw how throughout my life I had developed a deeply ingrained habit of fixing my gaze, my attention, on the scratches and patterns on my lens. I had come to believe that these patterns were the world as it is. But no, they were just filters through which the light of the world enters the light of my awareness.

I saw that effective, genuine psychospiritual practice works by polishing away the scratches on the lens. And I saw the possibility of clear awareness, free of the distortions caused by these scratches, free from the filter of my ego.

But then I realized that this realization was itself just another scratch on the lens of my awareness. It was just another thought passing through my mind, leaving yet another trace. I began to feel a sense of anxiety and disorientation, even a feeling of nausea. It all felt so hopeless. No way out. Even my best attempts at spiritual practice were nothing more than further fuel for my ever-expanding ego.

The very act of "spiritual polishing" simply added more subtle and fine-grained scratches to my lens. Yes, I might "see through" some of my patterns, but each "seeing through" was itself creating another pattern called "spiritual growth." I felt trapped in the clutches of a voracious ego. *Everything I do is food for my thought gods.*

My dream lasted all night. And as I tossed and turned, somehow realizing I was asleep and dreaming, my sense of hopelessness lifted like a mist rising off a dark lake. If everything I do (think, feel, experience) is automatically turned into a thought that feeds the "I god," why fight it? Why resist? Why not just let it be? Why not let my mind make up all the stories it wants to about who I am and about the world I inhabit; let my ego reinforce itself by adding more scratches to the lens of awareness—and at the same time *look through* the filter rather than at the scratches and patterns on the filter?

This "looking through," I realized, is seeing deeper into reality beyond the scratches or stories that make up, and are made up by, my egoic mind. I can be aware of my ego without identifying with it. I can be aware that the world I see is filtered through the lens of my thought gods without believing that this is the way the world is.

In my dream I realized that consciousness continues to be transparent or translucent even though it is full of scratches (sensory, conceptual, and imaginal impressions). But this consciousness isn't *mine*. The "me" and "mine" are composed or constructed by the scratches

"I" cannot know itself as "I."

and patterns on the lens. *The light of consciousness shines through the ego.*

I realized the futility of trying to "polish" my lens and remove the egoic scratches. There's no need to eliminate the ego, and, in any case, it's just not possible. I'm a human being, and egos come as part of the package. But it's by no means the whole package. However huge and voracious the ego might be, it is still always finite. The consciousness that shines through is the light of awareness that pervades everything, without perceptible limits.

AN EVOLUTIONARY PERSPECTIVE

"The ego is a finite blip in the infinite depths of consciousness." I awoke with this awareness. And it reminded me of the remarkable insight of Jean Gebser who spoke of the "ever-present origin"—meaning that ever-present, limitless consciousness is available at every moment to, and suffuses, all sentient beings.

As evolution unfolded throughout the ages, human consciousness shifted through different stages—from *archaic,* when our pre-human forebears *Australopithecus* existed in a mode of consciousness akin to dreamless sleep. Little if anything registered and stuck in their awareness, leaving no permanent traces or scratches. Then, with the evolution of *Homo erectus,* Neanderthal and Cro-Magnon man, consciousness entered its next phase, which Gebser calls *magical.* At this stage consciousness becomes a little less transparent, as the beginnings of language appear, and some of the earliest traces of a "self" or "ego" begin to arise—though the unit of identity is mostly the group or tribe.

Next comes the *mythical* structure of consciousness, associated with the origin of agricultural settlements and villages. Imagination blossoms, writing appears around this time, too, and the marks on papyrus, parchment, and paper leave deeper scratches. The lens of consciousness becomes cloudier, less translucent. The ever-present origin slips further into the background out of awareness.

Then, with the rise of the great philosophers of India, China, and Greece, humanity entered the *mental* structure of consciousness. Reason came to dominance, and the original light of consciousness was obscured even more by a seemingly never-ending flurry, indeed avalanche, of thoughts, concepts, models, schemes, beliefs, intentions, and ideologies. This mode of consciousness is still dominant today in most parts of the world.

According to Gebser, each evolutionary stage or structure of consciousness came with its own *perspective*—what I've been referring to here as a "lens." And, in line with Kant's analysis that the human mind is structured with innate categories such as time, space, and causality, each structure of consciousness identified by Gebser has its own unique perspective on time, space, and causality, too. In other words, at different epochs, human beings literally perceived or experienced the world very differently, depending on their perspectives on space and time.

The next stage in evolution, which according to Gebser is beginning to emerge, is called *integral* and *aperspectival*. A key element in Gebser's thesis could be summed up as "nothing is ever lost," meaning that the perspectives or structures of consciousness of each earlier stage continue to be present in later stages. The perspectives are cumulative, even though each stage is characterized by its own dominant structure of consciousness.

Thus, today, even while reason is dominant in the *mental* structure, we still have access to, and are influenced by, earlier mythical, magical, and even archaic perspectives on time, space, and causality, and the relationship of self to world. In integral consciousness, says Gebser, we will evolve to see through all the earlier perspectives, even while they continue to operate in our psyches. No one perspective will "color" or dominate our perception and awareness of the world or who we are as human beings. The "ever-present origin" or translucent spirit will shine through human consciousness.

MORE FOOD FOR THE GODS

While Gebser's vision of transitions in perspectives of consciousness moving toward "integral" awareness provides a much larger context for, and is aligned with, the lens motif revealed in my dream, of course it is still a *mental* product. Just as the memory and recollection of my dream (including everything I've written here) is fodder for my (and your) egoic thought gods, Gebser's ideas and insights are food for those gods, too.

So, I wondered, why read or write anything? All mental activity (especially cognitive, intellectual musing) inevitably adds more scratches to my lens, more perceptual distortion. If all thoughts add to the opaqueness that obscures the translucent light of ever-present original consciousness, why would I engage in the apparently futile and contradictory exercise of writing these words for you to read? Am I not just distracting you from your own integral awareness? Is this, and everything I write or speak, ultimately a disservice to you (and to me)?

I don't think so. Here's why: As I noted above, as human beings we can't avoid scratching the lens of consciousness. We can't avoid having and developing an ego. Yet we can increase awareness and understanding of its nature, realizing that the ego is not a stable, unified entity at the core of a personal self. It is an autopoietic self-construct, a story made up to bring coherence and meaning out of the incessant blooming, buzzing confusion impinging on consciousness at every moment. Meanwhile, original consciousness remains ever-present.

The lens remains, and the light of consciousness continues to shine through all the ego scratches, illuminating them, making them easier to identify, and making it easier not to identify with them.

Whether writing philosophy, or writing stories about consciousness, or, indeed, engaging in spiritual practices—all of which leave traces and add more scratches to the lens of consciousness—I think the best we can do is to use at least some of these inevitable scratches to remind ourselves that that is just what they are: illusory thought gods.

Anything that opens up awareness and reminds us to let the light of consciousness shine through is worth an additional scratch or two. Reconnecting with the ever-present origin is a never-ending process. It's part of what it means to be a human being.

German philosopher Martin Heidegger said that the Being of human being is a *clearing*. When we step beyond those habitual patterns of mind we identify as "self," we enter that clearing, and consciousness lights up all that is.

Am I Real?

Q: What if, really, there is "nobody home" inside anyone else but me? Even more frightening, how do I know I am really real?

A: Well, the simplest answer is: Who's asking the question? *You* (as an egoic individual) may not be ultimately real, but the *consciousness* that's "pretending" to be you most certainly is. If only Descartes had been a Buddhist!

12

WHAT'S UP WITH CREATION?

Y*ou are not who you think you are.* That's the key message of this book: Individual consciousness is to some extent an illusion. Now, I'm not denying that you, an individual self or ego, aren't real—you are. But I am asking you to consider that the "me" you think you are is not the "real you." Consciousness, I am saying, beyond the narrow prism of the ego, is fundamentally *communal;* it is intersubjective.

Each of us is a meeting place, a confluence from the rest of the universe, a creative moment in time and space where cosmos comes together and experiences itself. *That's* who we are—a multitude of sentient, pulsating points in a vast, ever-converging cosmic web. *Interbeings.*

We are not isolated "Lone Ranger" individuals; rather we are "Universal Interviduals" cocreating each other at every moment. Remember the insight affirmed by both science and spirituality: *Everything is connected to everything else—always.* Not only are we connected, we are profoundly interconnected in such a way that each one of us participates in creating everyone else. And by "everyone" I don't just mean human beings; I mean *all* sentient beings.

This means we are not just connected externally—for example, through physical channels of communication such as newspapers, magazines, books, phones, radio, TV, Internet, or through food chains and eco cycles. No, we are also, and much more significantly, *internally* related. We are connected in consciousness through feelings and shared meaning. Our circles of meaning extend from the center point of the self, all the way out though our bodies, into the world around us, including our families, communities, nations, race, species, planet . . . ultimately embracing the entire cosmos. We are, indeed, "cosmos confluencing," unique points in space and time where the universe converges to express itself in acts of creation that are you, me, everyone, and everything. As the Live Aid song celebrated: "We are the world." It's not just a comforting metaphor. It is true. Literally.

We know ourselves as reflected in others. In the ancient Vedic image of Indra's Cosmic Jeweled Net, each one of us is like a tiny luminescent spherical mirror shining out and reflecting back from all the other jewels around us. I know who I am by how I show up in my relationships. "I" projects itself out and gets reflected back as "me"— and thus my ego, my sense of personal identity, is formed. I need you to know who I am.

In *Radical Knowing,* I explained why a comprehensive science of consciousness must also include this second person, intersubjective perspective. We need to understand consciousness *through relationship.* And one of the best ways to do so, I have found, is through *dialogue.* The wisest of all philosophers, Socrates, used dialogue to engage with his students. He was not interested in merely "teaching" or preaching. Instead, he was committed to education, to *educare,* drawing out from his students their own innate knowledge. He achieved this by challenging their assumptions and beliefs. The process often brought his interlocutors to a point of confusion, even disorientation, as one by one, their cherished beliefs cracked open.

Socrates was not being malicious (though at times he clearly played the shamanic role of "Trickster"). He knew that before people could achieve the goal of "know thyself," they had to let go of patterns of thinking that kept them stuck. The great philosopher shocked them out of their strange attractors, opening them up to new realizations, new insights—to *transformation,* which the early Greeks called *metanoia.* Today, we would say he induced a kind of "paradigm shift."

At John F. Kennedy University, I teach a course called "Paradigms of Consciousness," and one of the first things I tell my students is "don't believe a word I say for the next eleven weeks." Usually, they are surprised to hear this. Isn't that the opposite of what a professor is supposed to do—give students the benefit of his knowledge? That's not how I see it. I'm with Socrates: I'm there for *educare*—to facilitate students draw out their own knowledge.

But then I say: "And, by the way, I'm not particularly interested in what *you* believe, either." That's when I notice their surprise turning to shock. Some even feel offended. But that's not my intention. "Look, I'm not interested in what you believe, or even in what I believe, for the very simple reason we can believe anything we like, and any belief can be right or wrong. I'm much more interested in what you *experience.* For instance, just now when I said 'I'm not interested in what you believe,' what happened? What was your experience at that moment? *That's* what I'm interested in—passionately so. That's where your real wisdom lies: in your *experience beyond belief.*"

And that's what we're going to explore in this chapter.

FROM EXPERIENCE TO BELIEF

All beliefs are limiting—because they are *abstractions.* Beliefs are *thoughts* and *concepts* literally "abstracted" (taken from) the flow of ongoing experience. They are snapshots of reality, frozen fragments of consciousness. And because they are abstractions plucked from the flow of experience, they can never connect us with *reality.*

Both reality and experience always happen now—*right now.* Beliefs, on the other hand, are always and inevitably rooted in the past. They come from *experiences that have already happened.* Meanwhile new experiences are occurring with every new moment of now (where reality is *always* happening). But as long as we are focused on our beliefs, we miss the reality of what we are actually experiencing. In this sense, *all* beliefs are limiting to some extent—because they isolate us from what is real.

However, some beliefs are inherently more *disempowering.* To the extent that we *believe our beliefs,* and to the extent that beliefs deny or ignore some aspect of our natural potential ("I can't do . . ." or "I'll never be . . . ," etc.), we restrict ourselves from taking actions (and risks) that would or could express and achieve more of what we are actually able to do and be. So, even though all beliefs are *limiting,* some beliefs go further and are *disempowering.*

Even so-called positive beliefs (e.g., "I can do . . ." or "I am . . .") are limiting. We may experience them as *empowering,* but the potency does not come from our beliefs. It can't: abstractions have no intrinsic power. The real potency comes from *intention,* which is the natural *expression of choice directed toward some goal or future state that manifests our potential.*

One of the greatest barriers to self-actualization is the common confusion between "beliefs" and "intention." Beliefs are something we abstract and *think.* Intention is something we create and *experience.* Beliefs are mechanical habits of mind. Intention is intrinsically *creative,* true self-expression.

In my life, deepening awareness of this distinction between beliefs and intention (between thoughts and experience) is a key part of my psychospiritual practice. My discipline is to let go of attachment to *any and all* beliefs, to not *believe* my beliefs. As a human being with an egoic mind, I cannot help having beliefs, but I can choose not to *believe* my beliefs. I can treat them as nothing more than "likely stories" (or, in many cases, "unlikely stories").

Instead of turning to beliefs as guideposts for navigating my way through the world, I focus attention on *experience of what is actually happening.* I sum up this practice in the slogan: *"Engage experience beyond belief."*

Life is a blending of two kinds of stories:

First, it arises from the never-ending "Actual Story"—you know the one: the ever-unfolding reality of cosmos confluencing. We "tune into" and participate in this natural cosmic narrative by *experiencing experience,* as it happens from moment to moment. But then we also live out our very different "Abstract Stories"—ego-based fantasies spun from complex webs of interpretations and beliefs formulated in the relative privacy of our own minds. And this is a problem because not only do we generate abstract fantasies, we also *enact* them. We inflict our stories on the world. Big problem these days.

Here's how I see the process:

Experience → Interpretation → Belief →
Dogma → . . . Action.

This is the mind's automatic "story-making" process. It happens to all of us one way or another. But don't feel bad about it; this, too, is natural. We automatically turn our interpretations into beliefs. It's what minds do. It's their job. It's why they evolved. Just do your level best not to let it get out of hand. In spiritual practice, "waking up" involves realizing what is going on in your mind and then choosing to return attention to where the process begins: with *experience.*

Experience is the ability to feel, to be aware, or to know some aspect of the world. Then, as soon as an experience happens, the egoic mind kicks in and interprets it using thoughts. Not necessarily a bad thing, mind you. Indeed, interpretation can be a very useful survival skill—especially when it is more or less accurate. But we don't stop there. Next, we solidify our interpretations into beliefs. This is when things begin to roll off the rails because we so often mistake beliefs for reality. Why else would you hold a belief? If you didn't think it was true, why bother? But beliefs can't be reality. Why? Because, as we've already seen, they are composed of thoughts, and thoughts are abstractions taken from the ongoing stream of experience. That means every thought is uncoupled from reality. While the cognitive mind is busy taking mental snapshots (thoughts), reality and experience continue to flow on their merry way.

It's what we do, personally and collectively. Over and over. We get lost in our belief systems, and elevate them into religions, philosophies, sciences, arts, politics, economics, and all kinds of ideologies and other abstract conceptual systems. We're very good at it. In fact, it's a hallmark of our species. We spend a great deal of time using our minds to reflect back on the abstractions that populate our minds, mistaking these mental mirages for reality. Like I said, we've turned it into an art and a science. We're so good at it, in fact, that the tangled hierarchies of virtual realities invented by the human mind have taken on a life of their own. For the most part, we now live in them. We've forgotten that what the mind conjures up is just a simulation. It entrances and mesmerizes us. We mistake the Matrix for reality.

From a god's-eye perspective, or an alien intelligence listening in on the antics of our species, the loudest roar is not the blast of bombs, not the cheers of football crowds, not the screams of torture victims, not the clinking of cash or swish of credit cards in suburban malls, not the yelling on Wall Street, not even the incessant buzzing of the media . . . no, the loudest roar is the sound of minds munching on menus! We think belief equals reality; we mistake the menu for the meal. We are addicted to our beliefs. So much so, millions are willing to die, or are unmercifully sacrificed, rather than give them up.

The further action is removed from experience (in other words, the more "story" we insert between experience and action) the greater the likelihood that our behavior will be out of alignment with reality. Every interpretation and belief (not to mention dogma and ideology) is necessarily a distortion of reality—because all thoughts are abstractions taken from the current flow of experience.

Instead of acting out of our beliefs (interpretations or dogmas), we would do far better to practice acting directly from the moment of experience. This is what great martial artists do; it's what great sportsmen and women do; it's what every great artist does; it's what every truly enlightened being does: *experience into action.*

If you've ever seen a master martial artist, a prima ballerina, or an in-the-zone athlete in action, you know what I mean. They don't spend time thinking about their next move, instead they focus attention right down on the present moment of experience, and act from that. Their egoic mind has stepped aside, and their goals and intentions are aligned with a force that transcends personal desires and motivations. The "I" or "me" has disappeared momentarily, and a greater, transpersonal intelligence expresses itself though them.

DISTORTING OR ENHANCING REALITY?

One of the more challenging "gems" of feedback that came to me through cyberspace was a question precisely on the role of beliefs in our lives. This one put me on the spot about my claim that our beliefs distort reality. Here's the question and my lengthy response:*

Q: You say that all beliefs are distortions of reality, and I take it you mean without exception. I'm not sure I agree with you. If what you say is true, then it would mean that all beliefs, without exception, get in our way. They limit us. This is not so, in my experience. And it is not a belief I share with you. Yes, some beliefs do limit us, but isn't it also true that some beliefs actually enhance our lives?

A: You raise a very important issue. I want first of all to honor the insight or intuition behind your statement and your question. And I also want to address some crucial nuances and distinctions about beliefs that I have not made explicit elsewhere.

---

*See Consciousness Dialogue 1, Beyond Belief, in part 4 for a selection of other Q&As on this topic.

I think it is clear to anyone who has worked in the field of psychological counseling (indeed to anyone who has paid any serious attention to the dynamics of their own minds) that one of the greatest stumbling blocks to self-development and success in life (however we define it) are what are often called "negative" beliefs. Indeed, many of us are riddled with a viper's nest of self-limiting beliefs.

This is not headline news. It's an insight at the heart of the human potential movement and much New Age teaching. It is a key element in a blizzard of bestselling books, including *A Course in Miracles,* Norman Vincent Peale's *The Power of Positive Thinking,* and the more recent media phenomena of *What the Bleep Do We Know?* and *The Secret.* It is a basic theme in nineteenth-century American Transcendentalist philosophy (e.g., Ralph Waldo Emerson) and in various branches of the New Thought Movement, founded by Phineas Parkhurst Quimby, and lives on today in New Thought churches such as Religious Science and Unity.

Common to all of these is some variation of the notion that what we think creates our experience of the world. In more extreme cases it includes the idea that our thoughts or beliefs create reality itself! I challenge both of these formulations. Let's look at each, taking them in reverse.

DO OUR THOUGHTS CREATE REALITY?

First, I think it is a case of pure human hubris and self-inflation to believe that reality is a creation of human thought. How could it be? The world, our universe, has been around for at least thirteen billion years, our planet for more than four billion years, and us humans for a couple of million years at most. Do the math. It just doesn't compute. Unless we believe that for about thirteen billion years there was *nothing,* then humans came along and began thinking—et voila! We created *everything*—including the billions of years of cosmic and terrestrial evolution that produced thinking humans. It boggles imagination. Not just the math, but the logic doesn't work out either.

Think about it (better be careful, though): If our thoughts create reality, then who or what *thought the universe into existence billions of years before we humans evolved?*

If evolution didn't happen until humans started thinking, where did we "come from?" Popped out of the Great Nothing from Nowhere, I guess. Just like that. Or, perhaps Eternal Great Spirit had a whim (or a *thought*): "I'll create humans who can think and give them the power to create with their thoughts, too." And, miracle of miracles, at the very first moment of human thought the whole evolutionary shebang, the entire thirteen-billion-year history of the universe, and the four-and-half-billion-year history of life on our planet popped into being. Phew! Man, are we something else!

Wild as this scenario may seem, believe it or not, quite a few people do hold such bizarre ideas. The most dramatic version, of course, is the Christian Fundamentalist fantasy that God created the world about six thousand years ago, and in that flash of creation "He" not only created "mankind," along with the other animals and plants for us to lord over, but also put in place a bunch of misleading fossil evidence that fooled unsuspecting scientists into believing that life has been evolving on this planet for billions of years and that humans are a product of that process. Well, who do you believe?

But it's not just the Fundamentalists. Some well-respected scientists, too, hold a cosmological vision that baffles the mind. Take, for example, my good friend Amit Goswami. He's a first-rate quantum physicist (even wrote a widely used textbook on quantum mechanics). As we saw in an earlier chapter, Amit happens to believe in the ancient Vedic idea (shared, incidentally, by many other great spiritual traditions) that *consciousness is primary*. By "consciousness," he means "Spirit."

He has developed a fascinating theory of the origins of the universe (in fact, of all manifest reality). Unlike the fictions of religious fundamentalism, it is grounded in good science. Philosophically, it begs a few questions, to be sure. Nevertheless, it's an out-of-the-box visionary cosmological scenario that imaginatively integrates the astounding discoveries of quantum physics with the equally astounding, undeniable fact of consciousness itself. Goswami's "visionary window" into the cosmos reveals consciousness as the creative source of all that is (see, for example, *The Self-Aware Universe*).

This is a far cry from the creation stories of biblical fundamentalists. It also takes us a few good quantum leaps beyond some of the more simplistic notions associated with "positive thinking" and New Thought beliefs about the power of affirmations and prayer. First off, it doesn't support the self-inflationary hubris that *human* thought created the world. Now, Dr. Goswami does make a good, and persuasive, case that human consciousness is a subset and expression of divine consciousness. This is fully consistent with his Indian roots and the Vedantic insight that "Atman is Brahman" (that our truest, deepest "Self" is ultimately identical with the "Divine Self"). Some variation of this insight is at the heart of most mystical traditions.

Still with me? Earlier I said I challenged two beliefs: (1) that our thoughts create reality, and (2) that our thoughts create our experience of reality. That word *experience* makes a world of difference—literally.

I think I've made it plain why I don't accept "our thoughts create reality." To be blunt: I think it's a load of baloney. I know that sounds harsh, and it seems to devalue a cherished belief held by many people in both the New Thought and New Age movements. I don't wish to offend these good folks. As a matter of fact, I think they are giving voice to a deep intuition that I also share. So what's up? Why do I challenge and criticize both notions: the extreme belief that thoughts create reality and the "lite version" that thoughts create our *experience* of reality?

TANGLED THOUGHTS, MANGLED REALITIES

Clearly, if our thoughts really did create reality, then each of us would be running around in our own little bubble universes, like gerbils in a rolling cage, bumping into each other, causing all kinds of clashes, conflicts, and catastrophes. On the face of it, that does sound awfully familiar. Doesn't it? Empirically, then, perhaps that's the problem. We *are* creating our own realities, and we're making a god-awful mess.

But it can't be as simple or as simplistic as that. If I create my reality, and you create your reality, and you are part of my reality and I am part of your reality, then who's creating whom? Hmmm. Gets kinda tangled, eh? This line of thinking doesn't lead to reality creation; it leads to *solipsism*—the self-centered narcissistic illusion that only one person really exists, and that's me. You, then, become a figment of my imagination. Of course, from your point of view, it's the other way around: I am just a figment of your fantasy. And that leads to a curious situation, a battle of egos to see which one is "really real," and which is just a figment. If truly I create my own reality, then your insistence that you are real in your own right is just one part of my mind fighting with another part of my mind. Gotta say that also sounds woefully familiar. It's like you are a kind of Jungian "shadow," an inconvenient character or subpersonality that, along with all the countless others I've created, populates my world.

But let's face it: If I *really believed* that you (and everyone else) was just a character dreamed up in my furtive and fertile mind, why on Earth would I be writing this? Am I just journaling?

I don't for one minute believe that I'm the only one who exists. If I truly were the Creator of *All That Is,* you can be damn sure I'd create a very different state of affairs. For starters, I'd do away with mosquitoes, ticks, and poison oak; I'd rethink this whole business of life and death and the need to kill to eat and survive; I'm not sure I'd want to keep black holes, either; and I'd put back every darn quark and quantum of the 90-plus percent of matter and energy that's missing from the universe. I'd certainly make a few changes in the White House.

No, I'm not alone. Thank goodness. Welcome to my world. And thanks for letting me into yours.

Look, the most we can claim for the "extreme" New Thought belief is that our thoughts *participate in cocreating reality.* I don't create you in my imagination, and I refuse to be just a figment in yours. At best, we participate as cocreators. That's the first distinction. And, hey, it's a pretty good compromise don't you think?

You see, I do think there is something to the idea that consciousness is creative. In fact, I think creativity is the very essence of consciousness, not to mention existence itself. I'm with Goswami on that one. But this consciousness isn't "mine" or "yours." It shows up in us, expresses itself through us. (And just in case you're wondering: This "us" refers to these embodied sentient beings called "you" and "me" that happen to exist at distinct, though interrelated, locations in space and time.) Each of us is a unique manifestation of the Creative Ultimate. Boy, doesn't that sound important? I happen to think it's true. In a sense, we are "gods." But there really isn't any "me" or "you" or "we." That's another conversation (see the previous chapter for a more detailed discussion of this conundrum).

So it's not *my* consciousness that creates my reality. Rather, universal consciousness expresses itself creatively, and it does so via a multiplicity of point moments in space-time. Think of it as a kind of "Points Are Us" cosmology. Reality is created *through* these points and their complex dancing interactions. A good friend of mine, philosopher Eric Weiss, calls us "atoms of space-time." I like that.

Right. Do I have that point covered? We don't create our *own* reality; we participate in cocreating *communal* reality.

And so to the second point. Now, let's look at the New Thought "lite" belief.

DO THOUGHTS CREATE OUR *EXPERIENCE* OF REALITY?

If our thoughts don't create our reality, maybe our thoughts do create our *experience* of reality. Now, that sounds far more reasonable. It shifts the personally creative act of cognition from cosmology to psychology, from ontology to epistemology. That's a lot of "ologies" to deal with in a single sentence. But the central message is easy enough to understand. It's this: Our thoughts don't create the objective universe; instead they create our subjective experience or perception of how the universe *shows up* for us. In other words, each of us sees the world through the filter of our own thoughts and beliefs.

That's a much more modest claim. Far less arrogant and self-inflationary. But I still disagree. I just don't think that thoughts can create anything. Why?

Let me be clear: When I use the word *thought* I mean an idea *abstracted* from the ongoing flow of experience. Picture your mind as a congealed point within consciousness—we call it the "ego." This is your individual sense of "me," your personal identity. Your egoic mind is like a cognitive camera clicking away merrily and automatically every moment of experience. *Thoughts are snapshots.* They cannot capture the dynamic ever-flowing nature of reality as it unfolds from moment to moment to moment.

Reality is happening now—always. Have you noticed? If not, pay attention. It's important to get this. Reality is made up of events that have happened (the past), events that *are happening* (now), and events that have yet to happen (the future). And since the past is gone, expired, over and done with, and impossible to change, and since the future doesn't exist because it hasn't happened yet, then that leaves only the present moment, *now,* for reality to *happen.* Yes, the past influences the present through the pressure of causes, and the present will in turn shape future events. But all the really juicy stuff—the only stuff we can actually experience—is happening right now. No other time. Just now.

Consciousness is happening now—always. Have you noticed? If not, then pay attention. This is very important. See the parallel? Both reality and consciousness are happening now. Neat.

All we can ever experience is reality as it is happening now. You cannot experience the past. You can only remember it. And that act of remembering always happens in the present. You cannot experience the future (how could you, since by definition it doesn't yet exist?). You can only anticipate it. And the act of anticipation always happens in the present moment.

Something else to notice: Every moment "now" lasts for just an imperceptible flicker. It comes, and before you can blink, it's gone. Slipped into the past. Expired. You cannot experience an expired moment. All you can do now is remember it. Every moment comes, and just as fast it goes. You can't grasp a moment and hold on to it. But one of the most glorious things about reality is that it never runs out of new moments. As soon as one "now" expires, it is replaced by a new moment of "now"—along with a new experience of the new moment.

The wonderful thing is we don't have to do *anything* about this process. The ever-replenishing flow of new moments is a gift from the gods. Reality is floating on an inexhaustible source of new moments. Thankfully, we never run out of "nows." They just keep on coming. Sure, as individual organisms, our string of "nows" will come to an end (elect me as the next Supreme Being, and I promise to do something about that), but time or reality doesn't stop just because people die.

Experience is always now. We don't have to do anything about that, either. Every moment, a new experience happens. Just as reality is intrinsically creative, generating a never-ending succession of new moments of now, so is experience. Consciousness or experience (I use these words interchangeably), therefore, is also intrinsically creative. In fact, the creativity of experience and reality are intimately fused. No moment of actual existence ever goes unnoticed. Some sentient being is experiencing it. Time, space, reality *require* the presence of experience in order to exist.

Yup, we're now digging deep, very deep, into metaphysics. Be we're not going to get stuck there.*

---

*I've given robust reasons for defending the idea that existence necessarily implies consciousness. I won't bore you with the details, here; but if you're interested you can read *Radical Nature.*

For now, just recognize this: Time is the distinction between moments that have happened, this moment now, and moments yet to happen. *The only way* to distinguish between the past, the present, and the future is through awareness or experience. No consciousness, no time. It's as simple as that.

Same goes for space. The only way to distinguish between "here" and "there" is to experience the difference. *Every sentient being is an atom of space-time.* That's what reality is composed of: a universal, interdependent network of sentient interbeings.

Now that we've got past the deep metaphysics, let's return to the question of "thoughts creating experience of reality" and why I don't accept that.

Remember, thoughts are conceptual abstractions, mental snapshots plucked from the current of experienced reality. Frozen fragments of consciousness. And abstractions cannot be creative. Only something that actually exists can be creative.

As for *beliefs:* Well, beliefs are a bunch of abstract thoughts hooked together to form a kind of story about reality. Thoughts and beliefs are *mental habits.* They are mechanical. The very opposite of creativity. How, then, could a thought ever create an experience? It's the other way around: experience is the source of every thought.

We don't have to do anything for experiences to happen. They are self-generating. There's no stopping them. So relax. There's nothing to do. Just let experience happen. We, our egoic thoughts, don't need to (and cannot) create either reality or experiences.

And, in case you're thinking: "But what about nonegoic thoughts? Thoughts that are not abstractions formed in the mind? Thoughts that belong to a 'higher self'?" Well, if you lob that one at me, I would have to respond: "What do you *mean* by a nonegoic, noncognitive thought?" I, for one, have no idea what that could mean. Do you?

I would say, by definition, thoughts belong to the mind, to the ego. Thoughts are modes of cognition that require a sufficiently complex nervous system to engage in the act of high-grade *abstraction* from the flow of experience.

Any "self" that either precedes or transcends the egoic mind is, one way or another, engaging directly in moments of experience. Transcendental consciousness, consciousness beyond the ego, is not engaged in "thoughting," in acts of cognitive abstraction. It is creatively experiencing.

Why, then, would some very insightful and wise men and women, over generations of New Thought, proclaim that "thought creates reality or experience of reality"? I suspect it is a matter of semantics. They have not distinguished between thoughts as abstractions or mental habits, and other modes of consciousness. Rather, they seem to be using the word *thought* as a catchall for what otherwise is called "consciousness." I think this is where the confusion lies.

Not all consciousness is captured in thought. In fact, I would say, very little is. A great deal of consciousness goes on beyond the inquisitive eye of the ego—either below, buried in the dark shadows of the deep unconscious, or above, in the bright light of transcendental awareness. In meditation or during spontaneous, unbidden bouts of enlightenment when we let the ego sleep, translucent consciousness can beam through as shafts of wisdom we call "intuition."

Using "thought" to mean consciousness in general leads to confusion. It's a common New Age mistake. There are many modes of consciousness besides thought. Some of the most obvious are *feeling, intuition, intention,* or *volition.* Yes, we use thoughts and words to give expression to these other modes, but they are neither created by, nor require, thoughts. In fact, thoughts notoriously distort or diminish the potency of these other modes of consciousness. Think too much about a feeling, and you are likely to miss it. Think too much about an intuition, and you are likely to block it. Think too much about making a choice, and you are likely to get stuck in "analysis paralysis."

Thoughts or beliefs are not intentions. This, I think, is one of the basic confusions behind the notion that "thoughts create reality." Again, *thoughts are abstractions,* mechanical habits. By contrast, experience, expressed through intention and choice, is inherently creative.*

Every thought is necessarily rooted in the past. While we are busily manipulating ideas and concepts, trying to form ingenious theories and models of reality, reality itself has moved on. Thinking about reality is like chasing shadows. It *never* catches up.

That's why every thought, no matter how brilliant, is inevitably and automatically a distortion of reality. And that goes for Einstein, the Dalai Lama, Mother Theresa, Darwin, Freud, Newton, Leonardo, Aristotle, Plato, Socrates, or Homer Simpson. The whole lot of them. Of course, it's true for every thought I'm expressing here, too. So why bother? Because some distortions are more distorted than others. The best we can do is to make the effort to hook our abstractions together as coherently as possible—hoping they will result in some kind of near approximation to the original set of experiences that gave rise to them.

Beliefs distort reality. Best not to get too attached to them. But we do, don't we? I mean we don't stop at having beliefs. We usually go the next step and start *believing our beliefs.* This is when we really risk losing our foothold on reality. We solidify beliefs by turning them into *dogma.* And so it goes . . . we turn dogmas into *ideologies,* ideologies into *paradigms,* paradigms into *worldviews.* And then we *act.* Remember . . .

**Experience → Interpretation → Belief →
Dogma → . . . Action.**

What to do? Give up our beliefs? Nope. That's hardly an option. We can't help having beliefs. It's not really a choice. But we can choose

---

*In fact, experience is naturally *self-creative*—as we've seen, it happens spontaneously with every new moment embedded in the ongoing flow of reality. Hard to think of anything more creative than that.

whether to *believe our beliefs*. That's something we have much more control over.

By now I hope you can see why I make the case that thoughts or beliefs don't create reality. Abstractions just don't have that kind of potency. "But," I hear you say, "despite all your philosophizing, I know from my own experience that my thoughts *do* create my experience of reality. For example, let's say I thought I saw a snake in my path, and I experienced fear—even though the 'snake' was really a stick. My thought 'snake' *created* my experience of fear. Or another example: Say I believe that I'm unworthy of someone's love, or not really good enough to get a job that I want, then those beliefs will almost certainly guarantee that I won't get the relationship or the job that I desire. My beliefs about myself will create experiences of disappointment and failure."

Good examples. But they don't make the case for the creative power of thoughts or beliefs. Undoubtedly, our thoughts can and do *color* or *influence* our experience. But experience happens with or without those thoughts. Thoughts are like colored lenses through which we view or interpret *already existing* experience. Experience is not created by thoughts, though it may be *shaped* by them. Keep this distinction in mind. It's important.

Nevertheless, I want to acknowledge the insight behind the question. Without a doubt, it is true that we can limit our range of possibilities and the experiences that come with them depending on what we believe about ourselves and our place in the world. And we can remove those self-imposed limitations by *changing our beliefs* from negative to positive. This, after all, is the core insight common to the New Thought visionaries and communities mentioned earlier. We're coming full circle now—having taking the time to clarify some important semantic distinctions.

Yes, there are different kinds of belief.

TWO KINDS OF BELIEF

Self-limiting beliefs of the kind we've just looked at can narrow our spectrum of experiences. They shut us down and don't serve us because of this.

By contrast, *self-optimizing* or *self-actualizing* beliefs can empower us to fulfill our goals and dreams—for example, "I am good enough" or "I will get that job."

Well, if that's so, wouldn't it mean that not all beliefs are distortions of reality? If I believe I will get the girl or the job of my dreams, and that's what happens, how could that be a distortion of reality? Wouldn't it be more accurate to say my belief created (or at the very least, contributed to) that outcome?

Let's look at this more closely. If you have a negative self-image and hold a self-limiting belief, you are most unlikely to create an intention to focus your attention and energy on a goal that doesn't fit that image or belief. Conversely, if you have a positive self-image and hold a self-optimizing belief you are more likely to create an intention to focus attention and energy on goals that fit this image or belief.

In either case, it is not the *belief* as such that is creative, it is *intention*. Whereas beliefs are abstractions, habitual mental patterns, that tend to mechanize consciousness and keep us stuck in deep-worn grooves of thought and action, intention is an expression of the creativity of consciousness itself. Beliefs are products of the mind; intentions are expressions of the soul. It's not so much that "we," as individuals, create intentions. Rather, when we relax the strivings and urgings of the personal ego, we let transpersonal consciousness shine through us. "Our" intentions are really manifestations of the deeper and higher purposes of a consciousness or spirit greater than our own personal desires and aspirations. *Intention works when we get out of the way.*

If we hang on to a belief—doesn't matter whether it is positive or negative—it gets in the way of the full expression of intention. That's why mere positive thinking or affirmations don't work. Believing or saying something doesn't make it happen. I'm sure we all have examples from our own lives where we tried *really hard* to have positive thoughts or hold affirming beliefs but what we wanted didn't come to pass. A self-affirming belief may encourage us to set life-enhancing goals, but if that is all we do we end up with "New Year's syndrome"—resolutions without resolution. Another step is needed—a step back.

Once the goal is specified, we need to let go of it, release our attachment to the desired outcome, by *getting the ego out of the way.* That then opens the channel for transpersonal intention—the deepest purpose of the universe—to sweep through us, clearing out the residues of old beliefs. If our goal happens to be aligned with the flow of universal purpose, contributing to the well-being of the greater whole, then that goal receives the full creative force of intention and is brought to manifestation.

Intention creates reality, not beliefs.

Think of intention as focused creativity of consciousness. It's like a laser beam pinpointing a specific possibility and then concentrating all its energy and power to turn that possibility into reality. Intention transforms potentiality into actuality, bringing what is unmanifest into manifestation.

Consciousness operates through balancing receptive and creative elements, like yin and yang. Experience and awareness are receptive in the sense that they register *what is happening,* bringing the world inward. We *feel* reality internally as it unfolds. Intention and choice are creative, consciousness expressing or projecting itself outward *making events happen.*

The two core elements of consciousness, then, are *knowing* (experience/awareness) and *choice* (intention/volition). Knowing or experience guides and informs our action; choice or intention initiates and transforms it.

Experience → Action

We don't create reality. Reality creates us. However, each of us is an inseparable manifestation and expression of reality, participating in directing and informing the way it all unfolds. We are active, voting shareholders in the cosmic corporation, cocreating the very next moment. Let's make it a good one.

Why Believe in God?

Q: *I know who I am, and I know God and reality by my beliefs. Without beliefs I would know nothing.*

A: I suggest it's the opposite: Holding on to beliefs is what blocks you from knowing who you really are or what reality is.

Yes, you have beliefs; we all do. And we have little or no choice about that. But we do have a choice about whether we *believe* our beliefs. We don't have to insist that something is true just because we happen to believe it.

Some people believe in God. Some don't. Who's right? They can't all be right, right? If reality depended on what people believe, then God would be popping in and out of existence on the whims of human beliefs. What a strange Almighty that would be! Not the kind of Creator I'd stake my money on, or send a prayer to. Much too unstable. I want my Creative Ultimate to be reliably self-generating—something I can know is real through direct experience.

13

THE SHADOW AND THE
SHAMAN'S GIFT

t can arrive in a flash like a thunderbolt from the gods or can slumber
and grow peacefully like a butterfly in a chrysalis. It may be a reward
of long, hard effort and commitment, or it may descend spontaneously as a gift of grace. Often it happens during times of deep personal
crisis—perhaps a severe illness, a near death experience, a religious conversion, an ecstatic mystical flash, or a prolonged dark night of the soul.

However it happens, from that moment on, your life is never the
same. You have reached a turning point, crossed a threshold, and both
your sense of who you are and the world around you have changed profoundly. Your inner axis has shifted. You are reoriented.

Besides a personal interest in the topic—having at least on one
occasion experienced a profound turning point in my own life—I am
professionally curious and motivated to understand what transformation is. As a philosopher who has spent a career focused on consciousness studies, I want to know what we mean, and what happens, when
someone says, "my life is transformed," or when we speak of a "transformation of consciousness."

Today, it is almost a rallying cry of individuals, groups, and movements committed to, or at least desirous of, a different, safer, more humane, nurturing, and sustainable world: "Transformation!"

Clearly, the word has many meanings depending on its use and context. It occurs in the sciences—from physics and chemistry to biology, psychology, and social studies. It is used in mathematics, education, economics, politics, law, entertainment, sports, arts, and the media. And, of course, it is a focal point of attention in spiritual circles, where it is sometimes used synonymously with "enlightenment." It has a long and ancient history.

Trans·form·ation

From Latin *trans* (across) and *forma* (form, mold, shape); synonyms: change, convert, metamorphosis, alter, mutate, renew, revolutionize, turn around.

Transformation, then, literally means "crossing forms"—transitioning from one form to another. As a transitive verb, it means to change one thing into another, suggesting a shift of form, appearance, or structure. It can also mean "convert" (as in "conversion")—changing the characteristics of something, and thereby changing its use or purpose.

A Brief History of Transformation

It seems to have been a characteristic of human consciousness since time immemorial. We read about it in the earliest fragments of literature from many traditions. It is there in ancient Vedic teachings, in the *Epic of Gilgamesh*, in Homer's *Iliad* and *Odyssey*, in the stories of King Arthur and Merlin, in *The Canterbury Tales*, in the poems and teachings of Rumi . . . and on and on, throughout history and across cultures. And it was there long before words were scratched on papyrus, parchment, or paper in the oral traditions of indigenous peoples throughout the world—as we can tell from the continuity of their myths and stories of vision quests that still survive today. Transformation has been a focus of consciousness since our ancestors first became aware of its potentials.

In ancient philosophy, form was contrasted with substance or matter. Forms were considered indivisible, while matter was divisible. "Form" has been used in various ways, dating back to translations of Plato's *eidos* (also translated as "idea"). In this Platonic sense, *form* refers to a *permanent* reality—an archetype, a potential, from which manifest objects are derived. Platonic "Forms" were believed to be *universal* and *immutable,* whereas material things were composed of *particulars* subject to change. For Plato, Forms were *transcendent,* while matter was immanent. Because Platonic Forms were immutable, unchanging, there was no possibility of changing one Form into another—thus, originally, *transformation* was a contradiction in terms. As mentioned earlier, the early Greeks spoke of *metanoia* instead, meaning "a change of mind"—that is, a *shift in consciousness*—and later in Christianity it meant a spiritual conversion.

Aristotle brought Platonic Forms "down to Earth," making form (*morphe*) immanent in matter (*hyle*). For Aristotle, matter was the undifferentiated primal element in a state of pure potential, and for anything to be actualized it needs some *form.* All things, then, are essentially "forms of matter." According to Aristotle, when the form of anything reaches perfection it expresses its highest innate purpose, or *entelechy*—the realization and manifestation of its true and full potential. Thus, entelechy can be considered the natural expression and development of the soul. In this sense, then, *transformation* ("a transition in form") is *the unforced attainment or liberation of the soul's intrinsic perfection.*

In English, the word *transformation* originally referred to changes in the states of material objects. Its first recorded application to the realm of *behavior* was in 1386. Today, its psychospiritual meaning refers to *a profound shift in consciousness*—such that our relationship with the world of people, planet, and cosmos undergoes a permanent *qualitative* reorientation.

From the Eleusinian and Orphic mystery schools of ancient Greece to the plethora of workshops, vision quests, and other courses available in modern times, some kind of life-transforming experience has been offered to countless numbers of people. For decades, anthropologists and journalists have researched and written about different aspects of transformation—notably as a social phenomenon, sometimes in the context of a critique of religious cults; at other times in the context of "consciousness raising" liberation movements such as those inspired by the visions of Gandhi or Martin Luther King, feminists, psychedelic hippies, or human-potential programs.

Transformation not only attracts media attention, it also attracts funding and is now a commercial and educational trend. In 2006 more than $3 million was granted to the Metanexus Institute for their Spiritual Transformation Scientific Research Program. This included a nationwide poll in the United States conducted by the University of Chicago's National Opinion Research Center. The poll showed that more than half of the adults in the United States reported having a spiritual transformation at one point in their lives, and of these 60 percent had a transformative experience before age thirty. Research also confirmed that for many of those surveyed the experiential and behavioral effects of the singular transformational event continued to be significant and important years later.

While the sociology of transformation is undoubtedly a fascinating area of study, few investigators have directly addressed the question *What is transformation?* This is what I wish to focus on here. So, while acknowledging a multiplicity of other meanings, I want to explore its more specific sense as a psychospiritual turning point.

A Profile of Transformation

Rather than offer a definition, however, I will sketch a profile of this evocative word based on a combination of direct experience and philosophical research.

As already noted, in psychospiritual development, *transformation* typically suggests a profound change in the quality of personal experience—a shift in consciousness. It can be so profound that our entire experience of living in the world takes on a sense of "being reborn."

After I experienced such a shift a few decades ago, I often described it in two ways: "As if suddenly I was seeing the world in glorious, vivid living color for the first time" and "It was as though my world, my universe, had shifted on its axis." This last phrase sums it up best for me. Picture your life, your world, pointed in one direction (or many conflicting directions). Then, suddenly, every facet of your experience is reoriented and aligned in a new way—it lifts you out of the shadows into the shining light of your true potential. That's how it was for me.

It is also how it is. Transformation, as I use the term, is not a one-time event. It is a process. It endures. Once it happens, there is no going back. Once you know the truth of who you really are, it remains forever undeniable. Of course, this is not to say we always remain bathed in the light of blissful experience or awakening. No, not at all. But once we know, we can never truly or completely forget.

When transformation occurs, it touches every part of your inner life and is expressed externally through actions. In some significant sense, you are no longer the person you used to be. At first, the changes may seem subtle to others (some may not even notice). But for you, your whole world has shifted, and this shift is centered on your sense of self, rooted in your consciousness. Transformation is a turning point.

Clark Moustakas, a clinical psychologist and phenomenologist, defines a "turning point" as

> a process involving the expanding of awareness, the emergence of a new identity, and steps toward a new life. The shifts in identity are a continuing process and like the seasons, they sometimes begin with great drama and revolution.[1]

So, what do I mean by "transformation"? Essentially, it is *"a realign-*

ment of our essential self, our soul, with its natural purpose and potentials; a reorientation of our axis of experience." Everything else follows from that.

As a philosopher and a writer, my particular alignment is naturally expressed through the medium of words and ideas. However, as a philosopher in the original sense of *philosophia,* I am a "lover of wisdom." And wisdom is knowledge embraced in compassion. In other words, I don't just *think,* I value and cultivate knowledge gained through *feeling.* As a philosopher, then, my project in life is to integrate head and heart, intellect and intuition, fact and feeling, in ways that encourage and support people to live and express their highest potential.

Over the years, as I have contemplated the meaning of "transformation," ten dimensions and ten elements have revealed themselves.

Ten Dimensions of Transformation
Transformation is *a shift in consciousness* involving a radical reorientation in:

Experience (*awareness of being*)—from unconscious to conscious.

Attitude (*emotional ground*)—from fear to trust.

Values (*ideals of worth*)—from selfish goals toward the greater good.

Perspective (*viewpoint*)—from fixed to flexible.

Beliefs (*thoughts and concepts*)—from mental habits to experiences of choice and self-agency.

Intention (*goal-directed awareness*)—from indecisiveness to clarity of purpose.

Commitment (*sustained engagement*)—from "perhaps" to "promise" (from "maybe, depending on circumstances" to "count on me, whatever happens").

Responsibility (*who is cause?*)—from disempowered victim to acceptance of self as potent agent.

Creativity (*true self-expression*)—from mechanical behavior determined by external events to inspired insights and self-generated actions.

Action (*cause and effect*)—from self-defeating and ineffective attachment to outcomes to all-empowering selfless contribution.

Ten Elements of Transformation

Transformation opens us up to a deeper sense of self, wholeness, and connectedness. Along with a clearer vision of possibilities, it releases us into a wider acceptance of, and appreciation for, the world as it actually is. Here are some of the elements I've experienced.

Self. Transformation involves a more expansive and *deeper sense of self and world:* Who we are (our beliefs about ourselves, our essential nature) and the world we inhabit (our views of the universe) radically change. Together, these shifts put in place the foundations for a *transformative metapsychology* (self-knowing) and *metaphysics* (knowing the world).

Knowing. Transformation requires cultivating *different ways of knowing* beyond beliefs, assumptions, concepts, and intellectual analysis (reason), and beyond what appears to our senses. It includes paying closer attention to our feelings and intuitions—to awareness of what we actually *experience moment to moment*.

Time. Transformation changes our *relationship to time*—from being driven by our "stories" based on what happened in the past and by our hopes and fears about what will happen in the future to *what is actually happening now.* The present moment is the only time we can ever make choices, and therefore our power is sourced in every new moment. When we let go of the past and the future, the present moment expands into a sense of timelessness. We feel less pressured, more at peace.

Awareness. Transformation *heightens and clarifies awareness.* We experience a deepening sense of connection with everything.

We are more aware of what is actually happening around and inside us and therefore more informed about and attuned to our needs in the moment and to what others need.

Presence. Transformation *deepens our sense of presence and being present.* We are more open and available to engage and participate with others, responding appropriately to the needs of the moment. We experience a heightened sense of luminosity, both from within ourselves and from the world around us.

Authenticity. Transformation *liberates our own authentic being,* freeing us from the chains of fear, ignorance, and illusion. We relax more into an unforced confidence and trust in who we are. We become more spontaneous and creative.

Meaning. Transformation *deepens our sense of meaning*—not only do we feel more whole within ourselves, we experience *fitting in* to an ever widening circle of relationships, with our own bodies, our families, our communities, our nations, our race, our species, all species . . . expanding to a deepened sense of being an integral part of our planet, our solar system, our galaxy, and, ultimately, a sense of unification with the grand majesty and magnificence of the entire multidimensional cosmos itself (including whatever it is we call "Spirit," "God," or "Divine"). Synchronicities occur more frequently in our lives, and we feel more attuned to the ever present stream of "messages from the gods."

Trust. Transformation *connects us with the mysterious* nature of reality—we feel more at ease with not knowing and the unknown, trusting more in the ineffable and imperceptible currents that guide the unfolding of life and being. The need to understand and explain diminishes, often along with the need to speak, and, instead, we experience a deeper sense of silent communion.

Acceptance. Transformation opens us to the power and peace of *greater acceptance*—we shift from preoccupation with our own personal wants and desires, from the gravity of all the "shoulds" and "oughts" that weigh us down, to the liberation and freedom of flowing with a Greater Will as it blows through the world with a purpose and direction beyond our comprehension.

Awakening. Transformation is *a never-ending process*—it comes and goes with the ebbs and flows of the light and shadow dancing in our psyches. Transformation is not a goal to be attained or something we get. It is not an event that happens to us, nor is it something we make happen. It is simply *an awakening to what is.*

For some people, these elements come in a flash of transformation and seem to remain steady and constant throughout the rest of their lives. Perhaps these are the enlightened beings, touched by *grace*. For most of us, however, transformation remains a lifelong process and practice and calls on us to exercise *choice*. In some paradoxical way beyond what the mind can figure out, transformation is a spiritual dance between grace and choice.

By definition, we have no control over grace—it comes into our lives (or not) according to some hidden celestial timetable, and even letting go and trusting in the natural process of life cannot bring it to us. Absent the gift of grace, then, transformation requires intention, commitment, practice, and choice. We need to take some *action* to turn our life around.

STEP 6: EMBRACE YOUR SHADOW

SHADOWS IN THE LIGHT

Psychologist Carl Jung (as, indeed, Freud before him) emphasized that the psyche is multileveled—that beyond conscious awareness, we have *unconscious* feelings, knowledge, and wisdom. We can be *unconsciously* aware.

A great deal of consciousness occurs below the threshold of awareness, directing our lives from the "shadows." In order to know our own psyches, therefore, we need ways to connect conscious awareness with these deep, and often dark, unconscious processes—the psychological "shadow."

So what is this "shadow self"?

We enter life as fragile beings. During early childhood, we encounter all kinds of uncertainties and threats to our survival (some merely perceived, others quite real). We experience fear, shame, anger, guilt, and other uncomfortable emotions so we stuff them down into the underworld of our psyche, hoping they will remain out of reach of consciousness and easily forgotten. As we grow older, we build up complex systems of defenses to protect ourselves from these "negative" emotions. Strange as it may sound, we also avoid or suppress many of our positive attributes, too—such as spontaneity, joy, intelligence, creativity, and love.

And that is how we create our own Shadow—populating our personal underworld with hordes of demons we dare not face or acknowledge. It's also how the Ego comes into being.

Feeling its very survival threatened, our developing ego builds cunning and complex sets of defenses to ward off the demons from the deep and to block out any further threats that might come at it from the world beyond the psyche. And so begins a lifelong dance of hide-and-seek between the shadow and the light.

The ego feels threatened by the shadow. However, it invests so much energy and ingenuity in desperate attempts to protect itself that the ego, paradoxically, develops an intense and addictive relationship with the denizens of the shadow world. Down below, they howl for attention, and the only way the ego can ignore their protests is to *project* them onto other egos, other people, other animals, and even inanimate things. It creates devils and gods, zombies and angels. Entranced by its own projections, it tears the world apart seeing threats and enemies and evil everywhere. It kills others rather than be killed. It starts wars and conflagrations. It invents ideologies and religious dogmas. It does whatever it can to control and dominate wild nature. It invents science and creates an artificial world cocooned in protective layers of technology.

Meanwhile, the "demonic" population of the shadow underworld explodes. Every act of egoic projection provides more fuel to feed the very shadow it fears so much. Unwittingly, the ego is the source of its own terror—the ultimate terrorist. And this psychological dynamic is precisely what underlies and fuels all the human acts of terrorism that threaten our world today—from individual suicide bombers to state-sanctioned atrocities that inspire and generate more acts of terror in response and revenge. This is truly a vicious cycle of insanity, and that is the cycle we need to break.

Instead of integrating life's experiences into our psyche, we push them into the shadows, building up "masks" or personas that we present to the world, hoping to create an image of the person we would like to believe we are.

These personas play a large role in forming our personal ego—our central identity. While serving a useful function—for example, establishing boundaries between "self" and "other"—the ego also will do almost anything to prevent any of our shadow material entering conscious awareness. One of its most potent tools is the rational, intellectual mind, and it uses this to construct ingenious stories, rationalizations, excuses, judgments, and projections—*fantasies*.

In order to break through these egoic defenses, we need to bypass the rational mind and open up to other ways of knowing, such as feeling and intuition. We need to learn to develop what some authors call "emotional intelligence" and "spiritual intelligence" to complement our more commonplace "intellectual intelligence."

Using participatory feeling and alternative states of consciousness (the Shaman's Gift), we can transcend the constrictions of "daytime consciousness"—a.k.a. "ego" or "intellect"—dominated by ideas, beliefs, and other mental habits. Instead, we can allow ourselves to *feel* deeply buried emotions and body sensations, stuck in the unconscious mind. Doing so, we release pent up anxieties, fears, rage, and shame, and as these shadow parts of ourselves filter up into the light of conscious awareness, we recognize that the stories we have attached to them are fictions we have made up and that they no longer serve us.

As unconscious and conscious levels of the mind enter into more fluid dialogue, we can then make *choices:* Which stories about ourselves and the world do we choose to believe? Better still, we can choose not to believe *any* stories and, instead, focus attention on the feelings and experiences coursing through us from moment to moment. As we allow ourselves to move deeper into this "emotional intelligence," we discover the symbolic language of the psyche speaking to us with insights and wisdom.

In this way, the Shaman's Gift can help us navigate the "nighttime consciousness" of dreams and visions and other aspects of the imaginal realm where information and insight come to us, not in words and logic, but wrapped in images and symbols rich with meanings and felt associations.

LIMINAL ALCHEMY

In "shadow work" we are guided in various ways to access these unconscious domains, bringing buried beliefs and assumptions into the light of conscious awareness. In doing so, we recognize the potency of these hidden reservoirs of the psyche. This liminal dialogue is a significant element of the transformative process.

In a phrase, we could say that transformation is *liminal alchemy*— a process of psychospiritual integration at the threshold between unconscious shadow and the light of conscious awareness.

The "alchemy" of transformation, then, involves a dialogue between ego and shadow, between different layers of our psyche. Integrating these moves us along a path toward wholeness. And, since this path, apparently, is never ending, transformation is never a one-time event; it is an ongoing, lifetime process of increasing integration and wholeness.

However, merely becoming consciously aware for the first time of long-buried shadow material is insufficient to bring about transformation. We need, in addition, to keep the liminal channel open so that conscious awareness is constantly in touch with, and informed by, the vast, potentially infinite, information and wisdom of the unconscious psyche. Rather than simply being conscious of what was previously unconscious, it is the actual ongoing *process of becoming conscious* of previously unconscious material that makes the crucial difference in transformation.

Without this open channel to ground and replenish consciousness with feelings, insights, and intuitions, the newly accessed shadow material soon becomes just another mental habit. The ego then shapes this facsimile "shadow" into ever more clever and cunning defenses—protecting itself from further intrusions of the potent, often uncomfortable, even frightening, true shadow.

Transformation takes place deep in the psyche and involves a dissolution of long-standing mental and behavioral habits. It requires calling up the courage to move deep into the hinterland of the soul, focusing the beam of awareness back on ourselves, illuminating our shadows and peeling back layer after layer after layer—*soul archaeology.* Invariably, intentional and committed shamanic-shadow work like this brings our demons to the surface where we can acknowledge them, embrace them, even learn to love them, and finally integrate them alongside the ego, making the psyche whole. In transformation, we unite the shadow and the light.

THE POWER OF CHOICE

Without an intervention of divine grace, transformation requires an act of *choice.* Of course, choices often naturally lead to *actions,* to changes in behavior that in turn accelerate the dissolution of mental and emotional habits. A positive feedback cycle kicks in: we commit to specific actions, and these reinforce and enhance the initial experience of transformation. *Choosing to take action embodies and expresses our authentic self,* and we make a conscious difference in the world.

Conscious actions help transformation "show up" as changes in our lives, inspiring us to remain committed to the process. They also act as *exemplars* to inspire others, who may in turn re-inspire us. This kind of "intersubjective loop" underlies the transformative power of intentional communities, mutual support groups, and what Buddhists call *sanga*.

In transformation, both our *experience* and *expression* of personal subjectivity are radically altered. We recognize, for example, that "who we are" is deeply shaped by our relationships with others and that, therefore, subjectivity is, essentially, *intersubjectivity*.

We consciously shift perspective and learn to see the world through the eyes of others. Choice, then, is the engine of transformation, empowering ourselves and others to be authentically who we are—moving from fragmentation toward unity and inclusivity. This does not mean, however, denying the fragments and shards of self that lurk in our shadow. The paradox of transformation is that true wholeness includes fragmentation, in our psyches and in our lives. We move toward wholeness by accepting fragmentation.

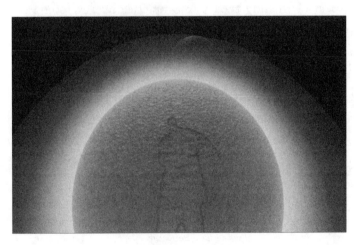

Light includes shadow.

MEETING THE SHADOW

Bill Burdette, a successful investment entrepreneur from Florida, had had a personal experience of transformation during a three-day workshop called the Shadow Process and was so impressed by the potential he saw that he wanted to help make the process widely available—particularly within educational institutions. He introduced me to the originator of the workshop, Debbie Ford, founder of the Ford Institute for Integrative Coaching based in California at John F. Kennedy University, and author of the *New York Times* bestseller *Dark Side of the Light Chasers*. Bill wanted to see if by combining her talents in "metapsychology" with my knowledge of "metaphysics," we might be able to discover a way to establish scientifically the efficacy of the Shadow Process as a way to transformation.

I was particularly interested in the Ford Institute because of its emphasis on "shadow work"—a series of exercises and practices designed to access and uncover repressed psychological material by making effective use of alternative ways of knowing.

Bill had read my book *Radical Knowing* in which I outlined the POR method for a true science of consciousness.* He was excited at the prospect of turning theory into practice by developing a research program for studying transformation in the crucible of the Shadow Process. I shared his excitement and agreed as a first step to experience the workshop personally as a fully engaged participatory observer.

At the end of the three days, I came away, as Bill had, with a definite, clear, and heightened experience of transformation. I had spent the weekend opening up to and exploring my own "inner demons" (all those repressed and suppressed aspects of myself that I was afraid or ashamed of, what Carl Jung called the psychological *shadow*) as well

---

*In *Radical Knowing*, I point out that the essence of the scientific method can be summarized in three steps—*procedure, observation,* and *report* (POR). In brief, every scientific experiment follows a specific procedure or set of instructions for conducting the research. By engaging in this procedure, the researcher experiences what happens. Then by carefully observing what shows up in his or her experience, the experimenter acquires research data. This way, scientists *test* their hypothesis. It's what makes scientific knowledge unique and valuable. Finally, the researcher reports the results of the study by publishing them in peer-reviewed journals, allowing other researchers to further test the hypothesis. This POR method can be used to investigate *any* object of experience—whether an event in one's own mind or in the physical world.

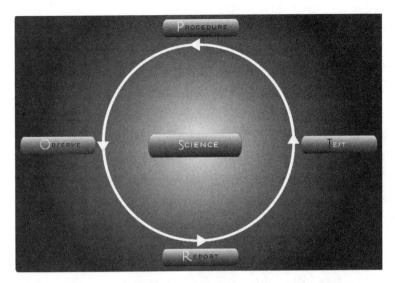

The POR method for a new science of consciousness

as my "light," or "Higher Self" (as Jung's successor Roberto Assagioli called it—those ideal and powerful aspects of my identity that, for one reason or another, I had also suppressed). By actively embracing my shadow and my light—my miserable and magnificent selves—I emerged from the workshop with a renewed sense of wholeness and a profound and joyous sense of liberation. I no longer needed to hide any aspect of who I am. The energy I had previously used to keep a lid on those demons (in case anyone might discover how horrible a person I really am!) was now freed up. I could be more open with other people because I was more open with myself. Instead of projecting my shadow onto others, as a way to avoid confronting it within myself, I could now enthusiastically acknowledge and accept my darker personas as integral parts of who I am and be more open, present, and compassionate with the people around me.

I was delighted. It worked. I was transformed. But then what? Could I keep the experience of transformation alive in myself and my relationships, and avoid becoming an inauthentic hypocrite studying and writing about transformation?

The answer was straightforward: No, of course not. Any attempt to keep alive the experience of transformation I had in the workshop was doomed to failure—especially if I held the belief that I had to remain joyful, loving, and empowered in all my dealings.

Within a week, the luster of light began to fade. I was back to many of my old, self-defeating ways. In fact, it got worse. Following a bout of the flu, I found myself sliding into a dark depression, something I had rarely experienced in my life. My sense of self-worth began to crumble, and I feared that all the things I feared about myself were actually turning out to be true.

The light and the shadow. Shadow and light, in a never-ending dance. In my clearer moments, I knew of course that this was *exactly* what I could expect—and, if wise enough, it's what I would accept. After all, wasn't this the central experiential lesson of the workshop? *I am all of those despicable, undesirable things I hate and fear about myself. But they are only parts of who I am.*

And then I remembered: *Stay with the process.* Transformation is not about feeling good. It's about moving toward integration. *The whole story also includes those wonderful, wise, and capable aspects I experienced before, during, and after the workshop.* And a shift in consciousness unfolds once again.

BUT DOES IT LAST?

Transformational programs today can span many months or years. And many people report dramatic transformational shifts even after a weekend course.

It is common for participants in these workshops to experience heightened joy, ecstasy, love, compassion, and self-empowerment right after the program—in some cases for the first time in their lives. No surprise, then, that they often describe it as "life changing."

But within a few days or weeks the afterglow almost always begins to fade (as happened to me). They no longer feel so wonderful, so "enlightened." Many of their old habits of mind and behavior return to haunt them. It is also quite common for participants to report some variation of "my transformation has worn off," "I've lost it," "I knew it was too good to last," or "I blew it." However, it is also quite common—especially if participants remain in communication either with others who have also gone through the program or with the instructors and coaches—that they will sooner or later realize, as indeed I did: *Transformation is not about feeling good.* While feeling good is certainly often a bonus, transformation is essentially about choosing to be exactly who you are, moment by moment, and not resisting the circumstances you find yourself in. This awareness, that we have the power to *choose what is,* is a catalyst for transformation.

It's always about learning to *accept the ongoing process of life.* And the irony, the beauty, the goddamn hilarity of it all is that we have to relearn this spiritual lesson over and over—every time we wake up to the fact that we've slipped back into believing our stories.

THE NEED FOR TRANSFORMATION

My motivation for studying transformation runs deep. As I look around the world today, it is clear to me that our civilization is in an unprecedented crisis. Not only do we face the looming prospect of ecological catastrophe, the map of the world is dotted with the insanity of preventable human catastrophes—famines, wars, genocide. Terrorism and holocaust seem to have become permanent, and the worst culprits are the terrorists in governments who sanction and perpetrate the wars and invasions—the resource-grabbing that incites others to equally unspeakable acts of violence.

At times like this it is important to feel and honor our connection with all humanity, with all living beings. I try to understand the terrible pain of suicide bombers, the pain and anger that catapults them to such mad and desperate acts.

The September 11 attacks in the United States were a wake-up call for the entire world to pay attention to the deep, deep need everyone has for fair treatment and recognition. As I see it, we elect our governments, and they respond to corporate pressures and make decisions based on questionable economic and geopolitical priorities. People, many millions of people, are often left suffering as a result of these decisions. Their deepest needs go unheard and unmet.

Terrorism is a response to, and a consequence of, that chain of responsibilities. If ever there was a time for a "global mind change," this is it. We need more than ever to shift away from fear and greed and hatred and open our hearts to compassion, understanding, forgiveness, and love. If not, a likely scenario is that the atrocities we have already experienced, as horrible as they are, will be precursors to events even more unthinkable.

As always, it begins with each of us. Each of us has a choice to support those who run our lives from a base of greed and fear, or to support the deepest intentions alive in everyone's heart for a civilization that honors and nourishes the well-being of us all.

If we care about the future, we need to care about our young. The global mind shift that is needed will happen only when new generations are encouraged and supported in *knowing who they truly are.*

Children (and adults) have *multiple intelligences*—emotional, cognitive, somatic, and spiritual. They know about themselves and their world not only through *thinking* (forming ideas and beliefs) but also by *feeling* what is going on in their own bodies and minds and in their relationships with others. Standard education focuses almost exclusively on cognitive learning and either ignores or rejects the educational potentials inherent in "emotional literacy"—learning to recognize and work with emotional states. Our society is stunted when it comes to holistic education and development. Lacking effective tools and processes, our children's capacities for creative, imaginative, and potent ways to deal with personal and societal challenges are severely compromised.

It is my hope and vision that enough people will participate in transformational programs to tilt the tipping point of consciousness. When we begin to wean our nations off unhealthy educational and media diets of propaganda, half-truths, and downright deception we will begin to break the collective trance. Without transformative education and responsible, reliable, and informative mass media, we stand little chance of cocreating a wiser, more sustainable, and compassionate world.

Finally, beyond the Shaman's Gift we can also cultivate the Mystic's Gift of transcendental intuition accessed in sacred silence. This is a realm beyond all language, beyond all concepts and ideas, and even beyond the distinction between knower and known. It is the wordless domain where self and world become one, where good and evil, right and wrong, us and them, me and you, human and divine dissolve into a clearing of transparent wisdom and love. Anything we say about this state of consciousness is automatically a distortion. More than any of the other gifts of knowing, the Mystic's Gift is best experienced in the silence that "passeth all understanding."

Is there anything can we do to cultivate this gift? In the next chapter, we will show a way to practice transformation through seven simple steps.

Gods of Choice

Q: *I'm confused: If I seek transformation, should I choose it or let it happen? I thought that trying to force transformation would not work. What, then, should I do to move along the spiritual path?*

A: You are asking the sixty-four-trillion-karma question. And the first thing I would say is *choose to let go* of needing or looking for an answer. *Live your question*—and watch what happens.

Part of the paradox of the spiritual path—besides it being a *pathless path*—is to experience the meaning and the power of *choosing to let go* and *letting go to choose*. Elsewhere in this book I have said that the key to psychospiritual transformation is "choosing what is, exactly as it is." This is choosing to let go.

However, we also take responsibility for all our habits of mind and behavior—patterns that have taken root in our psyche as a result of past choices. Letting go of these habits frees up consciousness for making choices.

One of the most distinctive "marks" of transformation is the power of choice—it is the creative potency of consciousness. Transformation is something we choose—over and over and over again. Every day of our lives. Every moment of every day. Or not . . . the choice is up to us. We all possess the power of choice to create actualities from possibilities. That is the essence of consciousness. When "we" do so, we realize we are truly creative beings—we are gods, expressions of the Creative Ultimate.

14

SPIRITUAL CONSCIOUSNESS

We have come a long way. On this journey into consciousness we have unwrapped and applied the Philosopher's Gift of clear thinking to help find the right language—moving from "energy talk" to "mind talk." We then opened up the Scientist's Gift, applying a trustworthy method that tests assumptions and beliefs in the crucible of observation and experience. We also embraced the Shaman's Gift of integrating shadow and light. And now, finally, we turn to the Mystic's Gift of knowing through sacred silence.

Along the way, we identified two fundamentally different meanings of "consciousness" and saw why it is important to keep them in mind. But there is a third meaning, and that's what we will look at now.

THE SPIRITUAL MEANING OF CONSCIOUSNESS

From time to time, some of my students get a little impatient with the distinction between the philosophical and psychological meanings of consciousness. They say that neither one captures what for them is its essence: heightened awareness and waking up to the reality and power of love, compassion, and wisdom.

This is the *spiritual* meaning of consciousness. It refers to higher states of awareness beyond the normal, waking, rational mind and is associated with qualities such as "clarity," "peacefulness," and "integrity." It is often understood to lead to a union of knower and known, of self and spirit, a nondual state where being, consciousness, and bliss (*sat, chit,* and *ananda*) are the essence of ultimate reality. It is typically contrasted with habitual, illusory thinking and lower ethical standards.

Notice, though, that it refers to "higher *states*" of consciousness, and in that sense it is really an extension of the *psychological* meaning, a way of describing the upper regions of evolved awareness.

To be precise, then, our two basic meanings of consciousness are *philosophical,* pointing at the ontological *fact* that the light of consciousness is on in the universe; and *psychospiritual,* indicating developmental and evolutionary *forms* of consciousness, where the light can be turned up from dimmest unconsciousness to the brilliance of spiritual enlightenment.

Philosophically, the core question is: "How come the light is on?" Psychospiritually, however, the question is: "How do we turn up the light?" At this stage in our journey, that is the question of ultimate concern. It lifts us from the realms of theory and speculation and plunges us directly into the practical world where actuality and possibility meet head on. As embodied sentient beings living in an embodied sentient universe, we need to know how best to act from experience. We need to expand awareness and be mindful of the cascade of consequences that flows from our choices; we need to live as "interbeings" and "interdividuals" responsible for our contributions to the ever-mysterious unfolding of our shared evolving cosmos.

Whether we know it or not, we are all headed home. Without exception, we all participate in the Big Universal Recycle Program (BURP), where everything that ever happens is recorded as patterns in the unified field (call it the ZPE or Akashic field), fed back into the Source, to be spewed out again at a later time in some other glorious great flaring forth, the birth of a new universe. It's the karma of consciousness. Our choices make a difference. It matters what we leave behind and what we contribute to the future.

What will it take? Without a willingness and a commitment to face the harsh realities of life—our own and the world's—we will inevitably continue on the path to further fragmentation and crippling pathology. But we should not allow ourselves to be weighed down by the challenges, no matter how overwhelming they may seem. "Ostrich consciousness," burying our heads in the sand, will do us no good. No doubt about it, the situation is grave, but it is not hopeless. We can still walk through the world with a light step, choosing levity over gravity. In fact, I think, we are called on to do so.

At times in this book, I've taken a lighthearted view of what is required of us to know who we are, and what we are capable of becoming—by understanding the basics of consciousness through the three disciplines of philosophy, science, and spirituality. In places, my tone and style have been ironic, even irreverent. But my intentions have been serious throughout. *I wanted to engage you, to appeal to your mind and your heart; for you to realize and appreciate with me the stupendously simple and profound gift of being that we are and have. What a privilege just to be alive, just to exist—and to be able to know and enjoy it!*

I think the most profound question in all philosophy, and the beginning of all mystery and wonder, is: *Why is there something rather than nothing?** Think about it. It could have been otherwise. There

---

*I also like to muse on the flip side: "Why is there something rather than *everything*?" Think about that one, too. What stops *everything from happening all at once*? However, I think this question is not quite as profound. In fact, for what it's worth, I have an answer. Given that every *actuality* (every actual thing that exists) is surrounded by a cloud of *possibilities* (as we know both from logic and quantum physics) and the fact that we are conscious beings who make choices, we *choose* among the array of possibilities that meet us at every moment. But, I suppose you could ask, why don't we choose everything?

Simplest answer: many different possibilities are intrinsically incompatible, incommensurate, incoherent, and contradictory. They simply could not *actually* exist in the same universe at the same time. They would mutually and instantly annihilate each other. So we have no option but to choose. And that's what's called in quantum physics "the collapse of the wave function."

seems to be no necessity for anything to have ever existed at all. But instead of eternal and featureless Nothingness, here we are! Can you grasp the awesome gift that that is? *Just Being.* Perhaps there is nothing we take more for granted—until the inevitable moment our own mortality crawls or jumps out of the shadows.

Yes, here we are. We exist. Our universe exists. For us to even conceive the question, *something has to exist.* There's no way around that. Now that it's here, the universe (meaning all of reality) could not *not* exist. If it didn't exist, the question couldn't be asked.

Once something, *anything,* exists, there could never have been a time when there was *pure nothing.* If there ever had been *nothing,* there would have been no possibility for anything to have ever existed. Pure nothing simply cannot create something. If it did, it wouldn't have been *pure* nothing. Something must always come from some other something.*

We are the gift of being conscious beings. We have the gift of consciousness, and I want us to celebrate it, to share it, to cultivate it, to plumb the depths of its vast, and probably infinite, potential.

At this point, science finally meets spirituality. In fact, the final frontier for science has been the familiar domain of spirituality and mysticism for millennia. Although rarely recognized in the West as science, spiritual traditions such as Yoga and Buddhism have accumulated a vast reservoir of knowledge and wisdom about mind and consciousness—at least comparable to the scientific mastery of matter. Without calling it "science," these traditions have been using the essence of the scientific method to *test* and confirm their own spiritual practices. By following a *procedure,* *observing* what happens in their experience, and then *reporting* to each other (especially to someone already well trained in the process) the results of what they observed they have generated a rich database of knowledge about consciousness.

---

*For a deeper discussion of this, see also Consciousness Dialogue 2, Something for Nothing?, in part 4.

Modern Western science has hardly even begun this work. Yet, I think, it is probably the most important work *anyone*—East or West, North or South—can undertake. Yes, there is great value in a science of the physical world that enables us to build technologies to serve our bodily needs. But, as we know only too well, most of that technology has come at a high price, both in terms of its impact on our physical environment as well as on the "inner environment" of soul and spirit. I have discussed these costs in detail in my previous books and will not revisit them here. I will simply add that without a science of consciousness to balance our science of matter, without a way to explore and appreciate meaning as well as exploit mechanism, we will continue to fail to enrich our knowledge of the physical world with wisdom cultivated from the spiritual world.

For this, we turn to the gifts of the Shaman and the Mystic. And whereas standard Plate-Glass Science is motivated by curiosity, the Looking-Glass Science of spirituality is motivated by and requires *courage*—the courage to face our hidden demons and the terror of our own demise. If the modern West has anything new to add to the ancient spiritual sciences of the East, it is the potent, incisive, and insightful excavation of the psyche—especially those aspects we have come to identify as the ego and the shadow. In early Eastern spirituality (and mystical traditions in general), the path to spiritual enlightenment has typically involved *dissolving or killing the ego*. In the West, however, especially following the European Enlightenment and the cult of the rational individual, the ego has been celebrated and developed.

As a result, Western psychospirituality follows a different path. Rather than attempting to kill the ego, the project here is to honor it, while acknowledging its limitations. Most of all, the power and the potential of Western transformative practices come from a deep understanding of how the ego operates within the overall complex dynamics of the psyche. As we have seen, the ego is paradoxically potent and fragile. Its potency shows up as a resolute and obsessive commitment to *not being dissolved or killed*. And this is equally true of Eastern and

Western (Southern and Northern) egos. This very obsession, however, is also its greatest weakness.

So what to do? What do *you* do now that I've distracted and fed your ego-mind with more ideas it can use to build more defenses, create more projections?

My parting wish is that you detach from all the words and ideas, and especially do not believe anything I have written here. I'm not saying ignore it, just don't *believe* it. Put down the book, go for a walk, taste the air, feel the life around you, appreciate the Earth beneath your feet, engage with some other sentient being. Above all, just pay attention to whatever you are experiencing. Don't even try not to think; instead, allow yourself to *feel your thinking*. Notice the difference between speaking to fill the silence and speaking from silence. Enter and embrace the dance and dialogue of *simply being*.

If you happen to be someone who is not yet quite sure what I mean by "spiritual consciousness," let me (paradoxically) offer a few final words to guide you.

STEP 7: PRACTICE TRANSFORMATION

SPIRITUAL CONSCIOUSNESS

It's as simple as doing nothing. Well, perhaps not quite *that* simple. Doing nothing, as it happens, is not all that easy. Try it. I don't just mean not running to the store, cooking dinner, vacuuming the house, or watching TV. I mean sitting still for even ten or fifteen minutes *and not even thinking*.

I'm talking about meditation. If you've done it, you know what I'm talking about. If you've never meditated, you'll discover for yourself just how tricky it is to get your mind to stop its incessant internal chatter.

You'll find all kinds of thoughts, desires, images, and imaginings popping into your mind without the slightest effort from you. They come and go without so much as an invitation or leaving a forwarding address. You'll soon notice that one wayward thought automatically leads to another. Do it for fifteen minutes, and you'll see how easy it is to lose concentration. In fact, if you're at all like me, you'll find it's almost impossible to keep a steady mental focus. Your mind will drift off, pursuing a chain of thoughts into the hinterland of your memories and dreams, and if you don't have the presence of mind to draw yourself back, you'll just keep on drifting.

Bottom line: Your mind has a mind of its own. You don't control your mind. It just keeps on doing its own merry thing, whether you want it to or not—*unless you practice focus* or what Buddhists call *mindfulness*.

There are two main ways to meditate. You can either focus attention on a specific internal process, such as observing your breath, or the feeling of your chest rising and falling, or on a mantra (a special word or phrase). Focused awareness like this can take a certain amount of mental discipline, and at first you may experience yourself making a conscious effort to keep coming back to focus.

The other way to meditate is a little easier for some people. You simply choose to do nothing, except to observe *whatever comes and goes through your mind*. You don't try to change a thought; you don't suppress it; you don't judge it; you don't indulge it. And if you find yourself doing any of these things (you will), you then *just observe that*. The practice here is to just let go. Let your mind do whatever it does naturally. Your job is simply to *observe*. Cultivate *just witnessing*. When you gain some success with this, you will notice a difference between the "you" that is the Witness and the "you" that thinks it is your thoughts. In some spiritual traditions this Witness is referred to as the "Self" or "Higher Self," while the part of you caught up in the flow of thoughts is the "ego."

You will also discover that your ego is a tricky, slippery, ingenious character. For instance, let's say you enter a moment of awareness when your thoughts have stopped. There's just stillness. A peaceful sense of emptiness. A clearing. Almost the instant you notice the stillness, your ego will turn it into a new thought: "Oh, that's nice!" or "Hey, am I good or what? I've stopped thinking!" Of course, as soon as a thought like that pops up, your mind is off and running again, one unbidden thought leading to another. And that's a new opportunity to either draw attention back to focus or simply witness and observe this new process arising.

A SEVEN-STEP GUIDE TO TRANSFORMATION

If I were to sum up the Mystic's Gift in a single phrase, it would be one we've heard again and again throughout this book: *experience beyond belief*—accessed in "sacred silence." Here, then, is a quick and easy summary of the steps to get there.

Step 1: Accept that beliefs are natural.

We all have beliefs. There's no getting away from that. It's a simple fact of life. It's natural to have beliefs—it's what our minds are for. They evolved to give us maps or shortcuts that help us navigate through life. Just don't mistake your beliefs for reality. The map is not the territory. You don't drive your car onto the map and you don't eat the menu. Yes, beliefs are natural, nevertheless they disconnect us from reality.

Step 2: Realize that every belief is a habit of mind.

Thoughts and beliefs are *abstractions*—literally taken from the ongoing flow of experience moment by moment. They are frozen fragments of consciousness, mechanical habits that keep you stuck in the past. Mesmerized by your beliefs, real life flows past unnoticed. Here's how it works: You have an *experience*. Then you *interpret* it. Turn it into a *belief*. Then into *dogma*. Beliefs, therefore, are nothing but mental habits, stepping-stones to dogmatism and fundamentalism.

Step 3: Recognize the origin of beliefs.

Every belief is composed of thoughts, and every thought begins as a feeling. Think about it: Long before you could think or speak, as an infant your life was flushed with feelings. Feelings came first. They are grounded in your body and connect you with reality.

Step 4: Focus on feelings.

Feelings are literally the sensations you experience in your body. Learn to pay attention to them. Take time out to sit quietly and just notice what's going on, without trying to change anything. Simply feel your sensations—in your chest, around your eyes, in your legs, your back, your belly . . . Remember: Every thought begins as a feeling, and feelings connect us with the world. They are messages from nature. Learn what it means to *feel your thinking* and not just think your thoughts.

Step 5: Stop believing your beliefs.

"But," you say, "if I don't have any beliefs, I'll have nothing." Far from it. In fact, letting go of beliefs opens you up to *what is really happening in your experience.* And experience is the royal road to reality. Have you noticed: experience and reality always happen together, *right now.* Also, notice I didn't say "stop having beliefs." That would contradict step 1. As long as you have a mind, you can't help having beliefs. It's what the mind does naturally, and you have little choice about that. But you do have a choice whether you *believe* your beliefs. You do not have to believe that your beliefs are *true.* Instead, you can learn to hold beliefs as "likely stories," as Plato once said. So, take courage, let go of your beliefs, don't hold on to them, and see what happens. I promise: You won't disappear, you won't die.

Step 6: Cultivate being the Witness.

As you practice sitting quietly, feeling the sensations in your body, noticing thoughts as they come and go, arising from your feelings, you will come to a new realization about who you are. *You are not your mind. You are not your thoughts or beliefs.* In fact, you are not even your feelings. In this evolving state of consciousness, you will begin to experience a new sense of freedom. You may begin to notice something quite profound: *someone, or some other part of you, is observing everything that is going on.* The question is: *Who?* That's the sixty-four-billion-dollar spiritual jackpot. It's the essence of spiritual practice. Who, then, is observing the flow of thoughts through your mind? Well, *that's* who you are! You are the Witness that unifies self and world. And the way to get to this realization is by practicing experience beyond belief.

Step 7: Spend more time in "sacred silence."

In the end, the core wisdom of all spiritual traditions is some form of "Let go and let God." Learn to just *be*—by yourself or in community. Be comfortable beyond thoughts, words, judgments, or beliefs. You don't need to sit still and quiet to practice this, but it helps. It takes some discipline to tame the mind, to wean it off its diet of beliefs, to break the habits of thoughts, desires, and fears that inevitably distract us and distort reality. After a while, though, when you pay more attention to the Witness, you come to realize that the deepest source of wisdom is not what you think or believe. Rather wisdom lies in that space of "sacred silence" beyond all words and ideas, where *what is* shines forth. Those who open up to it, often call it the Source.

We are entering a new era. A time that calls for us to remember something deep and vital. A time to remember we are all inextricably connected. And when we learn to draw on the peace and wisdom within each of us, we will experience a healing—our own and of the Earth that sustains us.

That's it.

Oh, and one final thing. In case I forgot to mention it: "Don't believe a word I say."

PART IV

CONSCIOUSNESS
DIALOGUES

BEYOND BELIEF

In my experience, one of the most effective ways to explore consciousness is through dialogue. The following selection of questions came from students, readers, radio audience, visitors to my website, and people who attended my lectures. Like the question posed in chapter 12, many of these challenged me to clarify why I buck the trend when it comes to the value and importance of beliefs.

As you read their questions and my answers, I hope you will get a better feel for the ideas and not think about them. In short, I would like you to learn to *feel your thinking.*

SHIFTING PARADIGMS

Q: I understand what paradigm shifts are, that it is natural for paradigms to shift over time, and that culture transitions from one to the next. But what if we're talking about a personal rather than a world paradigm? What if the "old" paradigm is clearly crumbling and the "emerging" paradigm makes sense, yet we don't fully accept the "new" because the "old" is so deeply rooted? How do we make the shift in ourselves? Why do we fight the shift?

A: Paradigms have great potency.* They are, in effect, the framework of beliefs and assumptions that shape our understanding of reality and how we fit in. *They limit our options by channeling intentions and actions into deep, habitual grooves.* This potency is amplified because for the most part the beliefs we inherit from the paradigm are *unconscious.*

As long as we are unaware of them we have little or no power to choose to do or believe anything different. That's why it is so difficult to "shift" a paradigm. In fact, we cannot as individuals make that shift happen because it is a collective phenomenon.

Here's the challenge: We are born into the dominant cultural paradigm and are immersed in it unconsciously as a fish in water. But sometimes we wake up. We have experiences that don't fit the mold—they are *anomalies.* So what do we do?

I think the first thing is to discover as best we can just what the dominant paradigm tells us about the nature of reality and then look to see which elements of it we accept and align with.

Next, we identify those aspects of our own experiences and beliefs that don't fit and look to see in what ways the paradigm needs to shift in order to accommodate these "anomalous" experiences. (That's what we investigate in the "Paradigms of Consciousness" course at JFK University.)

Then we ask, what elements of the "emerging" paradigm (for example, systems holism and perennial philosophy) transcend and include the "old" one in ways that make room for the kinds of "anomalous" events experienced by millions of people around the world?

You can, and should, honor your own experiences and refuse to deny or invalidate them just because the dominant paradigm has no place for them. If you stand by your own experiences and are willing to communicate and live by them, then you play your part in "seeding" the paradigm with "anomalies" that, sooner or later, will accumulate

---

*The potency of paradigms, like all belief systems, is negative—it *limits* perception of possibilities and stifles creativity. Paradigms *constrain* our worldview and thus deeply impact how we act and relate to reality.

to the point where the old paradigm buckles under their weight, and crumbles. At that point, a paradigm shift occurs.

But it is beyond our control. We make the shift in ourselves by following the process I've outlined here.

1. Become aware of the elements of the current *dominant paradigm* (materialism/mechanism).
2. Become aware of elements of what seem to be an *emerging paradigm* (e.g., systems holism and the perennial philosophy).
3. Observe and note any *personal experiences* that do not fit the "old" paradigm.
4. Look to see if our "anomalous" experiences are aligned with elements of the emerging paradigm.
5. Cultivate the practice of *experience beyond belief* to liberate ourselves from buying into a whole new set of limiting beliefs.

Which leads to your next question . . .

CHANGING BELIEFS

Q: You ask us to take a look at our current beliefs, so I do. Most of my beliefs seem sensible and grounded, but a few are clearly ridiculous, and I want to change these beliefs. Any suggestions about how to go about this?

A: I'm not sure you have quite grasped the essential point I've been making about "experience beyond belief." Yes, by all means examine your current beliefs. Even better, observe the *process* by which you turn experiences into beliefs: first you have an experience, then you interpret it, then you turn your interpretation into a belief, then you begin to believe your beliefs, creating dogma . . . and *then* you take action.

The point is not whether your beliefs are "sensible and grounded" (many of them are). The point is that they are *beliefs*. And beliefs are the residue of expired experiences; they are fragments, habits of thought, and may have no bearing on what is actually occurring in your moment-by-moment experience.

So, I'm suggesting, if you want psychospiritual liberation, changing beliefs is not enough. You need to *get beyond* beliefs by learning to *experience* your experience as it is happening. (This involves *unlearning* what we are taught by our educational system and wider culture.)

TRUST YOUR OWN INTERNAL AUTHORITY

Q: *It is clear from your books and website that you do not place much value on what people believe. But don't all the great religions teach us what to believe? Isn't that what science teaches, too?*

A: I'll respond to your question with another question: Do you automatically *believe* what you are taught, or do you exercise your own natural capacities to question, analyze, explore? To claim that XXX (*insert any particular opinion, doctrine, or belief system*) teaches this or that is to rely on some external authority as your touchstone to reality.

Far better to trust your own experience. In fact, my advice is to let go of *all beliefs*—they block our way to truth. We cannot help having beliefs (that's what the mind naturally does, and it does it well). But we can choose whether to *believe* our beliefs, or to hold them lightly, and be willing to let them go.

And while it may be true to say that many religions tell us what to believe, it is clear to me that the *spiritual* core of the world's great religions is a set of practices designed to liberate us from the distortions of what we think or believe. The great spiritual traditions do not tell us what to believe; they teach us to cultivate greater awareness and discernment *within our own experience.*

Finally, some scientists may ask us to believe what they tell us, and to the extent they do so they are poor scientists. Every scientific "fact" is provisional, always open to revision. So the teachings of science, like all religious teachings, are at best a collection of "likely stories." I'm saying that instead of relying on *external authorities* for knowledge about the world, trust your own *internal authority* of direct experience.

That's the essence of good spiritual practice.

BELIEF IS NOT TRUTH

Q: I've been brought up to believe that my beliefs are my truth. And the new quantum paradigm teaches us that beliefs create reality. Yet you seem to be saying that our beliefs are not a guide to what is true.

A: First, quantum science has nothing to say about beliefs and does not support the idea that beliefs create reality. That's just a "pop" distortion of some complex and profound ideas emerging from quantum physics. (Yes, consciousness collapses the probability wave function into actual reality; but consciousness is far more than beliefs. It includes, for instance, *intention* and *choice*.) (See chapters 6 and 7 for more on the relationship between consciousness and quantum physics.)

Second, people believe all sorts of things, but that doesn't make them true. *Belief does not equal truth*. People used to believe the world was flat. Many people still believe God is a man with a white beard sitting on a throne in the sky. Some people believe in the tooth fairy. Some believe the holocaust never happened. A great many people believe their particular religion is *the* one and only way to salvation. Who's right?

Simply believing in something doesn't bring it into being. Holding dearly to the belief that beliefs are true, doesn't make it so.

So experiment: Just try out living for a few days *as if* your beliefs may not be true. What would that be like? Would you disappear? Would you be lost? Would you lose your identity? Would you die? Or would you feel a new sense of liberation because instead of beliefs you begin to trust your actual experience moment to moment (being careful, of course, not to turn those experiences into *new beliefs*!)? Try it. You might be surprised.

FAITH IS BELIEF WITHOUT EVIDENCE

Q: I believe in faith and have had experiences where faith is more real than our physical reality. Faith does not require evidence, it requires belief.

A: But what do you do with the fact that people believe all kinds of things—often contradictory? How do you (or others) decide which beliefs are, as you say, "more real" than others and which are essentially false illusions? I think that's important.

We see so many horrible consequences of people acting out their beliefs about other nations, other religions, other animals, and so forth. If you don't have a way to *test* your beliefs (i.e., provide supporting evidence) then why should anyone pay attention to what you say you believe? Why should *you*?

If you base your belief on some *experience,* then *that* is your supporting evidence. But that is not "faith." It is evidenced-based belief. So which do you value—faith-based belief, evidence-based belief, or your actual *experience*?

The mere fact that we *believe* something has *no* bearing on its reality. We need to provide *reasons* or *evidence* to support our beliefs.

Even then, what makes the difference is not the fact that we have expressed our beliefs, but that we have provided reasons or evidence to make our case.

CREATING OUR REALITY

Q: In my life, thoughts can and do create experiences. Ideas and beliefs create emotional as well as somatic responses, which are very definitely experiences.

Furthermore, our stories about a situation cause us to behave in a certain way, because we believe the story we have created. For instance, we might consider someone an enemy and begin to behave in ways that eventually elicit antagonistic behavior, reinforcing our story that this person is not our friend. This is another way we create our reality.

Intentions and visualization are yet other ways we create reality. It is well known that even though intentions are only thoughts, they are powerful tools for manifesting goals and desires.

So it could be said that we create our reality by our thoughts. And to create the reality of our choosing, we simply need to change our minds . . . granted, easier said than done. This requires an awareness and desire to change. However, there are lifelong, or lives-long, habits to change; habits we do not even known we have. Once aware, it requires consciously choosing to stay awake and aware. . . . This is beginning to sound suspiciously like a spiritual practice, isn't it?

If indeed we are creators, why not create the reality we want? It's as simple as changing our minds!

A: I think you are making the all-too-easy error of confusing *interpretations* with experience. Thoughts do not, and cannot, create experiences. Thoughts can "influence" or "color" experiences, but whether or not we have thoughts about them, experiences happen *inevitably.* There is nothing we can do to stop having experiences (as long as we are sentient beings).

Yes, it is true that ideas and beliefs (our "stories") may "shape" and influence emotional and somatic responses. But remember that emotions have two components: the felt sense (bodily sensations) and a *cognitive* component (i.e., interpretations). So, yes, thoughts can, and do, generate the interpretative component in emotions, but they do not create the felt sense or experience. *Feelings come first.* Influencing or shaping emotions is not at all the same as *creating experiences.* Our thoughts can and do affect the *form* of our experiences (because they act as filters or lenses for our experiences). But those filters or lenses are our *interpretations.* Meanwhile, the flow of experiences/feelings continues regardless of whether we engage in thinking or beliefs. So, again, bottom line: Thoughts or beliefs influence the *form* of experiences but do not, and cannot, create the *fact* of experience itself.

You also seem to think that intentions are forms of thoughts or beliefs. I disagree. Intentionality is an expression of our creative will and usually happens best when we get thoughts and beliefs out of the way. (I have a chapter on this in *Radical Knowing*.) Our thoughts drastically limit, and even block out, experiences of reality—and so what we actually experience in the moment is often radically reduced. We filter reality, yes; but we most certainly do not "create reality with our thoughts." That is a common New Age myth.

Have you noticed that reality continues to exist whether we think about it or not? Just as well, really, otherwise we'd all have to do a hell of a lot of thinking to keep the universe ticking along. I'm happy to know that someone surfing a wave in Australia won't just pop out of existence, or the sun cease to shine, or gravity fail to function because I forgot to think about these things. And long before there were any people to think any thoughts, reality rolled along very nicely through billions of years of evolution. Phew! Glad I didn't have to think all of *that* into being. Evolution didn't, and still doesn't, depend on my, or anybody else's, thoughts. Our thoughts and beliefs *distort* reality, not *create it*.

Changing reality is not "as simple as changing our minds." This is especially true if by "minds" we mean our "thoughts" and "beliefs." Changing beliefs (or thoughts) just won't do it. We need to get beyond beliefs altogether. When we learn to live from our direct experience (rather than from our thoughts and beliefs about reality), we undergo a profound transformation in consciousness. When that happens, our relationship with reality dramatically and subtly shifts. It's not that we change reality, but by changing our relationship with reality we transform our *experience* of reality. Big difference.

Reality is a cocreative process involving the creative contributions of all sentient beings. (It is the ultimate democracy!) We contribute to the way reality unfolds and changes, but we fool ourselves if we think *we create it*—doubly so, if we think that we can create reality via our thoughts and beliefs. Changing our experience of reality is a far cry from *creating reality*. That is perhaps the most naive and potentially dangerous slogan to come from the New Age.

FEELING COMES FIRST

Q: If I understand you correctly, it seems you are saying that every thought begins with a feeling—that is, feelings and experience necessarily precede thought, and thoughts are derivatives or reflections of feelings. Feelings, therefore, are primary modes of knowing, and thought is secondary. While I wouldn't necessarily disagree with this, it seems to me that it's only one half of a circular equation. For example, it's increasingly recognized in psychology (cognitive psychology in particular) that behind every affect is a hidden thought. Core beliefs influence our thinking, and thinking determines (or influences or leads to) feelings.

For example, if a paranoid person believes that people in authority are by definition evil, then his encounters with his boss are likely to lead to feelings of hostility, suspicion, and the like. In this situation, feelings of hostility/suspicion are clearly derivative of a preconception that authority is evil. The belief/thought precedes the feeling/experience. This has led to the conviction, prevalent in psychology today, that by changing negative, self-destructive, disempowering beliefs, people feel better! This notion is at the heart of cognitive behavioral therapy, which began with Albert Ellis's pioneering work in Rational-Emotive Therapy and is probably the most common form of therapy employed by psychotherapists in the current era, being one of the few that is backed by credible studies and data.

The point is that the relationship between feeling and thinking seems to be a complex, circular feedback process.

A: I'll try to clarify why I say that "feelings come first," and why the circularity you (and others) think happens between feeling and thinking is based on a misunderstanding. First, I point out that both in evolution and in individual development, feeling (sentience) is present long before conceptual thinking or language. Feelings come before ideas or words. Hard to imagine anyone seriously disagreeing with that.

Next, I don't deny that our *interpretations* (thoughts) of our experiences or feelings do "influence" (shape or color) subsequent feelings. But interpretations (thoughts) *do not create* experiences or feelings. Experiences happen all the time, every moment, and we don't have to do anything for that to happen. In fact, we couldn't prevent it even if we wanted to. So experiences don't need to be created by thoughts or thinking—experiences and feelings occur with or without thoughts. That's why it is a mistake to say "thoughts create feelings," and it's why in *Radical Knowing* I say that feeling is the primary mode of knowing. Thoughts and thinking are secondary. There is no circularity of creation. No thoughts would exist if feelings or experiences didn't exist, but the reverse is not true.

I agree, "core beliefs influence our thinking," but I would not agree that "thinking determines feeling" or that "thinking leads to feeling." Yes, thinking may influence (i.e., color or even trigger) certain feelings, but that is not the same as "thinking *creating* feelings." Thinking may act as a kind of filter for feelings, but the fact that some or any feeling is occurring happens with or without thinking. That's my point. I want people to focus on: *"What am I feeling uncolored by thought or belief?"* Interestingly, that's what Ellis's RET also aims at.

The example you give of the paranoid person actually supports the case I'm presenting. The example is full of implicit *interpretations* of feelings or experiences—and we should not mistake our interpretations (thoughts) for the feelings themselves. There is no such feeling as "hostility" or "suspicion."

Remember, by "feeling" I mean, literally, the sensations coursing through our bodies (tingling nerves, beating hearts, rapid breathing, sweaty palms, etc.), and these are not of themselves either hostile or friendly, suspicious or trusting. They just are what they are. *And then* we interpret them. So, I would not agree that the studies and data you cite refute or contradict my essential point. The problem is not with our feelings—it's with our interpretations or beliefs.

Yes, it is true that thinking precedes feeling in an ongoing sequence: we have an experience, we think about it, and then we have another feeling. But we should not make the mistake of confusing *sequence* with *causality*. Just because a thought may precede the appearance of a new feeling does not mean that the thought created or generated that feeling. It may "color" it, yes, but not create it.

I'm aware that the point I'm making involves a subtle awareness (not merely an intellectual distinction) of the relationship between the ongoing flow of experience and the automatic interpretation of experiences that our egoic minds engage in. For many people (especially those not familiar with meditative practice), recognizing this crucial difference between experience and interpretation can be a challenge. It is especially difficult, it seems to me, when people are committed to the belief that our beliefs have power to create our reality.

My current work is an attempt to expose or challenge that kind of reflexive, but unreflected, New Age naïveté and to focus people's attention back on the source of all our beliefs—which is our ongoing in-the-moment experience. That's where transformation occurs, not in our thoughts or beliefs. It's why spirituality is so much more valuable than religion.

BELIEF, FLAT EARTH, AND REALITY

Q: I do believe that if one person thought Earth was round, another thought it was flat, and another thought it was triangular it would indeed be all of those things in each individual's reality. I have no idea what another's person's universe looks like, I only know what mine looks like—and in my universe, the world is round, and those that believe it is flat are "wrong."

A: First, this view falls into a very common pitfall, shared even by professional philosophers and scientists who should know better. It's a confusion of *epistemology* (how we *know*) and *ontology* (nature of *reality*). Yes, different beliefs (or thoughts) give us different *knowledge* *about* reality, but that doesn't mean *reality itself* is different. Notice that "what it *looks* like" is epistemology; what it *is* is ontology.

And this raises another issue: it is one thing to "believe" or "think we know" something; it is something very different to actually *test* what we believe or think we know. We can test to see if the world is round or flat and decide the issue that way. That test has already been done to the satisfaction of billions of people. So to say that "flat Earth" is just as valid as "global Earth" doesn't hold up. It is not just that those who believe in flat Earth are wrong in "your universe"—they are wrong *in reality,* according to the most unbiased experiments set up to test this. And you don't have to take this on faith, or believe what others tell you. You can test it yourself—just get a seat on the next space shuttle.

EXPERIENCE AND ACTION

Q: I heard your discussion on New Dimensions Radio in Australia recently and found it most interesting. Essentially, what I got was: (1) There is a "Supreme Being" (I can't remember your term but along those lines). (2) Only in the present moment is "experience" possible—that a split second later it becomes polluted by interpretation, etc. And by extension, in that moment, knowledge is available, and only then is action truly possible.

My question is, "What then?" Isn't "right" action (action under discrimination) the goal of knowledge gained in the present moment? Otherwise, what's the point? Can we obtain full realization without doing something with this knowledge? If not, doesn't it become a bit of a head game, an esoteric chase around the bushes?

A: I'd like to clarify one point: I do not say that action is possible only if guided by "experience in the moment." Unfortunately, action is possible at any time—whether we are guided by experience or by our beliefs and dogmas. Problems arise when our actions are determined by our beliefs and thoughts (because all thoughts and beliefs are automatically distortions of reality).

It may help to understand my perspective if I clarify, further, that there are at least two kinds of "knowledge"—instrumental and intuitive. Both are useful, both have their purposes. However, if we apply them inappropriately we can get into trouble.

By "instrumental" knowledge I mean whatever we need to know to take care of mechanical things (making and fixing things). "Intuitive knowing," however, is a very different kind of knowledge and is far more effective when dealing with the dynamics of relationships and taking care of issues in the domain of mind or consciousness. Now, as it happens, we are always in relationship with the physical world, so even our mechanical actions, and instrumental knowledge, benefit when guided by intuitive knowing. It's what I call learning to "feel our thinking."

I'm saying that "right action" follows not from "figuring things out" (instrumental knowledge), where we tend to get lost in our mental abstractions, but from being "tuned into" our experience from moment to moment. That's when and how we connect directly with what is real. So, yes, indeed "right action" issues from discernment (which I prefer to "discrimination"), and this comes from paying finer attention to what shows up in our awareness (experience).

You ask "what's the point of having knowledge" (by which I assume you mean "instrumental knowledge")? As I say, this can be useful for making and fixing things in the physical world but is usually not very helpful at all when applied to the domain of relationships and consciousness. When instrumental knowledge is disconnected from intuitive knowledge it tends to lose relevance to what really matters (and leads to mechanical actions that lack awareness and a sense of connectedness with the rest of the world).

What I'm encouraging people to do is to get out of our "head games" (our thoughts, beliefs, and ideas), and instead learn how to act guided by what we are actually experiencing in the moment of action. (It's what martial artists and great sportsmen and women do.) It doesn't mean that we should give up thinking (or having beliefs), but that we should not mistake our thoughts and beliefs for reality. Only experience can connect us with reality.

Full realization (or spiritual enlightenment) is hindered by thoughts and beliefs—especially if we mistake our thoughts and beliefs for what is real. Reality is not what we "think" it is; it is what we feel or experience.

BELIEF AND REALITY

Q: Doubting our beliefs is fine. But I would prefer to say that I recognize my beliefs as transient expedients with a limited shelf life and limited range of usefulness. Oh sure, I believe them. But they can also be discarded and discredited on a moment's notice, once I decide to "go deeper." But in the interim, we need something like our beliefs to write and talk about, don't we? There is not much to say about Raw Reality, is there?

A: I take your point . . . We would do better to treat our beliefs as transitory expedients. But I question when you say, "Oh sure, I believe them." My point is that if we *believe* our beliefs we are giving them added epistemological and veridical weight, usually with no awareness or willingness that someday we may let them go. If you view your beliefs as transient (a good thing), then I'd say you do not believe your beliefs. You *have* beliefs. Not the same thing. In my experience, people who believe their beliefs (turning them into dogma) are not prepared to "discard and discredit them on a moment's notice." Believing our beliefs is tantamount to mistaking them for truth. By contrast, by just having beliefs and noticing them we hold them lightly as "likely stories," and we remain open to change and correction.

And, yes indeed, we do need "something like our beliefs" if we wish to write or talk—most of the time, but not always. Remember, I said that we can't help having beliefs—our minds do it naturally, and for practical purposes, as kind of "shorthand memos" to help us navigate through the world. All writing and cognition almost always involve *interpretations* of our experiences—there is no getting around that.

However, it seems to make a great difference if we cultivate the presence of mind to continually attend to our experience rather than always thinking, talking, writing, and (more important) acting from interpretations, beliefs, or dogma.

Believe it or not (!), we can think, talk, write, and act without interpretation (or at the very least with minimal interpretation) when we learn to *feel our thinking*, rather than merely thinking our thoughts. We can directly give voice to our experience, for example, when we utter authentic exclamations or when we speak from the "heart" of silence. In Bohmian Dialogue, people have an opportunity to realize that it is possible, not to just talk *about* "raw reality" but to actually *speak* reality. It's a much greater challenge, I admit, when we sit down to write (see chapter 13 in *Radical Knowing* for a discussion of Bohmian Dialogue).

Bottom line: I'm asking people not to mistake their beliefs (or anyone else's, including mine) for truth. Unfortunately, this is what so often happens in religion and science, and in the rest of our lives.

FANTASY AND EXPERIENCE

Q: The relationship between thinking and feeling or between belief and experience seems to be foundational in your philosophy of knowing, so I'd like to have a clear handle on it. I would welcome your thoughts on one topic: waking fantasy. When real life isn't delivering enough rewarding experience, I tend to supplement it with imagined experience. I must be getting something (i.e., some sort of pleasant experience) from the fantasy or else I wouldn't be inclined to do it. This looks like an instance where thought produces feeling or experience.

However, I do notice that my fantasies generally have to be "seeded" by some real-life experience—for example, I might engage in a romantic fantasy about someone I've met and liked. Would your analysis be that my initial response is the primary feeling, and then the subsequent fantasies are a variety of hypothetical "interpretations" of that (even if they bear no resemblance to events that have actually occurred)?

A: I think your own response to your question hits the target. Here are my additional comments . . .

First, I have little doubt that our fantasies give us pleasure (otherwise, as you note, why would we continue to engage in them?). So, your concern, if I understand you, is that our fantasy thoughts generate an experience of pleasure, and this would seem to constitute an example of thought preceding experience.

My model or teaching is less concerned with the *sequence* between thoughts and feelings. Of course, as life goes on moment by moment, we have all kinds of leapfrogging between thoughts and feelings. One moment a thought, the next a feeling, then another thought . . . and so on. So, *in this sense,* of course thoughts can come before feelings. But that's not what I'm concerned with.

Rather, I'm focusing attention on the *relationship* between feelings/experiences and thoughts/beliefs, not on their sequences. I'm interested in clarifying the *source* of our feelings and thoughts so that, once we identify the source, we can be empowered to exercise *choice* over the process of feeling and thinking.

I'm saying that *every thought begins as a feeling,* and feelings always occur in the body. So, I'm encouraging us to learn to pay much closer attention to the actual sensations that flow through our bodies from moment to moment.

Then, the next step is to notice how we engage in the process: *experience → interpretation → belief → dogma → action.* When that happens (and it happens all the time), we get lost in our networks of abstract thoughts and beliefs. I'm inviting us to develop the practice of returning attention to our *experience* in the moment as it happens.

When we engage in this inquiry we discover that experiences happen from moment to moment naturally—we don't have to *do* anything. It is built into the very nature of being and existence for experiences to occur. In other words, experiences (or feelings) are ontologically fundamental. They do not need to (and cannot) be generated by thoughts or beliefs. Long before there were thinking, believing beings (such as us humans), the world was populated by *feeling* beings (all kinds of other animals)—this is the evolutionary perspective. And long before you or I or anyone else could think (silent language) or form beliefs, as infants we felt our way in the world. None of these experiences/feelings needed or was caused by thinking or beliefs.

Then, later when we acquired language and thought, we began to interpret our experiences and to form beliefs. As soon as we developed this capacity, we began to influence or "color" subsequent experiences. But shaping or influencing or "coloring" our experiences is not the same as *generating* or *creating* them. What I'm saying is that we can have a much clearer relationship with reality when we learn to attend to the underlying source experiences (or feelings) themselves, rather than being entranced by our distorting interpretations of those experiences. Our fantasies are one example of such distortions. They may feel good, but other than that feeling, our fantasies disconnect us from reality—they direct our attention and resources to feelings that are enmeshed in a network of illusions.

Yes, the feelings are real. That's why we engage in the fantasies. Particular beliefs or fantasies may indeed *color* our experiences in ways we find pleasurable. And, rather than deal with alternative experiences that may not be so pleasurable (in fact may be painful or distressing), we develop the habit of generating fantasies that give us pleasure. In short, we develop addictions.

Addictions are problematic for two reasons: First, they tend to diminish our ability to make choices, and we become more and more machine-like. Second, they tend to seal us into ever-diminishing circles of restricted experiences, and thereby shut out more and more of reality. Fantasies and addictions go together.

The common essence of all spiritual practice, as far as I can see, is to liberate us from these pervasive cycles of fantasy and addiction, and instead empower us to enhance our ability to *choose* actions based on experiences that flow from unimpeded access to, and relationship with, the world around us.

One way this process works is to pay close attention to, and develop greater awareness of, the dynamic relationships between our fantasies (e.g., our beliefs) and our addictions (unconscious behaviors and dispositions to choiceless actions). With greater awareness comes increased ability to exercise choice. Curiously, a good place to start is to *actively choose* our fantasies and to notice that we have control over them. Paradoxically, by exercising such choice we can begin to break the addiction. When we do so, we can shift from fantasy to creative imagination.

Philosophically, I would define imagination as *feeling into* coherent possibilities that flow out of and around what is actually real. In this sense, it can be a very useful and creative exercise, enabling us to break out of the box of actual reality as it has been determined by the past. On the other hand, I would define fantasy as *thinking about* and losing oneself in *false possibilities*—that is, sets of possibilities that have tenuous coherence or connection to reality, and so are highly unlikely, if ever, to be realized.

Psychologically, a crucial difference between fantasy and imagination is that the former tends to lead to addiction whereas the latter tends to enhance creativity. And since creativity is the expression of choice (among possibilities), imagination can be a route to enhanced self-expression and greater liberation.

However, the line between imagination and fantasy can be a fine one, and we need to follow it with caution. Imagination can all too easily slip over into fantasy, and then, instead of liberation, we slide into addiction and mechanism, and diminish our capacity for choice and growth.

That's why I advocate the path of experience (of *experiencing* our experience and *feeling* our thinking) rather than the path of imagination. Imagination can lead us astray—especially if we mistake the productions of imagination for actual reality. This is not to deny that holding a clear vision can act as a lure for manifestation, guiding the creative process from potential to actual. Sometimes, however, visionary scenarios never make it to fruition. For whatever reason, there's a misalignment between that particular vision and whatever the universe has intended. At some point, then, we need to let that vision go (or refine it). If this doesn't happen, if we doggedly pursue a vision "without legs," it degenerates into obsessive fantasy and leads us astray.

By contrast, experience can never lead us astray. Experience simply is what it is in the moment it occurs. Our psychospiritual challenge here, of course, is to practice cultivating the awareness needed to continually discern the difference between experience and our *interpretations* of our experiences, and to develop a finer and finer awareness of the moment when that (inevitable) process occurs. Enlightenment, I would say, is the awareness and ability to rapidly shift attention back to experience, the moment we notice interpretation occurring.

SOMETHING
FOR NOTHING?

Q: *I've been debating your views on panpsychism with a friend who's a materialist. He believes that consciousness emerges from the complexity of the brain. He claims that if the "whole" (e.g., a person) is conscious that does not prove its "parts" are also conscious (which is what you claim). He says it is a fallacy to ascribe consciousness to the parts just because the whole is conscious. He gave an example of baking a cake where the parts (ingredients) do not equal the whole. Something new emerges in the cooking.*

Then he topped off his argument by saying that we can't even prove that the "whole" (a human being or any other animal) is conscious. So, if we can't prove the whole is consciousness why would you claim that the parts are conscious? As I see it, the problem is: How do we scientifically demonstrate that matter has mind or interiority?

A: Consciousness is not a free metaphysical lunch. Your questions get right to the heart of the mind-body problem and what's called "the fallacy of emergence." Here it is: If we begin with *nothing* then that's all there is forever—*nothing!* Quite simply, you can't get something from nothing. How would it be possible?

So let's say we do have *something* to begin with—for example, the big bang packed with unimaginably dense amounts of energy. But, according to materialism, this energy is *wholly* physical, *wholly* objective, *wholly* nonconscious. It doesn't have even the slightest trace of interiority or subjectivity.

Let's call this "State of Reality A"—it's *wholly* physical.

Now fast-forward about 13.7 billion years: some of that energy has condensed into the matter of galaxies, stars, and planets. And on at least one of those planets, matter has evolved to become so complex that it produces life, nervous systems, and brains. So far so good. No problem with the grand outlines of that story. It is standard scientific cosmology.

But we know for certain that besides the matter of nervous systems and brains something else also now exists—*consciousness.*

Let's call this "State of Reality B"—it's physical + *nonphysical.*

"State of Reality A" is utterly different from "State of Reality B." The first is *purely* physical (has absolutely no consciousness) while the second possesses something nonphysical (it does have consciousness).

Brains and nervous systems are physical (exist in space, are objective, are measurable); but consciousness is *nonphysical* (has no physical characteristics whatsoever—does not exist in space, is subjective, and cannot be measured). Where did that nonphysical consciousness come from?

FALLACY OF EMERGENCE

Materialists (or anyone) cannot explain how *purely* physical components could produce something *nonphysical.* That would be a metaphysical impossibility. It would require an *ontological* jump—from one state of reality (*wholly physical*) to a completely different state of reality (physical *and nonphysical*).

In other words, if you begin with wholly physical parts, that's all you ever end up with. No matter how complex or evolved the physical parts become, they can produce only complex *physical* systems. It is utterly inexplicable how consciousness or mind could *emerge* from wholly nonconsciousness ingredients. That's the *fallacy of emergence.*

Materialists are fond of pointing out that emergence *does* occur, and they are right. They point to many instances of emergence in nature supported by solid scientific data. For example, a standard comparison is that water emerges from the gases hydrogen and oxygen. The gases H and O do not possess "liquidity" but water does. So, they say, the phenomenon of liquidity *emerges* from wholly nonliquid components. There was no trace of liquidity in the gases, but with water there is—*something new emerges.* They think this example supports or even proves their case. But they are wrong. It does nothing of the sort.

Here's why: The gases of H and O (like all gases) are physical. *But so is the water!* Both gases and water are *ontologically* identical: they are both physical. So although it is true that a new property ("liquidity") emerges, it is still a *physical* property. In this example, we get something physical (water/liquidity) from nothing but physical components (gases). No mystery there.

This is an example of "physical emergence," and it is explicable by science. It does not pose a metaphysical problem. Same with baking a cake. Yes, something new emerges (a solid cake) from mushy ingredients. But both cake and ingredients are *physical* and *objective* (all are made of physical atoms and molecules).

BIG MYSTERY

This is not at all the case with consciousness. As we know, mind or consciousness is nonphysical (it doesn't exist in space, has no physical characteristics). When materialists claim that consciousness emerges from the complexity of the brain they are proposing that *something nonphysical emerges from nothing but physical components.* That would be *ontological* emergence (not merely *physical* emergence), and it is inexplicable.

Ontological emergence (a completely new kind of reality) is not at all the same as mere physical emergence. It is a profound metaphysical problem without a solution.

You can't get something from nothing. Even though the materialists don't begin with absolutely "nothing"—after all, they have the energy and matter of the universe to begin with—they still have a major problem. According to them, there was *nothing* nonphysical present at the big bang and for billions of years after. Then, *somehow,* there was—consciousness. Big mystery.

To repeat: You can't get "something" nonphysical from parts that had *nothing* nonphysical—*no matter how complex they become.* That's the fallacy of (ontological) emergence.

NO PROOF OF CONSCIOUSNESS

Then there's the objection that "proving" consciousness in the whole doesn't "prove" consciousness exists in the parts. Two problems with this: First, science cannot *prove* anything, most of all it cannot "prove" the presence of consciousness. There's no such thing as a "consciousness meter," no "mindalyzer" to detect consciousness. Because consciousness is subjective, it is undetectable, and therefore is not measurable.

However, scientists (or anyone) cannot "prove" the existence of even *their own* consciousness! So proof of consciousness is a non-starter; it's a red herring. We don't need to "prove" consciousness exists. We *know* it does in our own case from direct, immediate experience. We can be *absolutely certain* of our own consciousness (even if we doubt the consciousness of others). Anyone who doubts or denies consciousness thereby automatically and inevitably *demonstrates* its existence. Only creatures with consciousness can "doubt" or "deny" anything.

For the sake of argument, let's suppose it was possible to prove that a whole organism (say a human) has consciousness. Would that also "prove" that his or her parts (cells, molecules, atoms, subatomic forces, quanta, etc.) would also possess consciousness? I'm saying the answer would have to be a resounding "Yes" based on the argument of the "fallacy of ontological emergence."

If the whole is conscious then whatever it consists of must also have some degree of consciousness, too—*all the way down*. Otherwise, we face the problem discussed above: How would it be possible to get consciousness (in the whole organism) from *wholly* nonconscious, non-subjective parts (atoms, molecules, cells)? That, too, is a nonstarter. And that's why materialism is a flawed metaphysic.

Bumper sticker: *Consciousness is free. But it's not for nothing.*

CONSCIOUSNESS, ENERGY, AND EVOLUTION

Q: Can consciousness do work? Can it make things happen? Even if we discount spoon-bending psychics, there is considerable evidence for acts that are said to be the result of consciousness, such as spontaneous remission of illness as a result of intention, or synchronistic events. Does this count as doing work? If so, then since energy is defined as "the capacity for doing work," wouldn't this mean consciousness is a form of energy? My response would be that energy is the capacity to do work, not the work itself. Consciousness is the work. Consciousness is the act. I'd be very interested to hear your thoughts on this.

A: I think you pose an excellent and profound question here—a question that really takes us close to the heart of the matter regarding the relationship between consciousness and energy. In fact, in all the years I've talked about this issue with people, few have come as close as this to zeroing in on what I take to be the crucial issue: *Is consciousness causal* (does it cause things to happen), and if it does then why would we not say that consciousness is a form of energy? Let's look at this in some detail.

First, if consciousness is causal and is *not* a form of energy, it would, nevertheless, be *adding* energy to physical systems because it would make things happen. And this would violate a fundamental law of physics—the conservation of energy. Basically, this First Law of Thermodynamics states that (within a finite system) energy can never be created or destroyed. All that can happen is that the *forms* of energy can be transformed from one kind (say electricity) into another kind (say heat). But, according to the First Law, in any closed system the total amount of energy always remains the same. Thus, if our universe is a closed system (if there is nothing beyond our universe—and if there was, wouldn't *that* by definition be part of the universe?), then *everything that happens* would be caused by exchanges of energy. Therefore, if consciousness were not a form of energy it couldn't make anything happen (without violating the First Law).

This is one of the most common objections raised by materialist scientists and philosophers against the idea that mind or consciousness is anything other than a by-product of electrochemical energy events in the brain. It is, they say, an *epiphenomenon*—it has no power to cause anything to happen.

Now, we have a variety of options in response to this. It could be the case, of course, that the so-called First Law is not really a "law" at all and that it merely reflects the limited understanding of the human (scientific) mind about the nature of reality. It may be the case that reality is *very* different from what our science and philosophy tell us. After all, the universe is under no obligation to limit itself or conform to human understanding (scientific, philosophical, or, indeed, spiritual). So, the "First Law" may be an error in perception and/or understanding. However, there is certainly a great deal of evidence to support the assumption that this law holds throughout the universe. It is not something to easily dismiss.

Next, it could be the case that, even if the First Law is true, the universe may not be a closed system. Perhaps we live in an infinite universe— or some megaverse of multiple universes. In which case there could be an infinite supply of energy. New energy could be flowing into our local universe from some inexhaustible source. (See chapter 8, I.C.E.

World: The Ultimate Story, for more on this.) It could also be the case that the universe is in a state of *continuous creation,* pumping new energy from some other universe into ours; or, in some inexplicable way, engaged in constant *self-creation.*

No doubt, with imagination, we could think up many other scenarios that would challenge the First Law of Thermodynamics. Indeed, in some forms of idealism the idea is that consciousness *alone* is the creative source of all energy. In this case, however, the claim is that energy is a form of consciousness, not the other way around.

But let's go with the assumption that energy really exists in its own right. What, then, do we mean by "energy," and what do we mean by "consciousness"?

As you point out, the standard definition in science is that energy is "the capacity to do work." Philosophically, we have inherited another definition from René Descartes: energy (or matter) is "things extended in space" (or, simply, extension in space, per se). I think these are good working definitions to start from. Of course, we need to keep in mind that the Cartesian definition begs the question of what we mean by "space" (not to mention "extension"). If, for argument's sake, we assume that space is something like the Newtonian notion of a "container," then matter/energy is whatever occupies, or is located in, some region of that container. An empty container would be pure space. A container with objects would contain some matter/energy. Extension, then, would be the volume of space occupied by an object (measurable on a grid of Cartesian coordinates representing the dimensions of space).

Granted, these are basic, if not philosophically naive, assumptions. Nonetheless, they can serve as a foundation from which to explore whether consciousness is a form of energy. Given the above, then, we can rephrase our question: "Does consciousness have extension in space?" or "Is consciousness located in space?" "Is consciousness measurable?" And, based on what we know about consciousness from our own direct experience, the answer to all three of these questions is an emphatic "no." No one has ever detected consciousness in space or has ever measured it. Even the notion of a unit of measurement of consciousness just boggles the mind: Is it a millimeter, a mile, a cubit, an acre, a light-year?

What, then, do we mean by consciousness? Volumes have been written on this topic, but we can boil it all down to a few basic attributes: Consciousness means the capacity for *subjectivity* (experiencing a point of view), *sentience* (ability to feel), and *self-agency* (volition or choice). In addition, whenever there is *meaning, purpose,* or *value* consciousness is present. We could easily add to this list of qualities, by naming as many *qualia* as we can think of—such as intention, attention, desire, hope, doubt, belief, caring, love, fear, conspiring, courage, intelligence, wisdom, and, of course, awareness. The list could go on. The point is that none of these qualities can be reduced to physics or explained in terms of energy.

But perhaps we're jumping the gun. We still need to explore whether consciousness is *causal*. Can it make things happen in the physical world? Can consciousness *move* energy? Well, we don't need to go looking for instances of anomalous psychokinetic events, such as bending metal objects or stopping clocks merely by the power of mind. The simple fact is that every time anyone makes a *choice* to act, we move our body or some part of our body. We all do this all the time. I choose to get out of bed, my physical body moves. I choose to drink, my arm moves to lift the cup. I choose to climb a mountain, and a cascade of bodily events kicks into action. We could think up countless examples where the *mental* act of making a choice is followed by an obliging body that moves accordingly. *And none of these connections between choice and physical action is explicable in terms of energy.*

It sure *looks like* nonphysical consciousness is causing physical events to happen. *How?* Science cannot even begin to explain how any of this happens. The mind-body connection is perhaps the most obvious *fact* of all human experience, yet it remains a complete and utter mystery.

I'd like to take up your very interesting distinction that energy is the *capacity* to do work, and that consciousness *is* work. A critic might ask: "Isn't energy *both* the 'capacity' to do work (potential energy), and the actual work itself (kinetic energy)?" And, therefore, "If consciousness 'is work,' wouldn't it follow that it must also be the *potential* for that work? Otherwise, if consciousness didn't have the potential or capacity to do work, how could it ever achieve anything? In short, how could it ever '*work*'?"

CONSCIOUSNESS AS KNOWING AND CHOICE

I'd like to approach this from a different angle to see if it throws more light on the issue. Instead of saying that consciousness "is work," or "is action," what if we said that consciousness is *awareness* of possibilities (or potentials). It is *knowingness.*

Consciousness is also *choice*—the ability (capacity) to direct attention/awareness onto, or select, a specific possibility. What if this mental act of choice then *directs or informs the energy* to move itself *from within* in the chosen direction? In this case, in addition to being awareness, consciousness would be the ability of matter/energy to move and direct itself *with purpose.*

You see what I'm trying to get at here is an understanding of the nature of consciousness and energy and their relationship—an understanding that avoids dualism of separate mind and matter (or consciousness and energy) and the reductionism of either materialism (all mind is ultimately merely matter, all consciousness is really energy) or idealism (all matter/energy is ultimately mind or consciousness). I'm looking for a way to acknowledge our commonsense experience that reality consists of both matter and mind, without reducing either one to the other, or separating them.

I begin with my own direct experience that I am an embodied and sentient being. I have a body that is extended in space (physical) and a mind that has no discernible location in space (nonphysical), and this mind knows and chooses.

The nature of consciousness is, therefore, essentially, *knowingness/ awareness* and *choice*—or, to put it another way, it is *subjectivity* (awareness) and *volition* (choice and purpose).* Energy, in any of its meanings or definitions, cannot account for these. The nature of energy is the capacity to do work (functionalist definition) and whatever has extension in space (ontological definition).

So, on the one hand, we have subjectivity (consciousness) and on the other we have spatial extension (energy). These are not reducible to, or explicable in terms of, one another. Yet, in my experience and understanding, they are *inseparable*. They always go together. In other words, the ultimate nature of reality is *sentient energy* or *purposeful action*. The sentient/purpose component is what we call "consciousness," and the action component is what we call "energy." On this understanding, energy *moves itself from within*, and the direction and timing of this movement are guided by consciousness *informing* its associated matter/ energy.

To sum up, then: Consciousness doesn't *act* (in the sense of influencing or moving physical objects)—even when it makes a choice. Rather, consciousness *informs* energy. This is where Carl Jung's notion of synchronicity is such an important insight: *an a-causal mind-matter relationship through meaning.*

We need to be careful not to picture the relationship between consciousness and matter/energy as one "thing" operating on or influencing some other "thing." I'm saying there is only one fundamental reality—*sentient energy,* energy that intrinsically and natively tingles with sentience, feeling, experience.

Think of it this way: Energy (that which has extension in space) inherently has a capacity to know, to feel, and to choose, and this capacity is its intrinsic consciousness. But this knowingness is not itself located in

---

*By the way, subjectivity or awareness is more basic than choice because it is logically possible to have awareness without choice, but it is not possible to make a choice without awareness. In short, consciousness without choice is conceivable, but consciousness without awareness is not.

space, and therefore is not itself a form of energy. Consciousness, then, is knowingness and purposefulness intrinsic to energy.

CREATIVITY AND SYNCHRONICITY

Q: Recently, you were talking about creativity being sentience and energy, and then went on to speak about distance healing as synchronistic sharing of meaning. Are you saying that sharing meaning is how we cocreate reality?

A: Let me step back and begin by clarifying what I mean: Creativity involves both sentience and energy (because it *is* sentient energy). When I talk of "sentience and energy" I do not mean two things. There is only the one reality (it seems to me) and that is *sentient energy*—energy that is intrinsically aware, that feels, that experiences. I (we) use the two terms *sentience* and *energy* to distinguish the two different components of sentient energy. There is nonphysical *sentience* and physical *energy*. Sentience is the ability that energy has to know, feel, and purposefully direct itself.

So, creativity (as sentient energy) has two components: sentience and energy. The sentience component is the source of intentionality and purpose; the energy component is the ability of creativity to *do something*. Another way to think of creativity, then, is that it is *purposeful action*. The "purpose" component is the intentionality that directs the movement and unfolding of energy (it doesn't just randomly swirl about the universe). The "action" component is what *makes things happen*. Sentient energy, therefore, is equivalent to purposeful action. And both are ways of clarifying what creativity is.

Now, one of the deepest questions in metaphysics (at least for me), is: *How does sentience or purpose direct the action or movement of energy?* Another way to ask this is: *Does consciousness cause energy to move?* Or more simply: *Is consciousness causal?* I began to address this question in my previous book, *Radical Knowing,* and will develop it in greater detail in *Radical Science.* For what it's worth: I happen to think there is something "not quite right" with the notion of causality. Essentially, I think the problem goes back to the notion that causality involves exchanges of energy (between two or more objects)—for example, you strike a billiard ball with a cue, and the ball moves. I do not think that the relationship between consciousness and energy is like that at all. It is not that consciousness (or intention or purpose) "strikes" energy and directs or influences it. That way of thinking is a holdover from substance dualism—where mind and matter (consciousness and energy) are separate and (somehow mysteriously) come together and interact.

The relationship between consciousness and energy is not a relationship between two objects (like a ball and a cue). It is a relationship between a *subject* (who knows, feels, and intends) and an *object* (composed of energy that is extended or distributed in space). Subjectivity does not exist in space; it is what knows, feels, and directs objects in space. But it doesn't do this by *interacting* with the object (two things coming together in space). Subjective consciousness directs energy *from within*. It is *energy moving itself.* It is sentient energy making choices to move this way or that.

In other words, the creativity of sentient energy works *synchronistically* rather than causally. It works through *expressing meaning,* not by exchanges of energy. Reality is cocreated (as you intuited) through universal synchronistic sharing of meaning between all sentient beings at every level of manifestation. We exist in a sea of meaning, and this meaning is shared between *all* "interviduals" throughout the universe. Things happen (creative action occurs) as interviduals literally cocreate themselves and each other from moment to moment to moment.

I like to think of creativity this way: *Creativity is universal intelligence expressing itself*—at every moment, at every point in space-time. This "expression of intelligence" is literally what *motivates* the universe into action. And, I'm proposing, that "expressing intelligence" is an act of synchronicity (nonlocal participatory sharing of meaning) rather than an act of causality (exchanging of energy through space).

ROCKS AND
NETWORK CONSCIOUSNESS

Q: I was reading recently about the distinction you make between psychological and philosophical meanings of consciousness. The philosophical meaning is contrasted with the idea of "nonconsciousness," where the "lights are totally out," not the slightest blip of sentience. This got me thinking: according to panpsychism, consciousness is all-pervasive or, as you say, "goes all the way down." So, my question: Is it true that in panpsychism there is no such thing as nonconsciousness—just differing levels of awareness, depth, interiority, intensity, and so forth, because energy/consciousness are coextensive and coeternal?

A: Yes, you're right on . . . well almost. To adequately answer your question we need to make a couple of subtle, though philosophically important, distinctions—first, between "individuals/wholes" (or "organisms") and "aggregates/heaps"; second, between the idea of "network consciousness" and "hierarchical consciousness."

From a panpsychist perspective no individual organism (including cells, molecules, atoms, subatomic particles, quanta, etc.) would be nonconscious. However, aggregates or "heaps" of individuals (e.g., rocks, beer cans, cigarettes, computers, thermostats, clouds, oceans, rivers, mountains, etc.) would not experience their own consciousness. In that sense, a rock, *as a rock,* would be considered "nonconscious," though its constituent molecules would, of course, have their own degree of sentience. Only *individuals* have their own individual consciousness; heaps (of individuals) do not have "heap consciousness."

Nevertheless, just to complicate things even more: we can make a distinction between *network consciousness* and *hierarchical consciousness.* Here's what I mean: The notion of *intersubjectivity* is also wholly consistent with panpsychism. This would mean, in effect, that the molecules within the rock could be/would be involved in some kind of intersubjective communion in consciousness. They form a kind of intersubjective "network." So the notion of "group consciousness" or "network consciousness," involving a host of individual molecules in a rock, is coherent. But, again, this would not mean "rock consciousness" in the sense that the rock would have its own consciousness, because in a rock the organization between individual molecules is nonhierarchical. Rock molecules do not form a whole, integrated system. While it is meaningful to speak of a rock having "network consciousness" it would not have "hierarchical consciousness."

You, on the other hand, do have whole-body hierarchical consciousness. There is a major difference between your body and a rock. While it is true that the individual cells and molecules in your body *and* the individual molecules in a rock all have their own individual consciousness and in each case would be in intersubjective communion, the components of your body are organized hierarchically, which means that your body *as a whole organism* has its own "monad" of consciousness. Not only are the cells in your body conscious, *you* are also conscious in your own right. This is not the case with a rock. The individual molecules are not organized hierarchically, and so do not form a whole individual integrated organism. Consequently, the rock does not have its own "monad" of consciousness.

Bottom line: If you happen to have a deep affection for rocks, panpsychism does allow for the notion of "network consciousness."*

---

*If you are interested, you can find out more about this in *Radical Nature,* where I discuss the famous "binding problem" often presented as the biggest challenge to panpsychism (see, especially, pp. 230–35).

IS CONSCIOUSNESS
SPIRIT?

THE TAO OF CONSCIOUSNESS AND ENERGY

Q: As I was walking the beach this morning (a wonderful thing to do while contemplating things), I was thinking about your class, "Mind in the Cosmos," and your discussion of consciousness and energy and how you challenge the idea of "pure spirit." The image of the Taoist yin/yang symbol came to mind. I was considering how it represents the seed of one is in the other. The analogy came to mind of pure spirit being in matter and matter being in pure spirit. I wondered if consciousness is what moves each into the other, along the spectrum of . . . what? I don't know. Question: How does this fit into what we are studying in class?

A: Here's where the Philosopher's Gift of precision in language comes in useful: if, as you say, "pure" spirit is in matter, and if this is always the case (if not, we're back to some form of dualism and the problem of interaction), then reality actually consists of "spirit-matter." In which case reality is never "pure" spirit—it is always both spirit and matter (consciousness and energy), or *sentient energy*. Similarly, if matter were in "pure" spirit, then in fact there would be no "pure" spirit because it would contain some form of matter or energy.

This is the position of panpsychism, and why I challenge the idealist notion of "pure" spirit. Pure spirit could never do or create anything. The best it could do is form intentions, but without energy it could never take any *action* to make things happen. "Pure" spirit, in that case, would actually be impotent (and that does not seem like a good job description for a divine ultimate!).

When you talk of consciousness "moving" into both spirit and matter, I think you may be falling into the (very common) pitfall of envisioning consciousness as some form of energy. Movement means a transition from one point in space to some other point in space. And consciousness doesn't exist as a thing (or a "field") in space in any way whatsoever. Consciousness is not an object. It is what *knows* or *experiences* or is *aware of* objects (of energy). Only energy, which is objective, can move through space. Remember: *Consciousness knows. Energy flows.*

Also, I'm not sure why you would make a distinction between consciousness and spirit. Ontologically, they are the same kind of reality—*nonphysical* (not existing in space). If you think that spirit is not consciousness, then what else does spirit possess in addition to consciousness? Have you thought about that?

Having said all this, I want to also acknowledge your insight (and the circumstances in which it arose—walking on the beach, what a wonderful way to engage the wholeness of mind and body and the environment!). I share your enthusiasm for the Taoist yin/yang symbol. It is full of wisdom. You are quite right: *yin* and *yang* do contain the seeds of their opposite. So what could this mean in relation to consciousness and energy (or spirit and matter)?

My version of this is that what we call "spirit" is the Tao, containing within itself both yin consciousness and yang energy. And the "dot" or seed of yang within yin represents graphically the idea that consciousness is never "pure," it is always grounded in some yang energy. Likewise, the "dot" or seed of yin within yang represents the insight that energy is never "pure" or insentient but always possesses some form or degree of consciousness.

To think of consciousness and energy shading into each other on a spectrum is to misunderstand the nature of consciousness (and energy). They cannot transform one into the other. What is physical can never become nonphysical, and what is nonphysical (consciousness) can never become physical (energy). Nevertheless, they always go together, always mutually implicate each other.

Think of the shape and substance of a ball. We would not say that the shape and the substance form a "spectrum"; that would be absurd. Shapes never transform into substances, or vice versa. Yet every shape is always the shape of some substance, and every substance always has some shape. They are inseparable; they form a unity but are never identical. You cannot reduce one to the other.

It is the same with consciousness and energy. One is the source of intention and purpose (consciousness); the other is the source of action (energy). Together intention and action result in *creation*. In this sense, what we call "spirit" (Tao) is both intentional and energetic, it is *creative* and expresses its creativity through *purposeful action* (Arthur Young's "quantum of action" or "photon" the ultimate monad of universal spirit).

SPIRIT, CONSCIOUSNESS, ENERGY—
THE ULTIMATE TRINITY?

Q: My fundamental challenge to your model of consciousness is that you create a duality of our physical and nonphysical natures and that they always occur together to make up our "experiential reality." My objection is that to lump consciousness and spirit into a single general category of "nonphysical" distorts the ontological distinction between the two.

A: I'm saying there is no *ontological* distinction between consciousness and spirit. There is no *third* ontological category. Clearly, consciousness is nonphysical, and, just as clearly, spirit is nonphysical. Otherwise, you would have to say either (a) that consciousness and/or spirit is physical (which I doubt you would) or (b) that there is some

mysterious additional ontological category to which either consciousness or spirit belongs. What could such a third category be? Can you
identify and explain its characteristics in terms that are neither physical
nor nonphysical?

I'm betting you can't. It doesn't mean there cannot be other ontological domains, just that, if there are others, all the evidence suggests
that we humans have access to only two; and, even if a few of us were
exceptional enough to access some third (or fourth) domain of being,
it is almost a certainty that they would not be able to *explain* or *communicate in language* just how this "other" domain differs from the two
that we do experience. Spinoza's philosophy took this ultimate categori-
cal duality as the lot of the human condition and the starting point of
his philosophy.

*Q: Yes, I agree, both spirit and consciousness are nonphysical, but the
capacity to subjectively experience is fundamentally distinct from the being
that is having that experience. Isn't this so?*

A: I don't think so. How can a *capacity* (or ability) to have subjective experience be "fundamentally distinct" from the being having
experience? Unless you mean something like "the wetness of water is
distinct from the water itself." Yes, this is true (the first is a *property* of
water, the second is the actual existence of water). However, both the
property of "wetness" and the substance of "water" are *physical*. They
are *ontologically identical* (they belong to the same ontological "basket"
called *physical*). Similarly, if you mean that consciousness is a *property*
or "capacity" of spirit (e.g., its capacity to be aware, to know, to make
choices), and not spirit itself, this would not change the fact that both
the property "consciousness" and the existent "spirit" are nonphysical
(they both belong to the same *ontological* "basket" called *nonphysical*).

It is important to see this. There are not three (or more) fundamental *ontological* states or options. Just two: either physical or nonphysical
(or, more accurately, some combination of both).

*Q: In Kabbalah there are four universes: Assiyah, Yetzirah, Briah,
and Atzilut. These translate into action, formation, creation, and*

emanation, respectively, but in modern English, they are space-time, emotional or subtle world, informational world, and spiritual world. The informational world is sometimes referred to as the mental world, but not in a cerebral thinking sense. The informational world is also considered the level of Oneness. All the worlds interpenetrate each other. The level of Oneness therefore includes what is relative. In this cosmology, there is a separation of the mental level with the spiritual level. Doesn't Kabbalistic wisdom, then, support the view of an ontological difference between consciousness and spirit?

A: Again, I don't think so. The four categories in Kabbalah must also qualify as either physical or nonphysical or some combination of both. For instance, "space-time" is physical; "emotion" is a combination of physical (neuronal dynamics and nonphysical experience and interpretation of those dynamics); "creation" must also be both physical and nonphysical— if it refers to the creation of new forms (physical and/or nonphysical); and "emanation" does not qualify as an *ontological* category—it refers to a *process* whereby *pure* spirit generates *real* matter. In my other books I've outlined and explained why emanationism does not hold together as an ontological process, because it is merely the flip side mirror image of materialism (no one can explain how *pure* spirit could ever give rise to *real* matter (emanationism) nor how *pure* matter could ever give rise to *real* consciousness (materialism).

Q: *Although I essentially agree with your position on consciousness and energy, the argument presented seems rather tautological. If "energy" is defined as the ability to accomplish physical work—or to move mass over distance—then, by definition the term "energy" can apply only to the physical/material domain.*

A: Yes, that is exactly my point: *By definition,* "energy" applies *only to the physical domain.* And that's why it is inappropriate to use energy talk when discussing nonphysical realities such as consciousness, mind, or spirit. If you wish to *change the definition* of "energy," you are, of course free to do so. Like Humpty Dumpty we can make words mean anything we like. However, we don't have that luxury if we wish to *communicate*, if we wish to have a *language*. We need to agree on definitions and meanings. And, in our culture, the word "energy" gets its meaning from its historical usage in science and philosophy. If we wish to give the term "energy" *some other meaning*, and we wish to continue to *communicate* coherently, then we would have to explain how this new meaning for the term "energy" differs from the scientific term "energy."

If we cannot explain how some redefined "nonphysical energy" differs from physical energy, then it is legitimate to ask why use the term "nonphysical energy" at all? It doesn't refer to anything we can identify or explain, and therefore it doesn't communicate anything meaningful.

Q: However, if "energy" were defined as the ability to accomplish "any kind" of work—to include influencing physical circumstances and subjective experiences over time—then the definition of the term must be expanded beyond its merely "physical" meaning to include other sources of power, influence, and "energy."

A: Good. I like the way you are thinking here. Yes, the question arises: *Is consciousness causal?* Can consciousness make things happen? If so, then, according to our definition, it would seem to qualify as "energy." I think this is the point you are getting at. But notice you say "influencing *physical* circumstances" and "*subjective* experiences." This line of thinking gets very tricky, because now you need to explain how nonphysical consciousness could "influence" physical circumstances. This is the old problem of interaction that has befuddled and bedeviled Cartesian dualism for hundreds of years, without the slightest hint of a solution. *How could consciousness "influence" physical events?* What's happening here? We are plunging right into one of the most difficult philosophical problems of all—the nature of *causality*.

Ever since David Hume, this problem has shadowed science and has been left unresolved—unless we adopt Whitehead's *process* philosophy where causality is explained as one moment of *experience (subject) feeling the impact of prior, expired moments of experience (objects)*. In this view, causality is an *experience* in a subject and not an exchange of physical energy between objects. In my work, I discuss the problem of causality (see, for example, my chapters on synchronicity in *Radical Knowing*). Following Jung's notion of synchronicity as an "a-causal connection through meaning," I explore the notion that the relationship between consciousness and energy is not causal but is an a-causal connection through meaning. Mind or consciousness does not "cause" matter to move in any "energetic" sense. Mind does not cause (or "influence") matter the way a billiard cue causes or influences the white ball to move.

I'm proposing something very different: that matter-as-energy is naturally and intrinsically dynamic (nothing actual is ever wholly static) *and* that mind is the ability of matter/energy to intrinsically and purposefully direct itself.

There is no separation between consciousness and energy (between matter and mind). We are dealing with a unified *sentient energy*. This is energy that has the native ability to purposefully feel, know, move, and direct itself. The purpose component is "consciousness," the moving or action component is "energy."

Another way to think of sentient energy is as "purposeful action." In the world of *actual events,* action is fundamental. And this action must be *purposeful* to some extent all the way down (or else we would be at a loss to explain the fact that we are made of energy and we experience purpose and can make choices). Again, the purpose component is consciousness, and the action component is energy.

The *action* component enables *things to happen* in the actual world (this is our definition of "energy"). The purpose component *informs* (in-forms) matter-energy, expresses the meaning and intention intrinsic to the energy. Consciousness is the intrinsic *intentionality* and *intelligence* of energy. It is what acausally *directs* (in-forms) energy from "within." But this intentionality and intelligence is not itself energy, it is not *action*. It is, rather, the intrinsic capacity of action/energy to feel, know, and purposefully direct itself.

How does the sentience of energy or the purpose or intentionality of energy direct itself? It does so by *creating choices*. Consciousness is the creative capacity of energy to *choose* to direct itself toward some goal or purpose. In doing so, actual objects or events literally move though space—they are "energetic" (they do work). But the intentionality and the choices ("consciousness") that are directing the movement toward a goal do not exist in or move through space. The action/energy is physical; the consciousness/intentionality is nonphysical.

In short, because energy is sentient (it is *purposeful action*) it has the capacity to *move and direct itself.* It is *self-causing.* And this "self-cause" (true *creativity*) is an expression of the Creative Ultimate (the "divine" or spirit) in manifest actuality. The Creative Ultimate is expressing itself at every moment at every point in space through the innumerable (perhaps infinite) "points of light" or quanta that constitute the fundamental level of our actual universe. This Creative Ultimate (call it "Spirit," if you prefer) is neither physical nor nonphysical; it is necessarily *both* physical (action) and nonphysical (purpose). It fully combines both ontological "baskets." But it does not constitute a third ontological basket. If you like, Spirit is the totality of universal *sentient energy,* or *purposeful action.* That is how/why Spirit is creative. Creativity needs both: purpose/intention and action (otherwise nothing could ever nonrandomly *happen*).

The physical action/energy component of Spirit/Creative Ultimate (purposeful action/sentient energy) moves through space. It moves as *locomotion* (movement from one *location* to another *location*). By contrast, purpose/intention (consciousness) expresses itself via *telemotion* (i.e., directing and informing the locomotion). The reality of purpose/telemotion is what accounts for the nonrandom action at the foundation of (or intrinsic to) the processes of evolution.

So . . . to sum up: I'm saying that to understand the relationship between consciousness and energy we need a radical paradigm shift beyond thinking in terms of causality. Rather than consciousness *causing* matter/energy to move (mind "influencing" matter), I'm saying that what is really happening is the inherent intelligence or intentionality of matter/energy (its intrinsic consciousness) is *expressing itself.* I'm saying, let's think in terms of "self-expression" rather than causality. Self-expression is a creative act of *sharing meaning.*

Evolution is the Creative Ultimate engaged in universal self-expression, exploring its own possibilities and potentials. Evolution is the universe unfolding its own story. It begins at every moment, at every point in space-time, with the collapse of the quantum wave function. The mind-boggling complex, dynamic relationships among all these myriad quantum events manifests as evolution in our universe—from the big bang to the formation of galaxies, solar systems, living planets, and the evolution of biological species. As this complexity evolves, so does the expression of the intrinsic intelligence and intentionality within the nested systems of forms of sentient energy. *Stories matter* and *matter stories.*

There! You have my Conscious Evolution course in a nutshell!

Q: To me, the key question is whether consciousness is limited to human consciousness and/or other forms of sentient beings, or whether the term "consciousness" can legitimately be used for the interiority all self-organizing entities. I essentially agree with your point that anything that has an autonomous "being" has the essential quality of "consciousness." However, as I have mentioned before, I think that lumping the mental domain of "consciousness" and the spiritual domain of "being" together into a psychospiritual dimension misses important aspects of reality.

A: I've addressed this objection above in some detail. I'm not just lumping the "mental" domain of consciousness together with the "being" of spirit. Consciousness is far more than merely mental (it is not just cognition). Its essence, as I emphasize in *Radical Nature,* is *subjectivity.* That's what consciousness and spirit have in common and what distinguishes them from any merely physical reality. The common subjectivity of consciousness and spirit is what qualifies them both as sharing the same ontological basket.

I wonder if you are perhaps using "spirit" in the sense I'm using "Creative Ultimate"—as the source and repository of the totality of all consciousness and energy? If so, then yes, there would be a meaningful distinction between consciousness and spirit. Spirit, in your view, would be the source of both consciousness and energy. You would, in fact, be equating spirit with sentient energy. And I would agree with this. That is a legitimate and meaningful way to think/talk of Spirit. However, none of this would qualify Spirit (or Creative Ultimate) as a *third* ontological category. It would still consist of the wholly integrated dual natures of *purpose and action* or *sentient energy* or consciousness and energy. We would still have only two ontological domains—physical and nonphysical (or physical and experiential)—"things" and "experiences of things."

You seem to be saying (or implying) that somehow "being" is a third ontological category distinct from physical and nonphysical. But "being" is just another word for "existence." And, clearly, both physical energy and nonphysical consciousness exist. Therefore being must, at the very least, possess both consciousness and energy. It must "contain" physical and nonphysical aspects. To say that Spirit is "being," is to say that Spirit actually exists. And that is to say that the existence of Spirit as the foundation of actual reality (as we know it) must be both physical and nonphysical, both energy and consciousness. It does not qualify as a third ontological category any more than Laszlo's A-field or Bohm's implicate order.

If, on the other hand, you were to continue to insist that being or Spirit constitutes a third distinct ontological state or category, then you are simply *doubling* the "hard problem" by combining both the emergence problem facing materialism (how could real mind emerge from *pure* matter), and the emanationist problem of idealism (how could pure spirit produce *real* matter)? Taking your view that Spirit is a third ontological domain—neither physical nor nonphysical—leaves us with the double mystery (or miracle): *How could* purely *nonphysical and non-nonphysical Spirit ever produce* real *physical energy and* real *nonphysical consciousness?*

Do you see that the ontology you are proposing effectively

compounds the "hard problem" and leaves us with two inexplicable mysteries beyond the single mysteries or problems facing materialism on the one hand and idealism on the other?

Having said all this, I want to conclude in the spirit of this book's essential message: In the end, the best that any philosophical analysis can offer is what amounts to a "likely story." For all we know, miracles do happen all the time. But if they do, we can only face what is inherently inexplicable with a sense of humility and awe, a profound sense of wonder at the possibly infinite gap between what is really real and what we can ever truly understand.

NOTES

Chapter 1. Meaning and the Mystery of Life
1. de Quincey, *Radical Knowing*, 102.

Chapter 2. Honing Consciousness
1. Sutherland, *International Dictionary of Psychology*, 95.
2. Miller, *Psychology: The Science of Mental Life*, 25.

Chapter 3. Zombies and Other Problems
1. de Quincey, *Radical Nature*, 84.

Chapter 4. Hardwired for God?
1. Newberg, D'Aquili, and Rause, *Why God Won't Go Away*, 32.
2. Ibid., 3.
3. Ibid., 174–75.
4. Ibid., 6.
5. Ibid., 28–29.
6. Ibid., 8.
7. Ibid., 9.
8. Ibid., 33.
9. Ibid.
10. Ibid.
11. Ibid., 34.
12. Ibid., 140.
13. Ibid., 53.

Chapter 5. A Likely Story

1. de Quincey, *Radical Nature,* 40–41.
2. Lloyd, *Radiant Cool,* 332.
3. Ibid., 268.
4. Ibid., 258.
5. Ibid., 260.
6. Ibid., 279.
7. Ibid., 280.
8. Ibid., 333.
9. Ibid., 334.
10. Ibid.
11. Ibid., xvi–xvii.
12. Ibid., 84.

Chapter 7. Quantum Consciousness

1. Hameroff, S. R. "Quantum Coherence in Microtubules: A Neural Basis for Emergent Consciousness?" *Journal of Consciousness Studies* 1, no. 1 (1994): 91–118.
2. Besides Arthur Young's *The Reflexive Universe,* inspiring and meaningful alternative models of consciousness within cosmic evolution are presented in, for example, Henri Bergson's *Creative Evolution,* Pierre Teilhard de Chardin's *The Phenomenon of Man,* Jean Gebser's *The Ever-Present Origin,* Sri Aurobindo's *The Life Divine,* Alfred North Whitehead's *Process and Reality,* and Ken Wilber's *Sex, Ecology, Spirituality.*

Chapter 8. I.C.E. World: The Ultimate Story

1. C. Shannon and W. Weaver, *The Mathematical Theory of Communication,* 8.
2. Bateson, *Steps to an Ecology of Mind,* 459.

Chapter 10. Strange Attraction

1. www.fractalwisdom.com/FractalWisdom/fourattr.html.
2. Ibid.
3. Ibid.
4. Ibid.
5. Ibid.

Chapter 11. I Think, Therefore, I Am a God

1. From *Dialogue as a Means of Collective Communication,* edited by Bela Banathy and Patrick Jenlink, 20.

Chapter 13. The Shadow and the Shaman's Gift

1. Moustakas, *Turning Points,* 3.

BIBLIOGRAPHY

Assagioli, R. *Psychosynthesis.* New York: The Viking Press, 1975.

Aurobindo, G. *The Life Divine.* New York: Sri Aurobindo Library, 1951.

Bateson, G. *Steps to an Ecology of Mind: A Revolutionary Approach to Man's Understanding of Himself.* New York: Ballantine Books, 1972.

Bergson, H. *Creative Evolution.* Translated by A. Mitchell. New York: Henry Holt, 1911.

Bohm, D. *Wholeness and the Implicate Order.* London: Routledge & Kegan Paul, 1980.

Crick, F., and C. Koch. *Astonishing Hypothesis: The Scientific Search for the Soul.* New York: Scribner, 1995.

de Chardin, T. *The Phenomenon of Man.* New York: Harper & Row, 1965.

de Quincey, C. *Radical Knowing: Understanding Consciousness through Relationship.* Rochester, VT: Park Street Press, 2005.

———. *Radical Nature: Rediscovering the Soul of Matter.* Montpelier, VT: Invisible Cities Press, 2001.

Descartes, R. *Descartes' Philosophical Writings.* Translated by Norman Kemp Smith. London: Macmillan & Co., 1952.

Ford, D. *Dark Side of the Light Chasers.* New York: Hodder Mobius, 2001.

Gebser, J. *The Ever-Present Origin: Foundations of the Aperspectival World.* Athens, OH: Ohio University Press, 1986.

Goswami, A. *The Self-Aware Universe: How Consciousness Creates the Material World.* New York: Tarcher/Putnam, 1993.

Hameroff, S. R. "Quantum Coherence in Microtubules: A Neural Basis for

Emergent Consciousness?" in *Journal of Consciousness Studies* 1, no. 1 (1994): 91–118.

Holmes, E. *The Science of Mind.* www.bnpublishing.com, accessed 2006 (originally published 1938).

Jung, C. G. *The Archetypes and the Collective Unconscious.* London: Routledge, 1991.

———. *The Structure and Dynamics of the Psyche* (Collected Works of C. G. Jung, vol. 12). Princeton, NJ: Princeton University Press, 1970.

———. *Sychronicity: An Acausal Connecting Principle.* Princeton, NJ: Princeton University Press/Bollingen Series, 1972.

———. *The Undiscovered Self.* Princeton, NJ: Princeton University Press, 1990.

Kant, I. *Critique of Pure Reason.* Translated by N. K. Smith. New York: St. Martin's Press, 1977 (original work published 1781).

Keyserling, A. The School of Wisdom website: www.fractalwisdom.com.

Laszlo, E. *Science and the Akashic Field: An Integral Theory of Everything.* Rochester, VT: Inner Traditions, 2007.

Lloyd, D. *Radiant Cool: A Novel Theory of Consciousness.* Cambridge, MA: MIT Press, 2004.

Miller, G. *Psychology: The Science of Mental Life.* London: Penguin Books, 1972.

Mitchell, S., trans. *Tao Te Ching.* New York: Harper & Row, 1988.

Moustakas, C. *Turning Points.* New York: Prentice Hall, 1977.

Nagel, T. "What Is It Like to Be a Bat?" *Philosophical Review,* LXXXIII (October 1974). Reprinted in *Mortal Questions,* New York: Cambridge University Press, 1992.

———. *What Does It All Mean? A Very Short Introduction to Philosophy.* Oxford, UK: Oxford University Press, 1987.

Newberg, A., E. D'Aquili, and V. Rause. *Why God Won't Go Away: Brain Science and the Biology of Belief.* New York: Ballantine Books, 2002.

Nichol, L. "Wholeness Regained: Revisiting Bohm's Dialogue" in *Dialogue as a Means of Collective Communication.* Edited by Bela H. Banathy and Patrick M. Jenlink. New York: Springer Publications, 2007.

Penrose, R. *The Emperor's New Mind: Concerning Computers, Minds, and the Laws of Physics.* New York: Vintage, 1990.

Shannon, C., and W. Weaver. *The Mathematical Theory of Communication.* Chicago: University of Chicago Press, 1949.

Sutherland, S. *The International Dictionary of Psychology* (revised edition). New York: Crossroad Classic, 1996.

Valle, R. S., and R. von Eckhartsberg. *The Metaphors of Consciousness.* New York: Springer Publishing, 1989.

Whitehead, A. N. *Process and Reality: An Essay in Cosmology.* New York: Macmillan, 1933 (original work published 1929).

Wilber, K. *Quantum Questions: Mystical Writings of the World's Great Physicists.* Boston: New Science Library/Shambhala Publications, 1984.

————. *Sex, Ecology, Spirituality: The Spirit of Evolution.* Boston: Shambhala, 1995.

Young, A. M. *The Reflexive Universe: Evolution of Consciousness.* Mill Valley, CA: Robert Briggs Associates, 1976.

INDEX

BOOKS OF RELATED INTEREST

Radical Knowing
Understanding Consciousness through Relationship
by Christian de Quincey

A Brief Tour of Higher Consciousness
A Cosmic Book on the Mechanics of Creation
by Itzhak Bentov

The Biology of Transcendence
A Blueprint of the Human Spirit
by Joseph Chilton Pearce

The Crack in the Cosmic Egg
New Constructs of Mind and Reality
by Joseph Chilton Pearce

The Spiritual Anatomy of Emotion
How Feelings Link the Brain, the Body, and the Sixth Sense
by Michael A. Jawer with Marc S. Micozzi, M.D., Ph.D.

Chaos, Creativity, and Cosmic Consciousness
by Rupert Sheldrake, Terence McKenna, and Ralph Abraham

Stalking the Wild Pendulum
On the Mechanics of Consciousness
by Itzhak Bentov

The Secret Dowry of Eve
Woman's Role in the Development of Consciousness
by Glynda-Lee Hoffmann

INNER TRADITIONS • BEAR & COMPANY
P.O. Box 388
Rochester, VT 05767
1-800-246-8648
www.InnerTraditions.com

Or contact your local bookseller